D1338284

Hannah Arendt and Political Theory

HANNAH ARENDT AND POLITICAL THEORY

Challenging the Tradition

STEVE BUCKLER

Edinburgh University Press

© Steve Buckler, 2011

Edinburgh University Press Ltd
22 George Square, Edinburgh
www.euppublishing.com

Typeset in 11/13.5 Goudy by
Servis Filmsetting Ltd, Stockport, Cheshire and
printed and bound in Great Britain by
CPI Antony Rowe, Chippenham and Eastbourne

A CIP record for this book is available from the British Library

ISBN 978 0 7486 3902 1 (hardback)

The right of Steve Buckler to be identified as author of this work has been asserted in
accordance with the Copyright, Designs and Patents Act 1988.

Contents

CHAPTER I

Introduction

My assumption is that thought itself arises out of incidents of living experience and must remain bound to them as the only guideposts by which to take its bearings.

I've taken an epigraph from . . . [Karl Jaspers]: 'Give yourself up neither to the past nor to the future. The important thing is to remain wholly in the present'. That sentence struck me right in the heart, so I'm entitled to it.

Hannah Arendt 1964

In an interview broadcast on West German television in 1964, Hannah Arendt, by then a famous political thinker, insisted that she did not regard herself as a 'philosopher' and had no desire to be seen as such: her concern was with politics. She was not even happy with the suggestion that what she did was 'political philosophy', regarding this as a term overloaded with tradition. She preferred what she took to be the less freighted epithet of 'political theorist'. There is, Arendt argued, a fundamental tension between the philosophical and the political; and the historical tendency to think about the contingent and circumstantial business of politics from a philosophical point of view, seeking to speak about it in terms of the universal and the eternal, has had unfortunate consequences. In the light of this conviction, Arendt said she wished to look at politics 'with eyes unclouded by philosophy' (Arendt 1994: 2). The aim of this book is to explore the implications of this statement as they make themselves felt in Arendt's work and to suggest that they underwrite a distinctive, potent and consistently challenging way of theorising politics.

Arendt was an unorthodox political theorist. Her work divided critical opinion and has continued to do so since her death in 1975.[1] At issue here is not only what Arendt said but also how she said it. Although she taught at major universities, Arendt always maintained something of a distance from academic life and was no respecter of its established conventions. She wrote in an eclectic style, involving a mixture of idioms and she did not shy away from investing her work with elements of paradox and perplexity. It is a stylistic mix that for some has been a source of profound insights, for others, simply baffling. In view of this, it is surprising that in the extensive critical literature on Arendt relatively little sustained attention has been given to the question of what her unorthodox style betokened in terms of method – to what Arendt believed political theory to be *for* and how, in the light of this, it should be undertaken. There has been a good deal of comment on the substantive content of Arendt's thought: her analysis of totalitarianism; her conception of politics and political action; her view of revolution; and her later writings on the life of the mind. There has also been much comment on her place in relation to other thinkers or themes: Arendt and Jewish thought; Arendt and German philosophy; Arendt and feminism. But little sustained and explicit attention has been given to the methodological issues that her work raises.

In another sense, perhaps, this gap in the literature is a little less surprising. Although she reflected and wrote extensively on the question of thinking and its relation with politics, Arendt's methodological commitments are neither immediately nor easily identifiable and her remarks on the subject were occasional and elusive. It is perhaps easier, initially, to say what Arendt was *not* trying to do. It is clear that she was not, in any accepted sense, a social scientist. The traditional appeal to empirical findings and explanatory hypotheses characteristic of social science amounts, as Arendt saw it, to a 'behaviourist' approach that falsely reduces political conduct to the measurable and the predictable. It is a standpoint that fails, she argued, to capture the authentic nature of politics, which she thought of as an intrinsically spontaneous and unpredictable engagement. It also colludes, she believed, with a propensity in the modern world for conduct to become increasingly routine. It is, in this sense, a form of social analysis that answers to, and helps perpetuate, tendencies inherent in modern mass societies, plagued by what she termed 'the rise of the social', for the primacy of material and technological interests, combined, correspondingly, with an increasingly managerial state, to render life routine and aspirations conformist. In these circumstances, 'behaviour has replaced action as the foremost mode of human relationship' (Arendt 1958: 41). We tend now to behave increasingly in the way that social scientists falsely assume we inevitably behave: 'the trouble with modern theories of behaviourism is not that they are wrong but that they could become true' (Arendt 1958: 322).

Equally, as noted above, Arendt distanced herself from the philosophical tradition: 'I have said goodbye to philosophy once and for all . . . I studied philosophy but that does not mean I stayed with it' (Arendt 1994: 2). There was, for Arendt, a distinction to be drawn between philosophy, on the one hand, and political theory, as she thought of it, on the other. It was a distinction that she wanted to draw as part of a conscious attempt to write against the tradition that saw reflection on politics as a branch of philosophy. This was a tradition, she thought, which had resulted in ways of thinking about politics that abstracted away from its real and particular character as a practice, seeking to dictate to it, as it were, 'from above'. On the traditional philosophical view, as Arendt saw it, the chaotic worldly realm presents a problem to be resolved through reflection upon abstract principles that would provide a recipe for eternal harmony. This tradition can be traced back to Plato, who sought to show 'how we can bring about in the commonwealth that complete quiet, that absolute peace, that . . . constitutes the best condition for the life of the philosopher' (Arendt 1982: 21). It is a tradition which potentially renders the contingent and 'noisy' business of politics superfluous. The tradition, since Plato, can be seen as constituting 'various attempts to find theoretical foundations and practical ways for an escape from politics altogether' (Arendt 1958: 222). It was for this reason that she regarded the philosophical standpoint as one that threatened to cloud her vision.

So Arendt was concerned to distinguish what she was doing from more conventional philosophical approaches, but she was reticent about characterising her own method. It will be the contention here that despite this reticence on the subject, Arendt adopted a distinctive and identifiable method. I will argue also that an understanding of this method allows us to see in her work a *deep* consistency, by which I mean that her methodological standpoint is not only manifest throughout the body of her writings but also shows a modal consistency with what she takes to be the character of the political as a central experience that needs to be thought about on its own terms. This in turn makes itself felt in the substantive treatments Arendt offers of the key experiential elements of politics, treatments that prove consistently non-reductive. Her unorthodox style, then, is far from capricious and in fact betokens an attempt to think about politics in a manner that encapsulates a fidelity to the political itself in all its contingency and humanity.

3

Given her reluctance to claim a methodological profile for herself, an account of Arendt's method must necessarily take the form of a recon-struction. In what follows, I will attempt to draw out and reconstruct, through readings of Arendt's works, a fuller sense of her conception of political theory as an engagement. I will seek to show that, for Arendt, to speak fruitfully about politics from a theoretical standpoint requires the adoption of a distinctive voice; one that incorporates a variety of idioms which combine to mediate the theoretical impulse and to bring our discursive resources into more proximate relation with the experience of politics itself. I will suggest that throughout her work, Arendt adopts this voice, modulated in crucial ways such as to provide an inflection that is peculiarly appropriate to the terrain of politics. And this distinctive way of speaking about the political, I will argue, poses a potent chal-lenge to established ways of theorising politics and presents a refreshing alternative to what have arguably become sterile debates.

The aim of reconstructing and characterising a distinctive method in her work is one that Arendt herself would probably have greeted with a degree of suspicion. Her reticence on the question of her method was something that she admitted could be considered a fault (Arendt 1979: 336). It nevertheless answered to real concerns that she harboured. She was reluctant to render herself liable to labelling in relation to estab-lished social scientific or philosophical schools of thought. Still less did she wish to be held up as providing a methodological model that could subsequently be applied in routine fashion: her injunction always was that we should think for ourselves. For these reasons, she preferred to let her approach disclose itself through her substantive theoretical engagements. However, I will argue here, in a manner that might allay suspicion, that the methodological approach discernible in Arendt's work, far from normalising her thought by assimilating it to established intellectual traditions, demonstrates its distinctiveness and throws into relief the challenge that it presents to more traditional ways of thinking. Equally, the method I seek to draw out of Arendt's work is not one that lends itself to mechanical reapplication: the modulated theoretical voice that she adopts constitutes, I will suggest, a discursive disposition which cannot be unthinkingly applied, incorporating as it does a sensitivity to the circumstantial that will not yield automatic results in application, and which therefore answers to the injunction to think for oneself. This does not mean, however, that there is nothing to be learned from a reflection on Arendt's approach: it might be seen as embodying a disposition that

4

can be emulated. It seeks to elicit, in this sense, a response that would see Arendt's own work less as an authority and more as an exemplar – very much in the way that Arendt herself responded to those whom she respected and chose to write about at length (Arendt 1968b).

In order to lay the groundwork for this analysis, it is worth focusing in a preliminary way on Arendt's conception of the relation between thinking and politics. In her early intellectual life, Arendt had no great interest in politics. Her early studies, under the tutelage of Martin Heidegger in Marburg and Karl Jaspers in Heidelberg, were orientated toward basic ontological questions, concerns that were combined with a strong interest in German romanticism. Things changed, however, with the rise of fascism in Germany, when Arendt was shocked into a preoccupation with political matters. The burning of the Reichstag in 1933 convinced her that one could no longer 'simply be a bystander' (Arendt 1994: 5). This did not mean that Arendt was inclined to become a political actor. She *did* act, being involved in a Zionist organisation in Germany (although she was never a committed Zionist) and subsequently, during her exile in Paris in the 1930s prior to her move to the United States, working for an agency helping young Jewish refugees. But she was never, she said, a 'political animal' (Young-Bruehl 1982: xxxix). She never craved the exposure in the public realm that she associated with the life of action; and to the extent that she later became something of a public figure through her work, she found such exposure distasteful. However, her attention as a thinker was drawn to politics. And at issue here was more than a simple revision of academic interest. It was Arendt's conviction that politics now merited *our* attention, and not just her own, because new considerations had come to light, revealed by the experience of totalitarianism. The turn to politics, in this sense, was not just a matter of interest but was also a matter of urgency.

The utterly novel phenomenon of totalitarianism brought to light, Arendt thought, the contingent and fragile character of the sphere of public action as a space of appearance and opinion. We can now see, she thought, that the public realm, if it is not sustained through active participation, may be lost entirely; and it is in this context that she sought a revision to the relation between political thought and the practical terrain of politics itself. The aim was to reflect upon the political in its fully contingent and circumstantial character, and thereby to understand better the potentialities and pitfalls of our ability to act in ways that are spontaneous and which can make a difference to our world. It was a study, by the same token, that would allow us to measure more effectively the full extent of what Arendt took to be the depoliticisation of modern society, a tendency which left us vulnerable to the 'anti-politics' of totalitarianism. The oppression and exile that Arendt herself suffered as a Jew in fascist Germany reflected in an acute form, she came to think, the experiences of disempowerment and homelessness that were characteristic of modern mass societies, with their conformist social imperatives and atrophied political culture, experiences upon which totalitarianism fed and took to extremes. In this light, for Arendt, it was an important feature of the engagement of political theory to find a voice in which to speak constructively about the problems that attend our threadbare political culture, themes that alert us to our vulnerability but which, on reflection, might also enable us to identify elements that would point to or illustrate the potential for more redemptive forms of action. The possibility of a political theory of this sort was tied up, for Arendt, with a departure from the traditional philosophical impulse to dictate to politics from a position of abstraction. The philosophical tradition that would seek to provide permanent answers to political questions and to identify the foundational moral principles upon which it can be thought to rest (principles abandoned with such remarkable ease under totalitarianism) now looks complacent. It may also, for Arendt, be a tradition of thinking that, historically, has colluded with the erosion of public space: in seeking conceptual finality, the tradition has embodied a kind of 'bypassing' of the political realm, a realm that is actually only sustained by the contingent exchange of opinion by active citizens.

Arendt did not think that there was no place for philosophical reflection in the manner of the tradition. It was more that we need to recognise now, in the light of recent experiences, that thinking about politics requires a different and more experientially sensitive voice: 'there may be truths beyond speech and they may be of great relevance to man in the singular, that is, to man in so far as he is not a political being' (Arendt 1958: 4).[2] And Arendt's work without doubt bears the marks of her philosophical background, particularly with reference to the tradition of phenomenology; but her specific orientation to the political and her adoption of an approach that reflected a desire to think in a way that incorporated a modal immanence with respect to politics makes it unhelpful to characterise her method in a way that depends upon resolving it by reference to broader philosophical approaches. Arendt's aim was to think in a mode that would reacquaint us with the distinctive fabric of political experience, gaining greater proximity to the political through the development of a manner of speaking that answers more closely to the discursive conditions of the public realm itself, recognising, as the tradition failed to do, 'that men, not Man live on the earth and inhabit the world' (Arendt 1958: 7).

The political, for Arendt, answers to the human condition of plurality. The public realm, where authentic politics takes place and freedom is enacted, is constituted by speech and action undertaken by plural beings in public view, interacting on the basis of autonomous viewpoints and freely-formed opinions. For this very reason, it is contingent: 'it comes into being wherever men are together in the manner of speech and action . . . wherever people gather it is potentially there, but only potentially, not necessarily and not forever' (Arendt 1958: 199). The public realm is not a given and so needs to be generated. This fragility has been thrown into relief by the erosion of the public sphere in modern mass societies and by the emergence of totalitarianism, which sought to destroy it altogether. In the light of this, there is no room for complacency in respect of how we think about politics. In particular, we must now avoid reductive ways of thinking that would seek to resolve the phenomenal character of politics into something more permanent by reference to eternal principles, natural categories or historical teleologies that would insinuate a sense that it is somehow guaranteed. Politics has no 'common denominator'; it cannot be indemnified theoretically, only sustained actively (Arendt 1958: 57). We need, therefore, to theorise politics in an idiom that answers to its distinctiveness as a practice and which bears, in its discursive character, the marks of a recognition that politics may be different from other human activities that can be thought to carry firmer guarantees of their place. This is reflected in Arendt's view that a true political theory must 'make the plurality of men, out of which arises the whole realm of human affairs . . . the object' and must speak accordingly (Arendt 1990: 103).

In what follows, I will seek to identify and explore what I take to be a consistent methodological commitment of this sort identifiable in Arendt's work. She sets herself against the dominant tradition by adopting what can be seen, at least from the point of view of that tradition, to be *mediations* of the theoretical voice which establish an authentically alternative way of speaking. The kind of proximity and immanence she seeks when thinking about politics do not cancel the distance that the theoretical standpoint adopts with respect to its object, a distance that provides the space within which suitable forms of ratiocination can occur: 'it is not uncommon for outsiders and spectators to gain a sharper insight into the actual meaning of what happens to go on before or around them than would be possible for the actual actors or participants, entirely absorbed as they must be in the events' (Arendt cited in Young-Bruehl 1982: xxxix). However, Arendt adopts a self-consciously mediated standpoint, modulating the voice of theory in such a way as to curtail the impulse toward philosophical abstraction, and correspondingly to curtail the temporal insensitivity that goes with it. I will seek to show that her approach incorporates two central mediations to the standpoint of the political theorist, which in turn lead to key modulations in the theoretical voice, mitigating its stridency and thereby developing a novel alternative. This self-consciously modulated way of speaking allows Arendt to retain a focus upon the phenomenological ground of politics itself.

I will suggest that this is achieved by identifiable mediations that combine to 'save the appearances' of the political. First, there is an epistemological mediation, serving to avoid conceptual closure, expressed in a situated, dialogic modulation of the theoretical voice, so that 'the results [of thinking] can be communicated in such a way that they lose the character of results' (Arendt 1994: 183). Second, and implied by the first, there is a temporal mediation, serving to avoid historical closure, expressed in a fragmented narrational modulation that answers to the recognition that 'political actions are meaningful regardless of their historical location' and that their resolution into a broader history represents the 'ruin' of their meaning (Arendt 1977: 81). These two forms of mediation provide for a way of thinking 'which employs neither history nor coercive logic as crutches' (Arendt 1968b: 8). This confers upon Arendt's thinking an intrinsically circumspect or 'tentative' character (Arendt 1979: 303). This is arguably in keeping with a concern to resist closure and to speak consciously in the light of recognition of irreducible plurality.[3]

I will seek to show that these mediations, embodied in Arendt's stylistic mix, constitute a method that displays the kind of deep consistency mentioned earlier. This is not to say that Arendt's thinking did not develop. Without doubt she progressed in terms of the substantive experiences that she addressed, and she refocused her interests. I will seek to demonstrate that there is, nevertheless, an overarching unity of purpose in her work, expressed through a methodological consistency. Having characterised this method in a preliminary way, attention will be given primarily, although not exclusively, to Arendt's most well-known analyses of aspects of the political in order to see how her method is applied. I will examine Arendt's approach to the totalitarian form of anti-politics in *The Origins of Totalitarianism* (1968a); to the nature of authentic political freedom in *The Human Condition* (1958); and to the capacity for new beginnings in *On Revolution* (1973). These cases illustrate Arendt's mediated and correspondingly modulated voice at work, and show how it delivers subtle and distinctive accounts of the phenomena concerned. In looking at these cases, we will see that the concern governing Arendt's approach is not that of the philosopher seeking conceptual finality, nor is it that of the political scientist or historian seeking explanatory closure of one sort or another. Her concern with politics developed, as we have noted, in the light of recent events that signalled a changed world, where our freedom is shown in its fullest contingency. Arendt's rethinking of political theory is therefore guided, I will argue, by a preoccupation with the present. The sense of continuity, or sometimes progress, that is insinuated by appeals to finality and closure do not match current experience and accordingly Arendt sought to think in a manner that avoided reductive resolutions of the political. In thinking politically, for Arendt, we dwell between past and future: recognition of this, again, is something that she thought answered to the newly revealed character of politics as undetermined with respect to the past and unpredictable with respect to the future.

An exploration of these themes brings out the distinctive nature of Arendt's contribution to political theory. It allows also for a critical assessment of some of the interpretations of Arendt's work that touch upon her method but which seek to relate her to more familiar approaches in political theory. There has, for example, been a tendency, not uncommon amongst commentators, to attribute to Arendt a method based upon narrative, held to be a potent alternative to the more mainstream analytical modes of theorising but which is by now itself somewhat conventional and provides for an unduly limiting characterisation of Arendt. By contrast, there has also been a tendency to assimilate her work more closely to the kind of thinking which seeks foundational principles that might ground a just political order, most often evident recently in deontological liberalism; an analysis that imposes an interpretive straightjacket that I will suggest curtails an appreciation of Arendt's achievement. Assimilations of these kinds, I will argue, fail to capture the innovative and challenging character of Arendt's thinking and constitute attempts to 'normalise' her work. By the same token, the discussion will bring out the scope of the salutary and potentially challenging alternative Arendt presents to the conventional methodological standpoints underlying much mainstream political theory.

What is the nature of this challenge? The dominant tendency is to frame the engagement of political theory in terms answerable to more 'basic' philosophical positions and, correspondingly, to derive appropriate methods from deeper epistemological presuppositions. It was noted some time ago by the political philosopher John Dunn, in terms which continue to resonate, that political theory framed in this way displays a characteristic disengagement from the experiential ground of its object, from real politics. For Dunn, 'most contemporary political philosophy . . . consists in . . . the bringing to bear of philosophy as an achieved academic practice upon the sorry conceptual disorder of public affairs' (Dunn 1990: 195). The result is an abstraction away from the recognisable terms upon which politics as a practice takes place in the world. Dunn's further point is that this tendency creates a sterility in political theory and in the methodological debates underlying it. In recent decades, for example, the principal methodological issues have arisen from contending epistemological positions associated with 'foundational' and 'anti-foundational' standpoints. Evidence of sterility here is to be found in the fact that not a great deal, in substantive terms, would seem to turn on these debates. The appeal to basic philosophical presuppositions, in the name of reforming the 'sorry disorder' of politics, has the effect of creating a theoretical distance between theory and its object such as to generate critical leverage; but a vocal distance of this sort, largely negating any proximity to the phenomenal character of the political itself, begins to look like an overrated virtue where significant epistemological disagreements do not issue much in the way of substantive disagreements and do not seem to warrant significant departures from what appears to be a broad consensus around conventional liberal democratic principles. If one considers the standpoints that have tended to inform contemporary debates, ranged across the epistemological divide, representing in various ways a deontological form of foundational liberalism on the one hand and non-foundational, communitarian forms of thinking on the other, there does not seem to be a great deal dividing them with respect to broad substantive political orientations. The implication of this is again well-captured by Dunn, who notes that the 'comforting resonance' between mainstream political theory and prevalent popular convictions may be 'less a token of the authority of political philosophy than of its radical domestication, its complete subordination to the dynamics of an existing ideological field'

(Dunn 1990: 195). Arendt did not concern herself a great deal with contemporary trends or influential schools of thought in political theory and she was completely uninterested in attempting in any way to locate her own work with respect to such trends or schools. However, it is unquestionably the case that her way of doing political theory resonates with the kinds of concerns expressed by Dunn and potentially provides a potent alternative to those approaches that have been prominent in the contemporary debate and which, in Arendt's terms, still answer in crucial ways to the philosophical tradition.

A further feature here, not unrelated to this consideration, is the lack of sustained attention that mainstream political theory gives to some of the problems that arguably attend modern democratic politics – phenomena such as civic disengagement, mendacious political discourse or widespread gullibility – features which, from the abstracted philosophical point of view, appear as problems too contingent to be met head on, but which were of deep and urgent concern to Arendt. If the theoretical distancing from its object, effected by making political theory answerable to basic philosophical concerns, proves somewhat nugatory with respect to its own critical promise, we may be led, as Arendt was, to a reconsideration of the relationship between theory and practice, or between thinking and acting. The proximity to the terrain of politics that Arendt's modulated voice achieves provides us with an exemplification of how to think about politics in a way that might allow a greater sensitivity to the texture of the political and, thereby, to allow more serious attention to issues about the health of our democratic political culture.

These themes will be developed in a discussion that will move through three stages. First (in Chapters 2 and 3), I will seek to draw out, characterise and explore Arendt's distinctive method. This will proceed from an analysis of her comments on the relationship between thinking and acting, and I will show that she sees the contrast between these two engagements in terms of a constitutive tension which underwrites the authentic viability of each. The connection between this and the modern vulnerability to totalitarianism will be examined and this will provide the basis for an understanding of how, in Arendt's view, modern political experiences have exposed the bankruptcy of our moral and intellectual traditions and, in the light of this, how a new sense of the potentialities and dangers associated with a contingent realm of political action has emerged. I will suggest that this realisation forms the basis for Arendt's desire to revise the manner in which we theorise politics, a revision that dispenses with prior philosophical assumptions and incorporates, in its formal character, a fidelity to the fabric of the political. These considerations, I will argue, make sense of the idiomatic characteristics of Arendt's writing that incorporate the key modulations to the theoretical voice in both epistemological and temporal terms, lending Arendt's approach a highly distinctive modal immanence.

In the second stage of the argument (Chapters 4, 5 and 6), I will examine the application of Arendt's method in respect of some of the key political phenomena that she addresses. I will analyse Arendt's exploration of the totalitarian form and will seek to show that her approach consciously avoids the kind of explanatory closure which would distract us from what she called the 'shock of experience', inviting us instead to engage in an ongoing reflection upon its implications for the crisis-ridden contemporary era (Arendt 1968a: viii). A further embodiment of Arendt's distinctive approach is to be found, I will argue, in her analysis of the concept of action, where she avoids making atemporal claims about human nature and instead looks at the issue wholly from 'the vantage point of our recent experiences' with a view to creating a space for dialogue that might renew, in the light of these new experiences, our sense of contingent political possibilities, and which might generate, thereby, the discursive resources suitable to addressing present problems (Arendt 1958: 2). A final substantive exemplification of Arendt's method will be explored in her account of the French and American Revolutions, showing her concern with the political significance of these phenomena 'for the world we live in' (Arendt 1973: 44). I will argue that her treatment of revolution, rather than seeking conceptual or explanatory finality, attempts to provide images of spontaneity that can form reference points for reflection and dialogue concerning the problem of new beginnings, bringing home to us the sense in which this problem is not one that can be solved theoretically, and pointing instead to the political realm of speech and action itself.

In the third stage of the argument (Chapters 7 and 8), I will explore some of the further implications of Arendt's distinctive theoretical approach. I will address the vexed question of what is sometimes seen as the 'missing' ethical dimension to Arendt's political theory. I will argue that Arendt's failure to provide an ethical blueprint applicable to politics is in no way an oversight. In a manner consistent with her more general method, she appeals neither to moral theory nor to tradition as sources of ethical constraint in politics, sources that might be susceptible to formulation in terms of a prior blueprint. Rather, for Arendt, it is in the very dynamic of political action and appearance itself that judgment arises as a form of constraint. In this sense, I will argue that the 'agonal' element in Arendt's conception of political action, far from preventing her developing a political ethics, provides the core of her ethical conception. These considerations will be supplemented by an account of what Arendt's approach implies for the role and responsibilities of the thinker in relation to politics. Through a comparison between the vocations of the actor and the thinker, an account of the burdens attendant upon attention to, and exposure in, the public realm will be provided. Arendt's comments on her own sense of the role of the theorist will be reviewed with these themes in mind.

The discussion will conclude with a review of the argument and will examine the challenges that Arendt's conception of political theory presents to more orthodox contemporary approaches, in both foundational and non-foundational forms. I will argue that Arendt provides us with potentially important correctives to the tendencies in modern political theory to resolve political questions, on the one hand, into questions of moral philosophy or, on the other, into questions of cultural convention. Each of these alternatives risks losing contact with the phenomenal terrain of politics itself, and therefore of losing the ability to deal profitably with the problems of the modern polity and our compromised democratic culture, problems that Arendt's method kept very much in the foreground.

Notes

1. For commentary on some of the controversies that Arendt's work provoked, see Young-Bruehl 1982: 223–33, 286–90, 305, 309–17, 337–78, 402–6, 412–30, 471.
2. When Arendt embarked, toward the end of her life, on what was to be her unfinished work on the life of the mind, she was, she said, returning to her first love (Young-Bruehl 1982: 327).
3. The argument here bears comparison with Margaret Canovan's characterisation of Arendt's method as combining the phenomenological analysis of experience with a fragmentary historiography. Canovan's principal concern, however, is with the substance of Arendt's work and she does not develop this methodological formula. (Canovan 1992: 4–5).

CHAPTER 2

Thinking and Acting

Toward the end of her life, Arendt's attention was focused very much on the study of the mind and mental faculties, culminating in her final, unfinished trilogy *The Life of the Mind* (1981). This has given some the impression that, following her early move away from philosophy toward politics, she later moved away once again from political questions toward a concern with the mental life. If this were so, then it might seem perverse to pursue the issue of Arendt's approach to political theory through a consideration of what she had to say about thinking, about matters that she took up once she had left political questions behind. However, the idea that Arendt made a second 'turn' of this sort is misplaced. Any survey of Arendt's work as a whole reveals the fact that a concern with the experience of thinking is a consistent theme throughout: from early pieces such as 'Understanding and Politics', first published in 1953, right through to 'Thinking and Moral Considerations' (1971), a piece which contained many of the ideas that were to inform *The Life of the Mind* itself, this thematic consistency is evident (see Arendt 1994: 307–27, 1971). This is not to say that Arendt's reflections on thinking did not develop. Her concern with the relation between thinking and acting was augmented, following her observation of the trial of Adolph Eichmann in 1961, with a commensurate concern as to the possible relation between thoughtlessness and evil, a question that she came to regard as being of central political importance (cf. Young-Bruehl 1994: 336; Bernstein 2000: 277). However, the preoccupation with thinking is consistent in Arendt's work, and her concern with this theme was equally consistently orientated toward the issue of the relation between thinking and the realm of action, and informed by contemporary political questions

14

rather than purely philosophical ones.[1] For this reason, an examination of how Arendt conceives of the relationship between thinking and acting is important in helping trace out the basis of her approach to thinking about politics.

Arendt's concern is with thinking as a form of reflection, rather than as technical or practical reasoning, and with its relation to worldly action; in essence, to politics. Her understanding of this relationship is by no means straightforward. There is clearly a sense, for Arendt, in which thinking and acting are closely interrelated, to the point where, at least in certain circumstances, thinking can become 'a kind of action' (Arendt 2003: 188). At the same time, there is also a sense in which thinking is far removed from the worldly realm: from a worldly point of view, we can generally see thinking as 'good for nothing' because 'it does not create values, it will not find out . . . what the "good" is, and it does not confirm but rather dissolves accepted rules of conduct' (Arendt 2003: 166, 188). In order to understand this seemingly paradoxical standpoint, we need to look at Arendt's conception of the standing of thinking in the contemporary world and the contrast to be drawn with previous conceptions. And this takes us back to her concern with the previously dominant philosophical tradition, the decline of which, she thinks, has had profound consequences, in intellectual terms, with respect to where we are now. The philosophical tradition that we have inherited can be regarded as misguided. What allows it to be thus regarded, however, are experiences that have conspired to create the modern situation, to create the standpoint from which we now have to look at these matters. These are experiences, moreover, in which the tradition itself can be seen to be implicated.

THINKING AND THE TRADITION

An understanding of the problematic circumstances now attendant upon thinking depends upon a sense of how the modern situation came about and, to this end, there is a story to be told concerning the collapse of the tradition. Nor is it just a story in the history of ideas. Thinking is an activity in the world amongst other activities: the story thus concerns construals of these activities and the relations between them. It invokes no causal historical logic: the attempt to invoke such logic is, for Arendt, a misguided enterprise and is in fact, as we shall see, indicative of the collapse of our tradition. Equally, the story that can be told offers no explanation through narrative completion or closure. For Arendt, the modern situation is characterised by a world changed in such a way as to defeat the narrative threads that might once have been offered by our historical tradition itself, something that the experience of totalitarianism makes apparent. Everything prior to the experience of totalitarianism Arendt looks on consciously with eyes that have seen it.

The tradition has shaped our sense of what it is to think and of how the practice of contemplative thought stands in relation to the realm of action. It was a tradition based upon the specific experience of the thinking ego; the sense we have that 'while a man indulges in sheer thinking . . . he lives completely in the singular . . . as though not men but Man inhabited the earth' (Arendt 1981/I: 47). In the light of this experience, the tradition, from Parmenides and Plato onwards, which established the long history of metaphysics, elaborated a relationship and hierarchy between the apparently unitary, authoritative voice provided by philosophical contemplation on the one hand, and the plural, opinionated voices of the many who occupy the practical world on the other. This was accompanied by a central ontological distinction between essence and appearance. Philosophical reflection, undertaken for its own sake and prompted by a sense of that which is essential and therefore eternal, transcended the fleeting realm of appearances. Contemplation provided access to a world beyond the contingent and the uncertain, and access therefore to ultimate truth beyond mere opinion. The ontological model underlying this conceptualisation was, as Arendt describes it, a 'two worlds' model, based upon a foundational distinction between the 'sensory' and 'suprasensory', such that 'whatever is not given to the senses – God or Being or the First Principles and Causes . . . or the Ideas – is more real, more truthful, more meaningful than what appears' (Arendt 2003: 163). For Arendt, this 'two worlds' view embodied a reification of the thinking experience; of the withdrawal from the ordinary course of events, and from the plural voices that sound around them. The special experience of the thinking ego, the non-appearing origin of thought, timeless and dimensionless, was taken as a basis for the assumption that such a withdrawal took one into a separate cognitive realm where phenomenal experience was reproduced and 'purified' and its eternal essence found. The philosopher's withdrawal into a realm of contemplation of the eternal was seen to give those who engage in it 'their share of immortality' (Arendt 1981/I: 47).

The nature of the experiential distinction drawn here immediately implied a hierarchy. The experience of contemplation provided a model for a kind of life – the quiet, contemplative life of the philosopher – that was intrinsically superior to the practical life (Arendt 1981/I: 44–7). It was a hierarchy expressed in Plato's cave analogy, drawing a contrast between the wise man who seeks truth in the light of the sun and the cave dweller who lives in a darkness illuminated only by fleeting images that are inconsistent and relative only to one's particular standpoint (Arendt 1990: 96). The practical life, lacking the certainty and the sense of permanence, the 'sheer quietness borne of the presence of truth' that contemplation can bring is equally 'laborious', a life where one is condemned to endless dealing with contingency and uncertainty (Arendt 1981/I: 6). In the absence of truth, one faces a context given only by the morass of variable opinions and interests that characterise everyday practical existence. This answers back to the underlying 'two worlds' conception: the contemplative life is not just *beyond* the practical, sensuous world but *above* it.

The hierarchy that the tradition established between different forms of experience and commensurate kinds of life also implies a further hierarchy. The life of contemplation is, of necessity, the life of the few; in part because only a few have the capacity (and the courage) to live it, and also because life lived as one of the many is intrinsically one lived in cacophonous conditions, where, if an orderly existence is to be possible, principles must be applied which pertain, as it were, from a position above the chaotic worldly realm, independent of a search for truth on the part of those who inhabit that realm (Arendt 1981/I: 81). The political implications of this conception are quite obvious: the recipe for a quiet polity, informed by wisdom, lies in the application of the results of philosophical contemplation to the disorder of the world in the form of a framework that defines the ideal political order and which carries intellectual authority rendering it independent of the compromising effects of plural opinion and conflicting interests.

This is an aspect of the tradition that arguably makes itself felt throughout the history of political philosophy, albeit in revised forms. However, there was an additional, and commensurate, political dimension to the 'two-worlds' tradition as Arendt sees it. The distinction between the 'chaotic' realm of mere appearances, upon which worldly interactions are based, and the realm of eternal wisdom, introduces equally a sense that the former constitutes a threat to the latter. For Arendt, the awareness of this threat is nowhere more evident than in the writings of Plato, informed by the trial and death of Socrates, accused by the Athenian state of corrupting youth as a result of his commitment to philosophical inquiry. So the worldly realm becomes a threat to the life of the philosopher not only in terms of the distraction caused by its haphazard changeability but also in terms of the suspicion in which those who seek to speak the language of eternal truth are likely to be held by the worldly – a factor also powerfully articulated in Plato's analogy of the cave (Arendt 1990: 94). As a result, if philosophy were to engage with worldly considerations at all, it must do so politically, by providing a recipe for eternal peace and harmony. Thus, for Arendt, Plato wrote *The Republic* in order to show how we can 'bring about in the commonwealth that complete quiet, that absolute peace, that . . . constitutes the best condition for the life of the philosopher' (Arendt 1982: 21).

In Arendt's understanding, then, the ambition of the philosophical tradition to legislate to the worldly realm, where politics pertains, has also been an ambition to quieten down this otherwise noisy realm for reasons that, on the 'two-worlds' view, answered to the (ultimate) interests of each side: legislation from above could mitigate the uncertainty and conflict characteristic of the life lived by the many whilst securing, by the same token, peace and security for the few. However, we can now see, she thinks, that this persistent attempt at metaphysical pacification may have had unfortunate consequences. The problem was internal to the tradition itself and the effects it had in the world. Emphasis upon withdrawal to a higher realm had a strong cultural impact that led to an 'unworldliness', marked by a failure to embrace worldly experience or to sustain the habits of being in a world of appearances. With the rise of Christianity, when 'philosophy became the handmaiden of theology', the image of contemplative withdrawal remained a touchstone for the best kind of life (Arendt 1981/I: 6, 139). The cultural impact of a mistrust of appearances and the recommendation of escape marginalised the capacity for freedom. The resultant conception of politics bound it to the practice of *rule*. What appeared to be the fragmented and chaotic political realm could be ordered by reference to the unitary voice of contemplative reason which legislates for a quiet life from a perspective wholly outside the political realm. The resultant image was one of command and obedience, again on the model of the experience of the philosopher, the one most capable of self-command. This ultimately lends a distinctively instrumental character to our politics. In Arendt's view it had been the key achievement of Plato to replace the image of politics as free action with that of politics as an instrumental undertaking, a matter of 'making' rather than acting, through the imposition of a blueprint. As Villa notes, this transposal may initially appear empowering, suggesting that the only limit upon the political agent is the available means to realise the end; however, in replacing the idea of action in a plural setting with a technical enterprise, to be undertaken by the expert, it is in fact deeply disempowering (Villa 1999: 196). However, the image remained dominant and its insinuation of the desirability of unworldliness helped rationalise the widespread abdication from the public realm that has been, for Arendt, a characteristic of our political history.

So there were deeply problematic aspects to the philosophical tradition. But in order to gauge the full significance of this, and where it now leaves us, we need to look first at Arendt's account of the decline and ultimate collapse of that tradition. The unpolitical promise of a quiet life through legislation from another world proved hollow; but the further implications of this need to be understood in the light of the intellectual and experiential currents that accompanied the very questioning of metaphysics in the modern period. For Arendt, we can detect the decay of the tradition historically at the point when philosophers themselves sought consciously to criticise its metaphysical basis. We see this most notably in the thought of Marx, whose rebellion against the tradition answered to aspects of the modern experience even before those aspects were fully manifest, a mark of his achievement (Arendt 1977: 31–5). In the work of Marx, we find a conscious attempt to reject the tradition by turning it on its head. For Marx, the elevation of contemplative thought over action had provided the basis for the ideological legitimation of prevailing socio-economic relations. A critical analysis of this form of legitimation established an agenda of action aimed at the revolutionary overthrow of an exploitative system. This was an agenda that could be defined and rationalised on the basis of a teleological theory of history, aimed at elaborating the historical dynamics which defined the practical route to the good society. Ultimately, however, Marx's rebellion against the philosophical tradition remained distinctively a *philosopher's* rebellion. In other words, his challenge to the tradition was one mounted from within the set of assumptions defining the tradition itself. There are three related aspects to Marx's thinking which demonstrate this in Arendt's view.

First, although Marx wished to overturn the hierarchical relation between thinking and acting that the tradition had instantiated, he nevertheless retains the idea that a hierarchy is to be asserted if the realms of thought and action are to be reconciled. In this sense, he retains the idea of an essential ontological distinction – a two-worlds conception

– that makes reconciliation a priority. Second, in privileging action over contemplation by means of a historical account that demonstrates how action, undertaken in the light of historically inscribed social positions, can realise the good society, Marx, far from liberating action as an autonomous capacity, rationalises it as a means to a predetermined end. In this respect, he reproduces in novel form the assimilation of acting to making, characteristic of the Platonic tradition. Third, as a result of this, the theoretically conceived ideal of the eternal city becomes something to be realised in action – but what is to be realised is an ideal expressed in terms of established verities of the sort that the tradition offered up as means of resolving the problems posed by the perceived haphazardness of the active life: an ideal of peace and plenitude that is depoliticised.

So Marx's rebellion against the tradition is framed in terms that retain central traditional assumptions. And this explains, for Arendt, some of the contradictions in his thinking. Marx 'leaped from philosophy into politics' in an apparent inversion of the tradition, but he did so whilst retaining the philosophical spirit (Arendt 1977: 30). Action became the answer but its demonstrability *as* an answer was in virtue of the theoretical gloss supplied by a dialectical theory of history, thereby 'making political action more theoretical . . . than it even had been before' (Arendt 1977: 30). In doing so, equally, the anti-utopian Marx places action at the historical service of a future utopia that bears comparison with the depoliticised ideal of the quiet life harboured by the ancient Greek philosophers of the Platonic school, where the tradition began.

Other great rebels, such as Nietzsche, Kierkegaard and later Sartre, challenged the tradition in different ways but in ways that paralleled Marx's failed assault: although they were rebels, 'they were still held by the categorical framework of the great tradition' (Arendt 1977: 28). They all, that is, maintained the conviction that the opposition between thought and action that the tradition took to be central required a 'resolution' through the dominance of one over the other. This particular sense of a resolution to the opposition between these two faculties, in fact, for Arendt, threatens to undermine each. At the same time, this is partly why, despite their failure, these rebels leave us 'better off'. The resulting hierarchies they introduced still contained, in a marked and prescient way, the idea of an *opposition*; which, in the light of the decline of the tradition, may strike us in a new way, not as 'two worlds' but as an internal differentiation in our experience: 'the very assertion of opposites . . . necessarily brings to light the repudiated opposite and shows that both have meaning and significance only in this opposition' (Arendt 1977: 35–6).We shall return to the more substantive meaning of this statement. For now, however, it is worth returning to the story that Arendt has to tell about our intellectual tradition and its demise; and in particular the contribution made by the rise of modern scientific thinking.

Here, the case of Marx is also instructive because his way of thinking and his particular rebellion against the tradition, invokes, in a politically relevant way, a form of modern scientific thinking. Marx's assertion of action as the means of the historical realisation of what previously could only be formulated in theory depended upon rendering thought and action relative to a socio-historical dynamic that was susceptible to scientific formulation. When Marx sought to abolish philosophy by realising it, he began subjecting thought as well as action 'to the inexorable despotism of necessity, to the "iron law" of productive forces in society' (Arendt 1977: 32). This social scientific motif resonates more generally with the rise of the scientific understanding that constitutes a further central element in Arendt's account of our tradition and its manifestations.

THE SCIENTIFIC MIND

A key part of the decline of the philosophical tradition, as it was inherited from the ancient world, was the rise of the modern scientific understanding, where the thinking activity was differently construed and in a form implying the questioning of metaphysics. Descartes, who was arguably the principal philosophical progenitor of the scientific point of view, argued that a solution to the continuing problem of doubt in the context of the apparent contingency of experience could lie in doubting itself. In this sense, he turned to the operations of the mind, the source of doubting, for a solution by reference to those products of the mind that provide us with results that are beyond question. The results were canons of scientific truth grounded in mathematical reasoning, in the 'faculty of deducing and concluding . . . a process which man at any moment can let loose in himself' (Arendt 1958: 283). This world view invoked an image of reality as consisting of hidden processes, governed by cause and effect, that could be comprehended by experiment and logical reasoning.

This new method of thinking, however, far from redeeming the promise of certainty in the wake of the implosion of the earlier philosophical tradition, reproduced that implosion in a new form. Scientific knowledge derives not from the direct evidence of the senses but rather from experiments devised according to the canons of the scientific mind itself; and so the scientific search for an objective reality 'confronts us only with ourselves' (Arendt 1977: 271). Fuelled by chains of calculative reasoning, scientific thinking models the world in ways that increasingly depart from anything that is familiar from meaningful everyday experience; under the influence of the scientific mind, the activity of thinking throws in its lot with a supposed ultimate reality that consists of processes that far transcend anything familiar, a reality that is not only resistant to visualisation but also turns out to be 'unthinkable' (Arendt 1977: 56). Once again, then, the attempt to generate knowledge through access to a cognitive field above and beyond the realm of phenomenal experience proves self-defeating: 'with the disappearance of the sensually given world, the transcendent world disappears as well, and with it the possibility of transcending the material world in concept and thought' (Arendt 1958: 288). Apparently, thinking only once more eroded its own experiential foundations by seeking to transcend the condition of plurality. The corresponding experience here is one of 'world alienation': the loss of the world understood as a meaningful context created by common understandings and comprehensible phenomena arising from the realm of appearances.

This difficulty has not led to the dislodging of the scientific attitude as the overarching intellectual motif. This is partly because science embodied not only a method of thinking but also the potential for a kind of acting, of changing the world (something which, in one guise or another and in one circumstance or another, it always has the potential to do). In its dependence upon the technique of experiment, the scientific attitude already insinuated an element of intervention with respect to the physical world. This mode of 'acting into nature' provided the basis for the rise of technology which, far from 'humanising' the world, rendered it ever more alien, unleashing man-made processes with the potential to run far beyond our control. In this sense, if science had the potential to be self-defeating, it did so through the threat of releasing forces of destruction. Again, for Arendt, there were profound political consequences attending these developments. Scientific knowledge depends upon the transcending of plural opinion and as such 'science moves in a realm where speech has lost its power' (Arendt 1958: 4). The result is a threat to the realm of appearances and so to public life. The claims to scientific knowledge of, and commensurate technological power over, nature are based upon the central theme of process which, again, contrasts with the spontaneous capacity for action. The image of politics as rule is reproduced here by reference not to metaphysical truth but to technocratic management and politics comes under the sway of projects in social engineering.

In a technological age, equally, the motif of process becomes influential with respect to our self-understanding, again making itself felt in the image of human history as a progressive process. Historical relations of cause and effect replace an understanding of human deeds as carrying meaning in and of themselves. So human activity becomes meaningful only to the extent that it can be understood as contributing to a process of historical development and this sets the terms for 'the modern escape from politics into history' (Arendt 1977: 78). The direct political result of this is vulnerability to totalitarianism. The helplessness of individuals in the face of overarching historical technological processes makes for a sense of 'superfluousness' that is taken forcibly to its limit in totalitarian regimes, which themselves place ideological emphasis upon historical and technological processes and which attempt to render persons, as thinking beings, superfluous to these processes (Arendt 1968a: 457). We now see how easy it is to lose our sense of ourselves, of our nature and potential, in the very process of being robbed of it (Arendt 1994: 316).

We can now see this in the light of the rise of the scientific world-view that seems at first to have happened in the abolition of the 'suprasensory', of metaphysics, leaving us only with the sensory world. But it is now apparent that things are not so simple. The abolition of the suprasensory jeopardises also the integrity of the sensory:

> once the precarious balance between the two worlds is lost, no matter whether the 'true world' abolishes the 'apparent one' or vice versa, the whole framework of reference in which our thinking was accustomed to orient itself breaks down. In these terms, nothing seems to make much sense any more. (Arendt 1981/I: 11)

This problem, brought crucially to light by totalitarianism, is the crucial defining difficulty in the contemporary period: 'our quest for meaning is at the same time prompted and frustrated by our inability to originate meaning' (Arendt 1994: 313). The central question here is what this prompts in terms of thinking in new ways, in a situation where we may have to measure without a yardstick, and important to this is how we rethink in a non-traditional manner the relation between thinking and acting. The break with tradition is not, for Arendt, simply a fact in the history of ideas but is part of our political history, an experience of a

23

changed world. Our commensurate concern now is not just with thinking about the world but with the position of thinking in the world.[2]

RE-THINKING THINKING

So, the legacy of the problematic history of the relation between thinking and acting, as expressed *in* both our thinking and our acting, remains with us. At the same time, the decline of our tradition presents us with a two-fold opportunity. First, the liberation that comes with that decline prompts us toward the possibility of rethinking our situation in terms not only beyond our tradition but beyond tradition per se. We can question, that is, the reliance upon traditional verities, a reliance that we now see may threaten our capacities both for free thinking and free acting. And this means that, intellectually, we can now 'look at the past with new eyes unburdened and unguided by any traditions and thus . . . dispose of a tremendous wealth of raw experiences without being bound by any prescriptions as to how to deal with these treasures' (Arendt 1981/I: 12). Second, the demise of the prevalent image of contemplative withdrawal held to be an experience available only to the few opens up the thinking activity to the many. Thinking may always involve a withdrawal of a sort but to the extent that we no longer see it, in the traditional manner, as an escape into a realm of special and exclusive insight, we can reconceive the thinking experience as one that remains rooted in concrete and common experience, to which we all have access (Arendt 1979: 303). This rethinking of thinking is therefore simultaneously democratising, such that 'every thinker no matter how eminent remains "a man like you and me", an appearance among appearances equipped with common sense' (Arendt 1981/I: 53).

The answerability of this reconceptualisation of the thinking experience to the shared capacity of initiation gives us a preliminary sense of the way in which, for Arendt, thinking may be seen as intrinsically related to acting, such that, as we noted, there may be circumstances where thinking becomes a kind of acting. We can now, in our precarious and liberated situation, see thinking as 'the other side of action' (Arendt 1994: 321). The liberation of thinking from the straightjacket of the tradition, from the injunction to search for an ultimate truth beyond appearances, allows us to understand the thinking experience more authentically as geared to the search for *meaning* in the world of appearances; and the generation of meaning in this context is rooted in the capacity for action. When released from the contemplative model, where speechless wonder is the motif, thinking can be seen as a mental dialogue of the self with the self; an activity 'in which I am both the one who asks the questions and the one who answers' (Arendt 1981/I: 185). So it is an individual experience that is nevertheless embryonically discursive and fitted for pertinence to the plural realm, the realm of action and appearance where the principal motif is dialogue: 'the thinking dialogue between me and myself suggests that difference and otherness, which are such outstanding characteristics of the world of appearances as it is given to man for his habitat amongst a plurality of things, are the very conditions for the existence of man's mental ego' (Arendt 1981/I: 187). I shall return to the question of what this means more specifically for Arendt's approach; the main point here, however, is that the criterion for this mental dialogue 'is no longer truth, which would compel answers to the questions I raise with myself' – instead, meaning is the issue. In formulating this view, Arendt appeals to the Kantian distinction between intellect and reason, albeit with inferences that Kant did not draw. The intellect can be understood as the capacity for cognition, for the acquisition of empirical knowledge; and this can be contrasted with the capacity to think, which 'is not inspired by the quest for truth but by the quest for meaning' (Arendt 1981/I: 15). Again, this allows a contrast with the tradition that sought criteria for thinking similar in form to those of the intellect, with the effect, for Arendt, of curtailing the articulation of meaning by forcing it to be answerable to the model of truth.

None of this means that thinking is no longer to be seen as dependent upon the capacity to effect a withdrawal from the realm of experience, from 'the exigencies of everyday life', which is otherwise ceaseless (Arendt 1981/I: 76). To think is always to 'stop and think' (Arendt 1981/I: 78). Thinking necessarily involves 'de-sensing': representing objects and experiences in the mind as 'thought objects' which can be brought into proximity with the abstraction of concepts, ideas and categories (Arendt 1981/I: 77). This withdrawal, however, owes its intellectual substance to its roots in the realm of appearances rather than to supposed access to a deeper truth beyond that realm. We can think, as it were, in the course of experiential 'exigencies': the de-sensing experience does not mean that we cannot think about 'a still-present somebody or something' (Arendt 1981/I: 78). The removal from the immediate experience of objects and events that thinking requires can therefore be achieved 'surreptitiously', in the thick of events; a fact that, for Arendt, demystifies the thinking experience and undermines its ontological distinctiveness: 'no matter how ... absent we are from what is close at hand, the thinking ego ... never leaves the world of appearances altogether' (Arendt 1981/I: 110, 2003: 165).

A recognition of the mutual bearing of thinking and acting is of particular moment, again, in view of recent experiences. The tradition, by making acting dependent upon contemplatively certified verities, did provide us with reference points and authorities by which to orientate ourselves in the world (albeit a depoliticised one). The demise of the tradition, therefore, threatened to leave us in circumstances where action (unused to its liberated condition) becomes thoughtless and thinking becomes increasingly irrelevant, where 'reality has become opaque for the light of thought and ... thought no longer bound to incident as the circle remains bound to its focus, is liable to become altogether meaningless or to rehash old verities which have lost all concrete relevance' (Arendt 1977: 6). And it is no accident that the redundancy of the tradition becomes fully apparent in circumstances that are equally conducive to the rise of totalitarianism.

It is of vital importance, in the light of this, that we appreciate and explore the mutual bearing of thinking and acting. Thinking requires a grounding in the worldly realm, whilst the resources that allow us to act coherently 'depend ultimately on the life of the mind' (Arendt 1981/I: 71). We can see thinking and acting, then, not as two worlds but as two contrasting but equally central aspects of our experience. The contrasting demands of thinking and acting may now be seen as characteristics of the condition of 'beings with a faculty enabling them to withdraw from the world of experience without ever being able to leave or transcend it' (Arendt 1981/I: 45). That they are not to be seen as representing two worlds does not reconcile them and they are best seen, in so far as they pertain to one and the same being, as existing in a tension, making contrasting demands upon one's resources: Arendt refers to the 'intramural warfare' between our engagement with the world of appearances on the one hand and with thinking on the other (Arendt 1971: 425). To talk of a tension between thinking and acting, rather than just a distinction, is equally to suggest that the two experiences have a common origin in our experience. For Arendt, each represents a form of 'free movement', making for the kind of escape from necessity that is characteristic of our humanity (Arendt 1968b: 9). The loss of established 'yardsticks' promises the possibility of a new, freely formed standpoint; a new beginning.

And this possibility, for Arendt, answers to the decisive human capacity for initiation: 'a being whose essence is beginning may have enough of origin within himself to understand without preconceived categories and to judge without the set of customary rules' (Arendt 2003: 321). In turn, understanding the thinking/acting distinction as an internal tension allows us to make sense of ways in which thinking may bear upon acting, their fundamental differences notwithstanding; this is best described as a 'constitutive tension', where the relation of tension is constitutive of each term in that relation.[3] The rootedness of thinking in the experiential realm of appearances, with the concomitant implication of the democratisation of the thinking experience, is especially significant if, as Arendt believes, thinking may be related to moral questions and to the capacity to tell right from wrong. This particular pertinence of thinking to acting can be understood in relation to the two central capacities that Arendt associates with the life of the mind: conscience and judgment.

THINKING AND MORAL FACULTIES

Although thinking produces no moral axioms, instead rendering all beliefs questionable, it may nevertheless activate conscience. As an internal dialogue of the self with the self, thinking enacts a bifurcation in consciousness, a 'difference within an identity given within consciousness' (Arendt 1981/I: 193). This differentiation depends upon the fact that we are also beings in the world (without which thinking would have no object) and it may become pertinent to what we do in that there may be some things that we might do that, in solitude, we cannot accept. There may, in this sense, be actions that, if committed, would create a situation where one could not live with oneself. The act of murder, for example, may create such a situation: 'who would want to live with a murderer? Not even another murderer' (Arendt 1981/I: 188).[4] Conscience may not be a guide to action, depending upon an experience too internalised to answer to the plural conditions of the public realm (a point to which I shall return); but it potentially furnishes us with a measure of reflective independence. The criteria provided by conscience 'will not be the usual rules recognised by multitudes and agreed upon by society, but [will determine] whether I shall be able to live with myself in peace when the time has come to think about my deeds and words' (Arendt 1981/I: 191).

In addition to conscience, thinking also underwrites the capacity for judgment. Thinking liberates us to look at things anew and so to subject them to reflective judgment in the Kantian sense: judgment in the absence of determining concepts or rules. This is not to say that judgment in this sense is purely subjective or idiosyncratic. The de-sensing dimension that we have seen to be central to thinking makes possible a 'stepping back' from the immediacy of experience, such that we are able to see things not only from our own point of view but equally in the light of the imagined standpoints of others: in judging, we exercise the imagination and allow it 'to go visiting' (Arendt 1981/I: 257). So judgment, then, transcends the particularity of individual prejudice or personal interest, not by reference to abstract concepts but to the putative standpoints of others. This is what gives judgment its objectivity. But it is not the 'safe' objectivity that comes with the appeal to authoritative concepts. Its objectivity is grounded in the capacity to adopt an 'enlarged mentality', taking into account the perspectives of others; and the result is not the authoritarian pronouncement seeking the certification of a truth-claim but the expression of an opinion that is an appropriate contribution to an ongoing discourse (Arendt 1981/I: 297). Judgment overcomes the subjectivity of our perceptions by the expedient of looking at the world mediated by the possible standpoints of others who look at it too. It is this, equally, that gives judgment its essential characteristic of communicability; it is a capacity that becomes 'visible' in the public realm as an opinion to be shared and discussed, a view that seeks the consent of others in non-ideally regulated discussion about how the world should be and what we wish to see in it. In this sense, the articulations of judgment contrast with the motif of compulsion that accompanies truth-claims, which short-circuit the discursive. The principal substantiation that judgment claims, comes by reference to examples, which themselves arise from acts of judgment, rather than acting as prior determinants.

The form of objectivity to which judgment has a claim is the non-traditional form of 'impartiality' with respect to differing points of view; a standpoint that we can see as occupying a space *between* rather than *above* contending viewpoints (Arendt 2003: 242). As a result, judgment, as Arendt understands it, remains closely connected with the realm of particulars – of objects, persons and events as they make themselves apparent to us in the practical realm (Arendt 1981/I: 258).[5] Judgment is the mental faculty that answers to the condition of plurality. Its basis and the source of its claim to validity are to be found not within the self but in the world, in our shared phenomenal experience. In this way, judgment finds its grounding in an appeal to what Arendt, again following and adapting Kantian thinking, terms 'common sense' – our common perception of a comprehensible and meaningful world that we share – the faculty that fits our senses into a shared experiential sphere and enables us to orientate ourselves within that sphere (Arendt 2003: 166).

It would be wrong, however, to overstate the substantive depth of common sense in Arendt's account. It remains a 'thin' notion, distinguishing her position from that of a 'communitarian' view broadly conceived. Common sense makes communicable judgment possible but it does not determine the content of judgment. The evidence for the existence of a common sense of this sort is in the existence of language, which delivers a communicable world in which we can exist intelligibly with others.[6] It remains instantiated, however, in the form of communicable opinions, whose communicability, whose fitness for discussion, is given in that it considers the standpoints of those who share our world with us. The specifics of Arendt's conception of judgment have been the subject of sustained analysis and may be of ethical significance in respect of Arendt's theory of politics; but I will explore these implications in Chapter 7. For now we can note that it represents a form of thinking that would seem to answer to the condition of plurality and so brings thinking into proximity with the realm of action.

THINKING, ACTING AND CONTEMPORARY EXPERIENCE

This is of significance with respect to Arendt's conception of the thinking/ acting relation, and how we are to understand this relation in the light of recent experiences which confirm the idea of a constitutive tension. Thinking and its product in judging, as mental operations, require a withdrawal from the realm of experience. Thinking, then, must always stand in a tension with the realm of practical experience; but we can now see, in the light of the demise of the tradition, that it has no other basis than that of the shared experiential realm itself. However, the dependence of the capacity to think upon the practical realm does not guarantee their possible 'reconciliation'. The lapse of the tradition has drawn attention to this. The tradition asserted an ontological gulf between thinking and acting which, ironically, made reconciliation possible through the legislation that one could provide for the other – whether the legislative solution was framed in Plato's terms or in Marx's. When we see thinking and acting as having a common root, as existential orientations available to thinking beings who equally, and correspondingly, inhabit a common world in which they appear phenomenally, we can begin to see the way in which each may be pertinent to the other, not in terms of a rapprochement but in a permanently problematised sense, challenging the complacency inherent in each. Thinking may challenge the unreflective process into which action may, by virtue of its nature, always fall as it sets off potentially uncontrollable chains of cause and effect; action may present a challenge to the life of the mind that shakes us out of the routine acceptance of intellectual traditions and customary ways of thinking.

The exposure of this thematic concern is doubly tied, for Arendt, to experiences of the collapse of our philosophical and moral tradition on the one hand and, on the other, to the events of the twentieth century that made this collapse evident to us, most specifically in the experience of totalitarianism, which brought to light how easily our established ways of thinking and the principles that were central to them could be jettisoned. Our tradition, in Arendt's view, has been informed by the temptation to search for results that would be reliable and would make further reflection unnecessary, such that we 'hold fast to whatever the prescribed rules of conduct might be' (Arendt 1981/I: 177). As we now know, however, the complacent view that abstract thought can supply us with results that will do in perpetuity, is only ultimately a recipe for thoughtlessness. And we have no better example of this than that of Nazi Germany, where, with great ease, new and traditionally counterintuitive principles were applied, suggesting that 'everyone was fast asleep when it occurred' (Arendt 1981/I: 177). The fact that, following the Nazi period, traditional moral verities were readopted with an ease comparable to their earlier abandonment only goes to confirm the fragility of our capacity to think freely. And it was the phenomenon of thoughtlessness that ultimately led Adolph Eichmann to commit 'evil deeds . . . on a gigantic scale, which could not be traced to any particularity of wickedness, pathology, or ideological conviction in the doer, whose only personal distinction was a perhaps extraordinary shallowness' (Arendt 2003: 159).

The loss or abdication of the ability to think is a central and decisive feature of our modern experience. Thoughtlessness points us equally to the loss of a common sense, also a feature of totalitarian conditions, and also, therefore, to the loss of the ability to judge. So we are now aware that the contingent intersubjective reference point of common sense that we may have appealed to in order to engage the capacity for judgment is also fragile.[7] Arendt invokes the idea of 'dark times', to describe a condition where we experience an erosion of the capacities both for free action and for free reflection on our experience; where these two capacities, as we have seen, become disconnected and where potentially, as a result, we conceive of a spurious reconciliation between them through legislation from one to the other. It is characteristic of Arendt's approach, however, that it is when central human capacities are most under threat, most in danger of emasculation, that they are most fully revealed in their true character, depth and significance. It is in our context of 'dark times' that autonomous and undetermined capacities for thought and action, crucially jeopardised, become most visible and worthy of comment. Correspondingly, the capacity for judgment, so often neglected in the tradition of political philosophy, shows itself simply because it is so much under threat. As Wellmer notes, Arendt's theory of judgment is also 'at the same time a theory of the corruption of judgment in our time' (Wellmer 1997: 35).

So, the question of how we think is simultaneously a question of how we approach the engagement of thinking in *our time*, knowing what we now know. It may seem initially perverse, therefore, that Arendt finds a model of the thinking experience in the ancient world. Socrates, in Arendt's view, appears to us as a key representative figure, instructive with respect to a reconnection with authentic thinking, and he does so because he represents an approach to thinking that *precedes* the tradition to which Arendt wishes to mount a challenge – despite the ironic fact that the most authoritative contribution to our depoliticising philosophical tradition is to be found in Plato, whose desire to transcend politics was a response to the death of Socrates at the hands of the Athenian state. The irony is sharpened and complicated in that Plato's Socratic dialogues themselves demonstrate the importance of what Socrates represents as a thinker, even though Plato's aim in transcending the realm of opinion and persuasion is anti-Socratic.

The dialogues are aporetic and demonstrate, therefore, a commitment to authentic free thinking. Socrates presents us with an example that provides a contrast in a modern context with the 'professional philosopher', who seeks authoritative final results. His desire was 'to check with his fellow men to learn whether his perplexities were shared by them . . . and this is quite different from the inclination to find solutions to riddles and then demonstrate them to others' (Arendt 1981/I: 172). Socrates' engagement was, in this sense, fundamentally discursive, taking the realm of opinion seriously and treating opinions as the subject matter of thinking; to be reflected upon, discussed and criticised. The purpose of the enterprise was not to destroy opinion through reference to higher truth but rather to bring out the elements of meaningfulness in our opinions through dialogue. In this way, Socrates' engagement with his fellow citizens in the marketplace introduced an instructive 'impurity' into thinking and into discourse (Villa 1997: 187). The salutary contrast here is again with the search for a pure or unimpeachable truth, a search that has subsequently regulated our tradition of political philosophy. In Arendt's account, Socrates, in combining the roles of thinker and inter-locutor, was able to stimulate the capacity for thought in others who may otherwise remain unreflective; to purge them of unexamined opinions; and to 'unfreeze the accepted concepts and definitions they harbour – and this without the aim of 'giving them truth', of replacing one set of verities with another (Arendt 2003: 173–6). In this, Socrates' engagement was given in 'knowing that we don't know and still [being] unwilling to let it go at that' (Arendt 2003: 175). As an exemplar of pre-traditional think-ing, Socrates provides us with a guidepost for post-traditional thinking. The discrediting of the tradition lends credence to Socrates' commitment to thinking as the 'unfreezing' engagement that is resultless and which produces only endless communication.

Interim Summary

In the light of Arendt's persistent engagement with the question of think-ing and acting, we can bring out a series of thematic emphases that pertain to the thinking experience which are entirely interrelated but which it is useful to disaggregate for analytical purposes. In particular, there are five considerations which prima facie do not always appear wholly consistent with one another but when taken together amount to a conception of the thinking experience that is coherent and which carries implications for an understanding of political theory.

First, we can see thinking as an experience answering to the condition of plurality. Thinking and acting are, for Arendt, fundamentally different and potentially at odds. Thinking answers to the condition of solitude, where one can engage in an emancipated dialogue with oneself, free from the conditions of action, of appearance before others. At the same time, however, this experience of withdrawal is itself substantiated by the expe-riences that arise in the realm of appearances, upon which one can reflect. In this way, thinking carries a pertinence to the plural realm of action. We can say that thinking, as an internal dialogue, *anticipates* embryonically the realm of action. We can also say that it *reflects* that realm residually in the context of withdrawal. Both statements are equally valid, and their equivalence reflects the fact that no hierarchy exists between thinking and acting. The tension between them can be seen, again, as intramural warfare. In their different and potentially conflicting ways, they answer to the existential condition of beings who act in a world of appearances from which they are capable of reflective withdrawal intrinsic to thinking. At the same time, thinking actually requires and implies linguistic interaction, which propels us back into the phenomenal world: 'because man exists only in the plural . . . his reason . . . wants communication and is likely to go astray if deprived of it' (Arendt 1981/I: 99). This confirms the pertinence of one to the other, simultaneously problematising and productive; but productive in what sense?

A second central theme here for Arendt is the very 'unproductiveness' of thinking: 'the quest for meaning [is] absent from and wholly good for nothing in the ordinary course of affairs, while at the same time its results remain uncertain and unverifiable' (Arendt 1981/I: 88). Thinking, for Arendt, is like Penelope's web: it needs, on each occasion, to be re-enacted from the start. However, if thinking is indeed, as we have seen, 'good for nothing' in the practical realm, it is so on the terms that the practical realm itself sets down; it achieves nothing, but this may be precisely the source of its power. As we have seen, in Arendt's account, where thinking is put to the service of worldly results as it was in the tradition, it fails us because it loses its independence, and therefore loses its potency as a human engagement that proves forceful in the public realm just because it does not conform. It is this non-conformity with the practical realm, a realm that so easily falls into routine conformity, that gives the thinking activity its active character.

Third, the above consideration underlies Arendt's view of thinking as 'active' in the manner of being *salutary*. The withdrawal from the course of events it requires means that thinking always constitutes an interruption: again, thinking demands a 'stop and think'.[8] The thinking activity places us in what Arendt characterises, in terms taken from Kafka, as a 'gap between past and future', a gap peculiar to the operation of the mind, where we are liberated from the otherwise continuous experience of events (Arendt 1977: 12–13). The idea of an interruption here again confirms a certain congruence between thinking and acting. Further, it is a congruence that allows for the challenging stimulus that each may

33

present to the other. Authentic action, the power of practical initiation, challenges our categories of thought; but equally, and especially where the capacity for action recedes or is under threat, original thinking may interrupt the routine that action can always instantiate.

Fourth, the salutary power of thinking depends upon its autonomous exercise. It is akin to a muscle that requires exercise if it is not to atrophy. In the situation that we now confront, informed by a sense that the tradition of political philosophy, which offered us apparently solid intellectual foundations, turned out to be unable to find application to or supply answers for the practical realm, this kind of non-indemnified exercising of the capacity for thought would seem to require thinking against the tradition, liberating us from the ultimately debilitating sense of certainty that the tradition offered (Arendt 1977: 14). It appears to require that we think, in Arendt's often quoted expression 'without a banister' (Arendt 1979: 336). And it is this manner of thinking, liberated from the con-straining requirement of the search for truth and the appeal to the author-ity of traditional verities, which releases the capacity for independent judgment and the authentic exchange of opinions.

Fifth, the fact that the anti-traditional theme in Arendt's account of the thinking experience is underwritten and justified by our most recent experiences with respect to the thinking/acting nexus and the political implications that appear to have followed from the traditional neglect of their interrelation, demonstrates the sense in which her reflections on this question are themselves contextually informed. This relates to what we have now become aware of: Arendt's approach, in this respect, finds something of a model in the thinking of her friend and mentor Karl Jaspers, whose thinking remained 'wholly within the sphere of our most recent experiences' and was orientated toward 'the world and the people in it' as we now know them (Arendt 1968b: 78–9).[9] Thus, for Arendt, thinking, including thinking about thinking, if it is to have any relevance to politics, is situated and poses itself against the claims of the 'eternal'. Arendt's anti-traditional standpoint, then, is consciously one that seeks to avoid providing precepts that might be invoked as the basis for a new 'tradition' that would supply, in the form of decisive formulations, a cognate replacement for the old one.

These interrelated features of Arendt's conception of thinking and its relation with acting combine to establish a distinctive position, resistant to the tradition and orientated toward the all-important concept of judg-ment. It establishes a contemporary, contextualised sense of the activity of thinking, released from traditional constraints and allowing us to adopt the position of judge with respect to human affairs without ever coming up with final verdicts but always with newly formed potential answers. I will now proceed to an analysis of what this means for Arendt's more specific way of doing political theory, and the character of the voice that she adopts as a non-traditional political theorist; something that lies already implicit in the reflections in this chapter. For Arendt, as we have seen, language is the central capacity that allows us to forge a link between the invisible realm of thought and the public realm of appearances (Arendt 1981/I: 108). In view of this, how the theorist speaks is a central key to arriving at an understanding of the nature and purpose of political theory as Arendt sees it.

NOTES

1. Steinberger puts it well when he says that 'current scholarship perhaps overestimates the sense in which *Life of the Mind* was for Arendt a departure, a return to "philosophy", and thus underestimates the sense in which it continues and supports her central project in "political theory"' (Steinberger 1990: 804). In similar vein, Vollrath comments that Arendt's question about thinking is not, what is thinking? But rather, what does it mean for the world that it includes persons with the capacity to think? (Vollrath 1977: 177).
2. On this, see Kohn (1997: 162).
3. I would concur with Biskowski's claim that the thinking/acting distinction has an important heuristic role in Arendt's work in alerting us to internal differences and tensions within our experience. I would depart, however, from his further suggestion that Arendt is 'too much in thrall to her own distinctions', such that she retains a categorical ontological distinction between the realms of thinking and acting, only reversing the priorities between them (Biskowski 1993: 872–3). As we have seen, Arendt interprets the 'philosophical rebels' such as Marx and Nietzsche precisely as retaining the ontological distinction whilst inverting the hierarchy, and so retaining the traditional terms of the distinction. By contrast, her own problematisation of the thinking/acting relation is aimed at questioning the tradition in which the distinction is framed whilst without thereby simply effacing the contrast. It is in this sense that I think the characterisation of Arendt's sense of the contrast as a 'constitutive tension' is useful. Equally I would question Villa's claim that there are 'moments' in Arendt's work where she seems to point to a 'rapprochement' between the *vita contemplative* and the *vita activa* (Villa 1999: 205). The term 'rapprochement' is difficult here, if the implication is of a kind of reconciliation between the two realms of experience. Arendt seems quite consistently to maintain that they are different in a manner that points to a tension, only insisting that the difference between them was not ontologically grounded in the sense offered by the tradition. The only exception to this, where something perhaps resembling a reconciliation is indicated, is Arendt's essay 'Philosophy and Politics' (1990), where the idea of dialectical discussion is invoked as a route to truthfulness.

35

What Arendt really means here is not entirely clear, but it could perhaps be understood as providing a reference point of truth that could be action-guiding.

4. On this point, Arendt draws upon Aristotle's view that it is characteristic of 'base people' to be 'at variance with themselves' (Arendt 1981/I: 189).

5. On the distinction between impartiality and traditional objectivity, see Vollrath (1977).

6. It can be seen, in this sense, as 'the epistemological condition of humanity *qua* human' (Burks 2002: 19).

7. The 'thin' character of common sense, as Arendt sees it, means that it cannot be reduced to a set of commonly held, or imposed, rules or understandings. But such rules or understandings may be generated through ideological manipulation. As Wellmer notes, common sense proves itself when it provides a basis for judgments that challenge established opinions and concepts (Wellmer 1997: 34).

8. I think that it is overstating Arendt's case here to say, as Steinberger (1990) does, that in the absence of original thought, agents become 'mindless zombies'. It is rather that where the capacity for independent thinking and judging is eroded, our reflections can become routine, uncritical and conventional, in the sense of answering in an undistanced manner to the processes in which we find ourselves caught up. This may equally express itself in the desire not to think about some things.

9. This feature also underlies Arendt's treatment of intellectual history, which some have regarded as cavalier. When Jaspers dealt with the 'great philosophers' he did so in a 'non-traditional' way, rejecting any reference to sequential logic suitable to generating a traditional 'history of ideas'. Instead, he 'converted the succession in time into a spatial juxtaposition, so that nearness and distance depend no longer on the centuries which separate us from a philosopher but exclusively on the freely chosen point from which we enter this realm of the spirit' (Arendt 1968b: 79–80). In this sense, Arendt has no problem with involving historical figures, no matter how distant, in the light of what we can learn from them with respect to themes that answer to our current concerns.

CHAPTER 3

Theory and Method

The first two aspects of Arendt's revision to the relation between thinking and the public realm enumerated in the previous chapter – the need for political thinking to be sensitive to the irreducibly plural character of the political, and the recognition of the fact that the latter constitutes a realm where thinking is, in the strictest terms, 'good for nothing' – establish the need for an approach capable of answering to the public realm, what we can characterise as an approach that, at least from the point of view of the tradition, incorporates an epistemological mediation. The idea of thinking as a salutary interruption with respect to the public realm also corresponds with this requirement, but already alerts us to another mediation in respect of the relation between theory and practice: one that emerges from the further features that we have identified from Arendt's account of the relationship between the two engagements. The sense that thinking is now required to be thinking against the tradition, without support of traditional intellectual reference points, and, along with this, the recognition of the fact that our very awareness of this requirement has been made available by our recent, world-changing experiences, allows us to consider a further mediation in the light of what unexpected events may have to say to us; what we can refer to, again in the light of opposition to the tradition, as a temporal mediation. I will suggest in this chapter that these mediations play a significant role in understanding how Arendt goes about the business of political theory.

The unorthodox character of Arendt's political theory has been widely noted and one of the most common ways to accounting for this is through reference to the narrative form as the basis of her theoretical engagement. It has been argued that Arendt's political thought can be seen as encapsulating a commitment to the narrative form as a methodological touchstone. This is an interpretation which may place Arendt outside the contemporary mainstream (or much of it), but it nevertheless arguably limits our sense of her approach. Disch, for example, emphasises the 'narrative strategy' that she sees Arendt adopting with the aim of engaging the critical faculties of an audience: an 'explicitly moral storytelling' (Disch 1993: 679, 682).

I will return in more substantive terms to the question of the role of narrative in Arendt's work later in this chapter. It is worth noting at this point, however, that it raises an issue that has more general significance in terms of Arendt's approach. The claim that the use of narrative constitutes a definitive *formal* characterisation of Arendt's method is unconvincing. It is only *one* formal device in her discursive armoury. As Pitkin points out, a lot of what Arendt does is simply not narrative (Pitkin 1998: 277). In fact, an important element in her work comprises the kind of discussion we would tend to associate with more familiar theoretical devices: she analyses concepts, draws distinctions, makes claims and draws inferences. These elements are, however, combined with other more unorthodox techniques to form a broad stylistic assemblage. This suggests that it is unlikely that any attempt to pin down and characterise Arendt's methods simply by reference to particular formal quality will succeed.

However, the very internal diversity of Arendt's approach points us in another, potentially more fruitful direction. The fact that Arendt seems to seek the curtailment of any one formal element through mediation by others may say something about the reflexive standpoint that her work embodies, the sense it incorporates of the relation between theory and its object. This re-engages the account of the relation between thinking and acting that we looked at in the previous chapter. We saw that Arendt's account of the tradition that privileged the contemplative over the active distorted our sense of the relation between the two and, we can now see, threatened to undermine both the relevance of thought and potency of action. This recognition encourages us, in Arendt's view, to reconceive the thinking/acting relationship as one of greater proximity, but a proximity that does not imply their reconciliation, which can only be asserted at the price of the effective annihilation of one term in the relation through its answerability to the other (and the loss of any sense of a tension between them). We are therefore pointed toward a sense of pertinence between activities that are nevertheless fundamentally different and may sometimes stand in a problematic relation.

Finding a non-annihilating sense of the proximity between thinking and acting is the fundamental challenge that Arendt seeks to meet. And from a theoretical point of view, we might express this generally in terms of finding an idiom in which to speak that, whilst incorporating a sense of the distance between theory and its object, providing space within which appropriate forms of ratiocination and critical reflection can occur, captures also a non-transcendent sense of proximity to the object. It is equally a challenge that comes into focus the more we think specifically of the relation between thinking and acting in respect of politics (always the concern underlying Arendt's analysis of the tradition). The requirement is to retain, in theory, a suitable fidelity to the experiential terrain of the political itself. And for Arendt, experience shows up for us the phenomenal nature of politics as a contingent realm of appearances characterised by plurality.[1] So we need to find a theoretical voice that incorporates fidelity to this terrain, that 'saves the appearances' of the political. For Arendt, this challenge is met in the context of a response to and a rejection of the tradition, whose nature and historical effects, after all, define the challenge itself. And in this context, against the backdrop of the urge to abstract away from the finely grained and contingent aspects of our experience by reference to the adoption of the transcendent theoretical voice, the imperative is to mediate that impulse and so to bring the theoretical voice into a more immanent relation to the experience of the political.

The concept of *mediation* – with its implications of intercession by way of bringing about a level of agreement between disputatious voices or standpoints – looks appropriate with respect to what Arendt is seeking to do in methodological terms, and is in conscious opposition to the strident, unitary voice of traditional theory. The corresponding concept, applicable more particularly to the theoretical voice and which might redeem this methodological commitment, articulating this sense of mediation, is that of *modulation* – a transposal that would seek to bring the voice in tune with another pitch or register. The concept has a metaphorical application, deriving from its origins in the sphere of music, but is appropriate in characterising Arendt's concern with how to use language and idiom in a theoretical sense that is resonant with its object. I want to suggest here that Arendt's approach involves crucial modulations aimed at realising a suitably mediated and so ontically *reformed* theoretical standpoint.

This sense of modulation answers to Arendt's sense of our condition as beings capable (principally through speech) of genuine public appearance, and also capable of withdrawal into the life of the mind (and where each of these experiences is dependent upon the other). As we saw in Chapter 2, the assertion in light of this of a two-worlds theory, where an ontological distinction is drawn is, in Arendt's view, a long-standing (and now evident) error; what she asserts instead is an experiential differentiation internal to our common ontological condition. This differential however has ontic implications with respect to how we theorise the public realm – implications that, as we have seen, lead her to resist the reduction of political theory to foundational philosophy. Thinking and acting need each other; but not in the sense that either resolves the other, rendering it routine and unproblematic (the promise of the tradition and also of its 'rebels'). Rather, the tension between them is permanent; but it is a tension that answers to our condition of spontaneity, where our experiences remain, as it were, permanently unresolved and our engagements unfinished. The modulation to the theoretical voice that Arendt seeks amounts to an attempt to find a way of speaking that accommodates a sense of this permanent tension. In more specific terms, therefore, Arendt seeks a voice that reflects a more proximate relation to the contingent and spontaneous terrain of politics.

This marks the search for a 'true' political theory that makes 'the plurality of men out of which arises the whole realm of human affairs . . . the object' (Arendt 1977: 103). We must now see political theory as embodying the search for contingent meaning rather than absolute truth (Arendt 1981/I: 62).[2] As such, 'it leaves no final results behind it and provides us with no solid axioms or moral truths' (Arendt 1971: 425). This aim of speaking discursively in the light of the realm of contingency makes sense of two specific forms of theoretical mediation incorporated in Arendt's work and which imply corresponding modulations to the theoretical voice. The modulations which are most evident in Arendt's work and which answer to corresponding general mediations appear intertwined, but here I will separate them out for purposes of analysis. Each implies the other and so neither on its own is sufficient to provide an account of the distinctiveness of Arendt's method. Each separately, and both together, gain expression in a range of stylistic nuances that I will review toward the end of this chapter.

THEORETICAL MEDIATIONS AND VOCAL MODULATIONS

We have seen that Arendt's approach to political theory involves the adoption of a reflexive relation to its object: 'political thought can only follow the articulations of political phenomena themselves, it remains bound to what appears in the realm of human affairs' (Arendt 1973: 19). To say this is to say more than simply that political theory should remain focused on its own sphere, as if it were to be seen simply as a ring-fenced subdivision of a broader philosophical enterprise. We noted in Chapter 1 that when Arendt took up political theory, she believed that she had left philosophy behind. An emphasis upon the connection between political theory and what 'appears' signals a connection with contingency of a sort that we are now aware of in light of the modern experience of a compromised public realm. And, as we noted in Chapter 2, looking back from this vantage point, for Arendt, we are aware of the extent to which our relatively depoliticised condition might be laid, in part, at the door of the philosophical tradition that spoke the language of absolute truth which, when applied to the political realm, promised resolution of the 'problems' of contingency, plurality and conflicting perspectives. If the traditionally formulated commitment to truth is the enemy of human affairs, then our attention is drawn to a need for an epistemological mediation to the traditional theoretical engagement, reflecting a commitment to a phenomenal sphere that rests upon contingent experience lodged in a condition of plurality.[3] This is reflected in Arendt's creation of means by which 'the results [of thinking] can be communicated in such a way that they lose the character of results' (Arendt 1994: 183). The mediation is evident in terms of what we can think of as a dialogic modulation of the theoretical voice.

To reiterate an earlier point, and by way of qualification, the claim here is not that the dialogic element provides a basis for attributing to Arendt a singular distinctive form. Much of what she says is not explicitly dialogic in form, unless it is taken as such in the same sense that all philosophical articulations might be thought of as contributions to a 'debate'; but of course this establishes nothing distinctive, and in any case Arendt was, in her writings, largely heedless of most contemporary academic debates (Arendt 1994: 3). Nevertheless, she does seek to engage in political theory as a dialogic enterprise, although in a rather different sense (Arendt 1977: 242, 2003: 98). We can again bring this out by reference to a contrast with the philosophical tradition. In the tradition, dialogue was understood as having, in principle, an end point in the form of truth. Thus understood, dialogue contributes to a discursive closure and therefore, ultimately, has the effect of rendering the expression of opinion redundant. For Arendt, on the other hand, dialogic thinking retains fidelity to the realm of opinion by resisting closure. The phenomenal character of the public realm, as given in the experience of plurality, requires that any proximate theoretical engagement with that realm internalise the recognition of a multi-perspectival dynamic that generates provisional senses of meaning. A dialogic modulation answers to this.

In the previous chapter, we noted Arendt's reference to Socrates as an exemplary figure when it comes to authentically free thinking at a point prior to, and in a form contrasting with, the epistemological strictures of the tradition. Socrates' constant questioning had the effect of unsettling unexamined beliefs and unfreezing orthodox conceptions; in his dialogic engagements, he had the ability to 'move freely' between the realm of thought and the practical, plural world (Arendt 1981/I: 167). Socrates is an illuminating case, but the example that he presents us with is only partially applicable in the contemporary world. Our recent experience, most thoroughly embodied in totalitarianism, of the loss of a connection between thinking and acting (with the commensurate corruption of each), and with this a realisation of the contingent and fragile character of the public realm, means that Socrates' insouciance no longer appears possible. Socrates was unaware of the problem of thinking and acting as we confront it now and was able to take the world – in the sense of a coherent realm of human engagements and institutions – for granted in a way that we cannot. In the light of our recent experiences, our attention is drawn, then, to the need for thinking that attends to the realm of human affairs; this implies the requirement that we adopt a more considered theoretical position, where dialogic thinking loses it 'pedagogical character' and where we are no longer satisfied with the 'priority of the questioner' (Arendt 1979: 183; cf. Dolan 2000: 273).

In view of this, Arendt finds ways of modulating a more abstracted philosophical voice in order to retain a dialogic fidelity to the realm of opinion. One thematic device that serves her purpose here is to be found in her consistent use of what we can think of as 'situated problematisations'. The particular problems, concepts, experiences and events that provide the substantial material of her political theory are framed and addressed in a way that answers to the specifics of our contemporary situation, in the context of our experiences and in recognition of what those experiences have newly brought to light (Arendt 2005: 108–9). These include the newly problematised relation between thinking itself and the world. This device of bringing us back consistently to the vantage point of contemporary experience has the effect of qualifying the traditional philosophical framing of questions pertaining to human affairs as eternal and thereby of exposing what we now see as their irreducibly *political* character. The resultant problems are, in this sense, framed as *ours*; and this is to save them for the realm of plural opinion.

A further, and commensurate, thematic aspect to this approach involves the recognition and preservation of unresolved tensions in a theoretical account. As we have already seen, tensions internal to our experience have a significant place in Arendt's thinking, and she resists the temptation to dissolve them by way of abstraction. This again, for Arendt, has the effect of stemming the traditional philosophical impulse, allowing us to face up to tensions in our experience, and their implications, as phenomena to be reflected upon and discussed, rather than as problems associated with the truth of the nature of 'Man' that exist to be ironed out. Tensions, for example, between thinking and politics, between freedom and liberation, between acting and making, all of which I will come to in due course, are related features of our situation which we should not, and ultimately cannot, treat as resolvable through the application of theory (Arendt 1977: 218; cf. Benhabib 1996: 177–84). A theoretical approach that, in the light of this, aims to 'heighten the intellectually irresolvable' mounts an appropriate resistance to closure (Arendt 1979: 185). And in the context of resistance to the tradition, the dialogical requirements that are implied, and possibilities released, find application with respect to an acknowledgment of the autonomy of the public realm, of the potency of spontaneous action; that is, to the potential of action to negotiate problems which, from a purely philosophical point of view, look insurmountable unless they are transcended theoretically (Arendt 1979: 185).

So there is, in Arendt's work, an epistemological mediation with respect to how, theoretically, we speak about politics such that the results of thinking shed their character as results and retain a dialogic modulation. This kind of mediation directly implies another, also characteristic of Arendt's work. A fidelity to the experiential terrain of the political, and the desire to save its appearances, are thematically answerable to our recent experiences and so to our current situation, the terms of which (theoretically and practically) have become apparent in the light of those experiences – a theme that corresponds with the use of situated problematisations that we mentioned earlier. Most prominent amongst these experiences, again, has been that of totalitarianism, which by exposing the decline of the public realm and threatening its complete eradication, teaches us about the fragile character of that realm, sustained only by mutual appearance, and problematises the manner in which we theorise it. It is this experience, by the same token, that has exposed 'the ruin of our categories' and so has also problematised not only how we theorise our experience but also how we contend with the past, always a central and difficult concern with respect to how we conceive of our present condition, and now acute in that the traditions the past may have been thought to deliver are discredited (Arendt 1968a: 460). For Arendt, we have experienced a break in the continuity of tradition which cannot be repaired by spurious reinventions, and this compromises any conviction or assertion that our self-understanding and our command of circumstances can be underwritten by reference to definitive reference points.

That the break here, for Arendt, is irreparable points to the fact that at issue is not simply a change with respect to how we go about things but, more than this, it is a question of how we can think *ab initio* about what we are doing or can do. And once, as it were, 'the cat is out of the bag' with respect to the contingency of human affairs, it cannot be put back. This implies the need for a temporal mediation in our thinking in comparison with the tradition – and it is one that, again, entirely corresponds with the epistemological mediation. If the traditional appeal to philosophically grounded truth no longer provides a route by which we can escape contingency, neither now does an appeal to the past, whether as a source of authoritative traditions or as the material for a confirming narrative. The temporal mediation implied reflects a modified intellectual relation with the past and is expressed in a corresponding modulation to the theoretical voice. This is evident, in general terms, in Arendt's work in what can be termed a narrational modulation, which establishes a non-traditional way of making the past relevant to the present.

The most fruitful examples of the use of narrative may be taken from pre-modern thinking. And Arendt characteristically looks to the ancient world for such examples. In particular, she refers to the Homeric tradition, where poetic narrative sought to preserve the meaning and uniqueness of events and made a claim to interpretive validity through the exercise of impartiality in the telling of stories, a feature that, as we saw earlier, is also pertinent to Arendt's conception of judgment. In recovering meaning, poetic narrative served to save events from the oblivion threatened by the passage of time and to preserve them as objects of remembrance (Arendt 1977: 45). The power of narrative to capture and preserve meaning in a non-reductive fashion is pertinent to Arendt's approach. However, again, the ancient model is limited in terms of its application to thinking in the modern setting. There is without doubt a strong narrative strand in Arendt's work, evident for example in her studies of the French and American revolutions of the late eighteenth century in *On Revolution* (1973) and also in her account of the conditions leading to the emergence of fascism in *The Origins of Totalitarianism* (1968a). More bounded narrative elements also make themselves evident throughout her work. Further, as Disch points out, Arendt's deployment of the narrative form is suggestive in that it answers to her rejection of explanatory accounts redolent of modern social science, replacing the latter's 'literal idiom' with the 'resonant voice of poetry' (Disch 1993: 674). Certainly, as we noted earlier, Arendt rejects the approach embodied in explanatory social science. The elements of narrative in Arendt's work are, in this sense, indicative of her desire to make a methodological stand against what she takes to be the 'behaviourist' agenda governing modern social scientific thinking. The question, however, is whether this strand in Arendt's work, and the implications for her general standpoint that we can draw from it, justifies the attribution to her of a narrative method. Two potentially related issues arise here, one concerning the character of Arendt's narrative voice and the other concerning its scope.

To the extent that Arendt deploys the narrative form, she does so in a novel fashion. She departs from more familiar invocations of historical narrative as a modality that, in its own terms, provides us with an account of events and experiences that itself demonstrates narrative completion (and in virtue of which can claim a modal equivalence with the finality that more 'behavioural' explanatory accounts promise). Narrative completion, from this view, can provide an explanation of its own sort. But this is not how Arendt uses it. As Benhabib points out, Arendt deploys the narrative voice in a manner that deliberately breaks the 'chain of narrative continuity' and so shatters the chronological structure that might provide a sense of completeness. The 'redemptive' aspect of narrative accounts rests rather on the disclosure of the fragmentary and ruptured character of our history, fractured by the moral reversal embodied in totalitarianism (Benhabib 1996: 120). In formal accordance with this sense of the methodological relevance of historical narrative, Arendt deploys it in sporadic and fragmented ways, resisting the urge toward narrative closure.

The rupture with the past that we have experienced now renders the aims of narrative plenitude and continuity misplaced. Furthermore, and related to this, traditional narrative affected the kind of reconciliation with events that looks inappropriate and potentially inauthentic when we are faced with the experience of totalitarianism, through which this rupture came to light and which remains permanently resistant to settled meaning and absorption into a finished narrative (Arendt 1977: 52). Stories do justice to agents by recognising and preserving their ability to reveal themselves, in speech and action, as unique – as distinct from all others. And each life-story enters into history as the 'storybook of mankind'. At the same time, this general story does not tell us all we need to know because 'mankind' is only an abstraction. This point is simultaneously an issue for politics because it implies a denial of what the tradition of political philosophy seeks, a truth underlying the realm of human affairs (Arendt 1958: 184). It is for this reason that Arendt's 'storytelling' amounts to nothing resembling a general, confirming narrative and rather consists in the fragmented deployment of particular narrative for purposes of exemplifications that provoke and provide matter for ongoing reflection.

The modulation to the theoretical voice here consists of resistance to the search for narrative continuity and the deployment of history through a focus on specific events and the potential illumination they can bring us in their uniqueness. From the point of view of a more traditional narrative approach, this appears as a deliberately fragmentary engagement with the past. It can be understood by reference to Walter Benjamin's image of the 'pearl diver': we delve into the past in order to recover events which, when wrenched from their inert historical context and looked at from the point of view of the present, provide us with the kind of illumination that comes with the appearance as singular occurrences (Arendt 1986b: 195). Their 'exotic' character as objects, and the resonant meanings that they disclose, provide us with no answers; but they constitute 'raw material' that we can consider and talk about. This fragmentary narrational modulation in Arendt's work once again aims at encapsulating a fidelity to the phenomenal and the contingent through resistance to closure and a settling of accounts.

It is a modulation equally that answers to the aim of mediating the standpoint of political theory in a temporal sense. It serves a mediation that, in respect to more traditional standpoints, re-opens our relation with the past and challenges the impulse to 'capture' it, an impulse that always threatens to curtail its meaning.

Behind Arendt's suspicion of narrative completion more particularly is the tendency that she associates with much modern historiography to wed narrative accounts to the idea of historical process, with connotations of inevitability. This sense of a process that at least in retrospect can be seen to exhibit an inexorability invites us to render historical accounts in terms of causality, 'an altogether falsifying category in relation to politics' (Arendt 1977: 78). The result, Arendt argues, is 'the ruin of the . . . particular through the seemingly higher validity of general "meanings"' (Arendt 1977: 81). Resolving events into a process that is amenable to explanatory models dissolves all sense of their uniqueness, wherein may lie their real meaning. It also implicates our understanding of the present, insinuating the view that our present circumstances and experiences are themselves the results of historical processes and are not, therefore, to be understood on their own terms (Arendt 1994: 319). The metaphor of 'wrenching' past events from their context answers to the aim of rescuing events from their place in a settled and finalised narrative in which they are buried. Second, the fragmentary modulation serves to rescue events in their particularity from explanatory reduction by reference to causal historical process. This also represents an anti-traditional modulation: Arendt's principal reference point in relation to explanatory modelling of the historical process is Marxism and, as we saw in Chapter 2, for Arendt, Marx rebels against the tradition from a position wholly *within* the terms of the tradition itself.

The significance of this temporal mediation to the theoretical standpoint in Arendt's approach does not only, however, concern our intellectual relation with the past. We have noted already that, for Arendt, the question of how we orientate ourselves to the past implicates our disposition toward an understanding of the present. A voice that resists narrative and explanatory ways of neutralising the singularity of past events also resists the tendency to see the present as an equally neutralised product of the past. In this way, Arendt's temporal modulation answers to a desire to treat the present as itself singular and to be understood on its own terms: the recognition of the uniqueness of past events corresponds with a sense of the uniqueness of present events. Fragmented narrational references provide illumination, but the principal focus is upon the present, itself distinctive and challenging. Despite her extensive use of history, Arendt's concern is always with issues and events that comprise our contemporary experience. And, as we shall see in the next chapter, the corollary to this is that a concern with recent experiences may lend past events a meaning (rather than just a causal significance) that we may not have previously known they had. An emphasis upon the sense of continuing mutual illumination between past and present in terms of the particular significance of events confirms the requirement to keep thinking, in terms of a search for meaning, rather than conceding the capacity for thought to reliance on settled historical accounts that 'fix' events and their meaning, determining how we are to see them.

This forms part of a consummate standpoint that Arendt seeks to offer. Her temporal mediation corresponds with the epistemological mediation. The unguaranteed sense of the relations between past and present allows an equivalent sense of the discursive openness with which we consider the present. So, these two mediations are commensurate and help us make sense of the style and purpose of political theory as Arendt goes about it. So far, we have examined them in abstract terms. I will shortly seek to exemplify them in more concrete terms; but first, there are some general issues to be considered in terms of what such a mediated approach implies.

THEORY AND OBJECTIVITY

One question that arises here concerns the issue of theoretical objectivity. We have seen that part of Arendt's objection to the tradition, and a reason for her desire to depart from it, is that it rests centrally upon a quest for truth. For Arendt, from the point of view of the public realm, truth-claims look coercive and threaten to close down the plural interplay of opinion. Arendt's mediated approach constitutes a way of speaking theoretically that acknowledges and is sensitive to plurality. This raises a question as to whether Arendt may be vulnerable to a charge of subjectivism and, related to this, whether she is able to claim any cognitive distance between political theory as she practises it and its object – the realm of opinion itself.

It is certainly not the case that Arendt believes there to be no such thing as truth, and indeed, truth of a sort is highly pertinent to the public realm. Here, she refers to empirical truths: shared acknowledgment of facts is essential to the possibility of a common world that we can inhabit and in which a coherent public realm can exist. Where factual truth ceases to be a matter of common acknowledgment, the potential for anomic isolation increases and the capacity of persons to understand their situation is threatened. Our sense of reality depends, for Arendt, on the confirming testimony of others who also see the facts of our situation; without this, where one is left alone with one's own sensuous experience, it is easy to doubt the evidence of one's senses. The collective implication of this is a potential erosion of our capacity to come to contingent, freely formed agreements in the context of a common sense – the capacity central to the exercise of freedom. For Arendt, it is not an accidental characteristic of totalitarian regimes that they seek to eradicate our sense of factual truth by systematic lying and the rewriting of history. So Arendt does not deny the availability of the political relevance of empirical truth. Her objection is to truth-claims, supposed to be pertinent to the public realm, that are normatively charged and which claim a metaphysical basis, whether traditionally philosophical or, more recently, of a scientific character, which in either case provide a coercive guarantee.

Objections have been raised to Arendt's position here in that it rests upon a distinction between analytical and synthetic truth that may now be regarded as questionable (see Nelson 1978). Her distinction, it has been suggested, depends upon an assertion of the independence of factual truth redolent of a 'positivist' position that would itself constitute a threat to the phenomenal fabric of the political, another means of transcending the realm of opinion. This criticism is misplaced, however, in that it involves a misunderstanding of the basis upon which Arendt appeals to factual truth. In accordance with her approach more generally, Arendt does not seek to draw a foundational philosophical distinction between analytical and synthetic: she invokes it as politically pertinent with respect to recent experience. She asserts the importance of factual truth in the light of the significance we know it has in resisting the decline of shared public perceptions in general and the anti-political conditions of totalitarianism in particular, where we find the attempt simultaneously to eradicate factual truth and to put in its place a sense of truth grounded in an ideology of history. In the light of this, we see the significance of factual truth in the maintenance of a public realm; to the extent that this might imply the assertion of an analytic/synthetic distinction, Arendt is prepared to deploy it 'without discussing its intrinsic [philosophical] legitimacy . . . we look into these matters for political rather than philosophical reasons' (Arendt 1977: 231).[4]

So Arendt affirms the importance of empirical truth and her doubts concern rather the assertion of theoretical truth-claims, at least in so far as they claim pertinence to the public realm. But this still leaves a question as to whether Arendt is able to claim a sense of objectivity attaching to political theory as she understands it; and it is arguably an issue that is only compounded by the manner in which she deals with the analytic/synthetic distinction, on a political rather than a philosophical basis. Furthermore, the fact that this way of abridging the question is consistent with the mediated approach that we have seen Arendt adopting hardly blunts the issue: she is methodologically consistent here but, as she would be the first to point out, consistency *on its own* is not necessarily a virtue. However, although Arendt's theoretical position does not claim the objectivity often associated with more traditional foundational positions, she appeals instead to the exercise of impartiality. This takes us back to the Homeric tradition from which, as we noted earlier, Arendt draws some inspiration and which 'precedes all our theoretical and scientific traditions, including our traditions of philosophical and political thought' (Arendt 1977: 262). The point here, realised through a narrative account, is to achieve an impartial position with respect to different standpoints whilst, by the same token, retaining a fidelity to the freedom of human agency, resisting the temptation to transcend the standpoints that agency embodies by reference to some 'higher' position, resisting, that is, the impulse to say what had to happen or what ought to have happened.

This appeal to impartiality provides a means of gauging the theoretical distance that Arendt's approach secures with respect to its object, whilst at the same time confirming its modal immanence or proximity to the experiential terrain of the political. The idea of impartiality also re-invokes the capacity for judgment introduced in Chapter 2. As we saw there, Arendt refers to a model of reflective judgment that does not rest on an appeal to an abstract model of universal reason and appeals instead to the ability to form an opinion whilst taking into account the putative standpoints of others. Arendt argues that 'political thinking' – by which she means the formation of opinion in the public realm – entails the exercise of the 'enlarged mentality' through which one imaginatively incorporates into one's judgments the possible perspectives of other individuals or groups and in the light of which one is liberated from narrow dictates of self-interest: 'the very quality of an opinion . . . depends upon the degree of its impartiality' (Arendt 1977: 242).

This sense of impartial judgment represents a model of political thinking appropriate to participants in the public realm. Political theory, as Arendt practises it, adopts a greater distance from politics itself and from the corresponding form of 'political thinking'. It appeals to an impartiality 'that differs from the qualified representative opinion [characteristic of political opinion formation] . . . in that it is not acquired inside the political realm but is inherent in the position of the outsider required for such occupations' (Arendt 1977: 260). At the same time, the distance achieved here is not one underwritten by the kind of ontological distinction proffered by the 'two-worlds' model, in virtue of which the political is viewed from the standpoint of the eternal. The engagement of the theorist entails a withdrawal from the political, but nevertheless, when engaged in this way *as* a theorist, 'I am not simply together only with myself in the solitude of philosophical thought . . . I remain in the world of universal interdependence' (Arendt 1977: 242). So Arendt seeks a perspectival distance from the political whilst resisting the adoption of a position 'above' the engagements of the public.[5] This formulation still requires unpacking, however, and this is best done by reference to some related aspects of Arendt's way of thinking which answer to the theoretical mediations and vocal modulations that we have identified as central to her method: first, her resistance to foundational theoretical recipes; second, her discursive orientation; and third, the (non-ideological) partisan position that she adopts, which draws us back toward the modal assimilation with the operation of 'political thinking', or judgment, that her political theory displays.

These features of Arendt's political theory are definitive of her approach and they reflect the combined negative and positive moments in her thinking, reflecting our current situation where we have to be both negative, rejecting the supports provided by traditional thinking, and by the same token to think positively about the political capacities that are brought to light by their denial in our recent experience. First, and in a negative sense, Arendt's thought adopts a distance from references to causes, principles or formulations of collective interests that, in traditional terms, might be thought of as reference points that would resolve the indeterminacy inherent in politics, but which modern experience tells us are more appropriately seen as ideological. Second, and in a more positive sense, her object remains the phenomenal realm of politics itself, taken on its own terms; answering to this inherently discursive realm, her voice remains discursive rather than conclusive. Third, these features coalesce in a theoretical standpoint that manifests a corresponding commitment not to a particular ideological agenda but to the possibilities of politics itself, possibilities which again impress themselves upon us because they have been under threat. In this sense, if Arendt's approach can be thought of as embodying partisanship, she is a partisan of politics. This feature of her thinking equally underwrites its critical potential

– a point to which I will return in Chapter 7. These related aspects to Arendt's way of doing political theory all reflect the general mediations embodied in her approach. They are also susceptible to exemplification through reference to some of the more specific stylistic dimensions to her work.

STYLISTIC MOTIFS

I will review briefly here three stylistic features of Arendt's work that supplement and transform the more traditional elements of conceptual analysis and logical inference that she deploys: first, the use of narrative; second, the use of poetic and metaphorical devices; and third the use of examples, particularly biographical reference to exemplary figures. These are related stylistic motifs but I will look at each in turn with a view, at this point, to considering how, at a general level, they help realise the kind of modulated voice that Arendt seeks.

First, and returning to an earlier theme, a feature of Arendt's writing that has often been noted is her use of the narrative form. We saw that though it may not provide a reference point for a complete formal characterisation of her theoretical method, it nevertheless features prominently and contributes significantly to her approach. Most obviously, for example, Arendt offers narrative accounts of recent political events; in particular of the revolutionary periods in France and America in *On Revolution* (1973). She also confirms the importance to be attached to narrative accounts in her reference back to the accounts offered of great political events of the classical period. As Disch notes, storytelling is a mode that answers to the requirement of impartiality: 'telling oneself the story of an event or situation from the plurality of perspectives that constitute it as a public phenomenon' (Disch 1993: 666). The deployment of narrative, in this sense, mounts resistance to explanatory devices familiar from modern social science, which seeks scientific objectivity rather than impartiality. It can assign meaning to events in their contingency and particularity. The narrative approach therefore resists the tendency of explanatory accounts to assimilate cases, rendering them suitable for inclusion under ossified categories, marginalising their specific meaning and obviating the invitation to reflective judgment on the basis of the particular case. In a more positive sense, narrative treatment replaces *ex post facto* explanatory categorisations of agents and events with accounts that incorporate a sense of the contingency of phenomena; in doing so, it also reflects more fully the sense of spontaneity that Arendt associates with the concept of public action, where agents can, as it were, bring something new to the table and can make a difference to the world in unpredictable ways. By the same token, it is an approach that corresponds with a recognition of the central category of 'natality' in respect of human action: a recognition that each of us enters the world as a unique individual, carrying with us the promise of something new and unprecedented.[6]

Her use of the narrative form is far from constant and is also far from complete. The narrative form as deployed by Arendt, is, as we have noted, decidedly fragmented, reflecting the element of discursive openness that the epistemological mediation in Arendt's work requires. As we noted earlier, Arendt refers to Benjamin's image of the pearl diver, wrenching the valuable material from its ossified context and finding, thereby, its true value. It is an image that indemnifies the idea of disjointed history, where we deploy specific narrative fragments that in themselves illuminate, in their particularity, acts and events and render them in a form pertinent to our own most recent experiences, reflecting the temporal mediation discussed earlier.[7] In this sense also, Arendt's use of the narrative form is consciously sporadic and so is necessarily mediated by other stylistic strategies.

This takes us to the second motif that makes itself felt in Arendt's work, in the form of the poetic and metaphorical references that pepper her work. Metaphors allow invisible thinking to become manifest in the realm of appearances: 'the transformation of the given raw material of sheer happening . . . is closely akin to the poet's transfiguration of moods or movements of the heart' and the poet's political function involves 'a cleansing or purging of all emotions that could prevent men from acting, out of which arises the faculty of judgment' (Arendt 1977: 262; cf. Bernstein 2000: 287). The poetic, then, in Arendt's thinking, displays its common origin with the narrative and its deployment equally serves to mediate the tendency toward the reduction of the political to terms answerable to the philosophical or the social scientific vocabularies that, from the point of view of action (and our capacity to appreciate it from a phenomenological point of view), are deadening hands (Arendt 1977: 262–3). Positively, it renders experience in its phenomenal dignity: poetic condensation of experience renders it memorable and draws our attention back to the autonomy of the realm of action (Arendt 1958: 169–70).

A cognate stylistic element is to be found in her emphasis on exemplification and the use of biographical treatments of exemplary figures. In general terms, her use of examples is of methodological significance and may also be of ethical significance – but I shall return to the latter point in Chapter 7. In terms of her broader method, exemplification represents a further way in which theory maintains its modally proximate relation with the public realm. Her examples provide 'visible' cases and give our thinking, always hidden from the world as an activity, a phenomenal embodiment. They equally have pertinence to the political realm through impressing upon us possibilities with respect to ways of being in the world. The pedagogical function of examples is grounded not in instruction, which implies the guidance of action by thought, or practice by theory, but is instead grounded in the concept of 'inspiration', that is itself pertinent to the public realm. 'Inspiring principles' which, aside from other motives or aims that propel people in the public realm, are visible in action and susceptible to judgment: 'teaching by example' says Arendt is the only form of 'persuasion', or practical guidance, that thinking is capable of delivering 'without perversion or distortion' (Arendt 1977: 247–8).[8] Specific exemplifications resist the imposition of broader philosophical or explanatory categories that always potentially rob enactments of human freedom of their uniqueness. In this sense, again, they engage the capacity for judgment, for assigning meaning to particulars in themselves.[9]

More specifically, Arendt deploys biographical accounts of exemplary figures, most notably in her accounts of those who have displayed the capacity for thinking independently in 'dark times' (Arendt 1968b). The significance of these accounts is twofold. To tell a biographical story is to release into the account we have of events something unique, answering to the capacity for spontaneity and for interruption that is central to the political. This does not mean that what they say *substantively* is irrelevant; but what they do say is also formally significant as representing the determination to retain the ability to think and to judge in conditions where thinking and judging are severely compromised. The relevance of this, for Arendt, is made potent for us in the contemporary context where we view the political situation in the context of totalitarianism. Once again, here, the significance of the biographical fragments that Arendt deploys is in terms of their inspirational, rather than their strictly instructional, import.

SUMMARY

The mediations, epistemic and temporal, that we have identified in this chapter, and the modulations and corresponding stylistic motifs that substantiate them, can be seen to redeem the more general points concerning thinking and acting, and the relation between theory and politics made at the end of Chapter 2. They establish a theoretical engagement that is answerable to the condition of plurality, mediating the traditional search for truth by reference to the commitment to impartiality, resulting in a non-definitive, discursive theoretical formation. The resistance that it therefore mounts to established accounts has the potential to be salutary in the sense of unsettling those patterns of thinking inherited from the tradition, and prompts us to think without the crutches that the tradition offers us. Once we are liberated in this way, we are equally free to think in the light of our own most recent experiences untrammelled by the insistent voice of the eternal.

So these are key motifs that reflect and substantiate Arendt's distinctive methodological approach. In the next three chapters, I will seek to illustrate them by reference to an analysis of Arendt's three most well-known works: *The Origins of Totalitarianism*, *The Human Condition* and *On Revolution*. In each case, I will aim to show, in the course of an examination of the substance of Arendt's discussions, how she achieves the appropriate epistemological and temporal mediations, reflected in corresponding modulations to the theoretical voice and, in turn, how the kinds of stylistic devices that we have looked at are deployed in order to realise these modulations.

In this chapter we have seen a recognition of the way in which our more recent experiences may change the political world and our understanding of it – and how Arendt seeks to incorporate this recognition into her conception of how to go about political theory. In view of this, it is appropriate next to move to a consideration of her most sustained treatment of what she takes to be the definitive experience that shapes our understanding of the modern world and of modern politics: that of totalitarianism.

Notes

1. This is of course a very curt formulation of Arendt's conception of the political, but it will serve at this stage as a benchmark against which to develop the methodological point at issue here. I will look more fully at her theory of politics in Chapter 5 in the course of examining her discussion in *The Human Condition* (1958), at which point it will be used to exemplify the broad methodological point established here.

2. Thinking can of course be employed in the acquisition of knowledge but when it is so employed, 'it is never itself; it is at best a handmaiden to an altogether different enterprise' (Arendt 1981/I: 61).

3. As Vollrath puts it, Arendt construes events in the public realm 'in a phenomenal sense' rather than construing them 'from an epistemic basis' (Vollrath 1977: 163).

4. It is also the case that, for Arendt, factual truth can come into conflict with the realm of opinion: it does so in that recognition of facts is not just a condition of public life by providing a basis for common sense but is also the basis of a voice that can speak *to* the public realm in a manner that transcends opinion. However, this potential clash pertains 'only on the lowest level of human affairs', that is, with respect to problems posed by the meeting of needs or the satisfaction of interests (Arendt 1977: 263).

5. As Vollrath notes, 'the observer must judge the political phenomena, that is, he must converse with others – with actors and observers – about the way in which the space of political phenomena is created, preserved, abolished and destroyed' (Vollrath 1977: 164).

6. For an extended treatment of these and related issues, see Disch (1994).

7. Kateb emphasises the importance of poetics and storytelling in Arendt as a route to meaning but points out that this potentially creates a problem when it comes to the metaphysical systems that she wishes to reject but which she seems to see 'as stories or analgous to or sufficiently like them' (Kateb 2002: 334). So is Arendt reproducing a form that she rejects? I think this point is mitigated again by the fact that her use of narrative is fragmented and resistant to completion and storytelling is therefore not definitive of her method. By the same token, her deployment of narrative is of a decisively different sort than the metaphysical stories that might be told which are taken to be sources of truth.

8. For a reflection on Arendt's use of examples and exemplary figures, see Parrikko (1999).

9. Ferrara notes that Arendt refers to 'schemata' as a key reference point in the representative thinking that forms a basis for judgment. By schemata, she means concrete examples that prove representative of the more general case. The analogy between examples and schemata, he suggests, 'obscures what it should clarify' (Ferrara 1998: 120). This is a forceful point: the analogy between examples and schemata – with, from an Arendtian point of view, jarring Platonic overtones – looks unfortunate and represents perhaps one of the weakest theoretical formulations in her work. This said, whilst the analogy may be unfortunate, it does not undermine Arendt's broader position. Despite her reference to schemata, her own use of particular examples, which are generally highly contextualised historically, remains true to her methodological commitment to a voice that engages the faculty of reflective judgment. The examples that Arendt draws from history and poetry seem to play their role of imparting discursively orientated meaning without dependence upon the sense of a blueprint that the concept of schemata would seem to insinuate. However, we do need to be careful in relation to the use of examples here and the 'representative' role that Arendt assigns to them. Whereas some conventional views would assert that the key criterion for effective representation is that of resemblance, in fact it is arguable that the relation is the reverse: the criterion for resemblance is representation (cf. Black 1962). Representation, in other words, can reveal points of resemblance that we might not otherwise recognise. Significantly, this engages with the Arendtian deployment of reflective judgment, where exemplifications may be identified which carry significance in virtue of the qualities of the case itself and how they are presented, rather than through their comparative assimilation with other cases that would justify their inclusion within a more general category.

CHAPTER 4

Theorising Dark Times: The Origins of Totalitarianism

In referring to dark times, where our capacities both for thinking and acting are compromised, Arendt makes the point that they are not new or rare; but our sense of them now comes in the context of totalitarianism, the horrors of which are unprecedented, showing us just how dark times can be (Arendt 1968a: ix). The experience of totalitarianism, as we have noted, was central to the development of Arendt's political thought, just as it was to the course of her life. She encountered first hand, and as a consequence of totalitarianism, two phenomena that she came to believe were decisive features of our recent experience. She suffered oppression in the form of a short period of imprisonment in Germany in 1933 and later internment in France in 1940 before her flight to the United States. Equally, in being forced to flee her homeland, she felt the experience of the exile, of one who has lost their place in the world. Years later, she commented that although when revisiting Germany she experienced joy simply at hearing German spoken around her in the streets, she nevertheless knew that, given what had happened, she could never again see it as her home; and so her state of exile was permanent. The twin phenomena of oppression on the one hand and homelessness on the other were, Arendt thought, key to the experience of people more generally in contemporary conditions, experiences which totalitarianism sought to press to the ultimate extreme (Arendt 1968a: vii).

In exploring the phenomenon of totalitarianism, then, we may be led to further reflection upon our broader contemporary experience; and in coming to an understanding of its novel and unprecedented character, we may come also to an awareness of the novel character of our modern situation, of the challenges it presents and of the human capacities that we may be required to draw upon if we are to avert the worst dangers that we face. She seeks to approach the phenomenon by 'retrieving the history and analysing the political implications' (Arendt 1968a: 460). So she combines a historical account of the origins of the phenomenon with a related analysis of its key political features and what it has brought to light in terms of the predicament of the political in the modern world. She proceeds from some typical theoretical questions: What happened? Why did it happen? How could it have happened? (Arendt 1968a: xxiv). And she seeks to answer these questions by means of an attempt 'to try and tell and understand what happened' (Arendt 1968a: xxiii). However, in terms both of the explicatory and historical dimensions that are invoked in this deceptively simple statement of intent, methodological mediations are involved. Arendt seeks neither a definitive analytical account of totalitarianism nor a complete historical explanation. She develops instead a complex set of thematic strands designed not to 'close the book' on totalitarianism but rather, as Villa notes, to begin an 'interminable dialogue' concerning the experience, its origins and its implications (Villa 2000: 2; cf. Canovan 1992: 7). It is vital for Arendt that we retain a sense of the sheer novelty of the phenomenon, and therefore of the continuing implications of the historical and intellectual rupture that it has revealed. We must avoid 'denying the outrageous, deducing the unprecedented from precedents, or explaining phenomena by such analogous generalities that the impact of reality and the shock of experience are no longer felt' (Arendt 1968a: viii). More traditional analytical and historical accounts of phenomena run the risk of 'familiarising' them through assimilation and burial in a final causal story.[1] Arendt's mediated approach seeks to preserve the phenomenon in its reality and sustain a sense of its impact.

In analytical terms, Arendt comes up with a broad provisional definition of totalitarianism as a regime that operates by the instrument of terror and which is built upon an abstract ideology invoking inexorable historical processes. I shall return to this later on, but for the present it is worth noting that Arendt's purpose here is not strictly definitional in a traditional sense (cf. Canovan 2000). Conceptual definitions generally seek to assemble identifiable analytical elements that combine to confer familiarity upon the phenomenon concerned, such that we are able, in a conceptual sense, to 'master' it. This sense of mastery by way of an analytical 'pinning down' of a phenomenon relies, in general, upon an assimilation of that phenomenon with previous, recognisable cases and many have been tempted to equate totalitarianism with 'past evils', familiarising it, even if it is regarded as a more extreme 'version' in relation to cases with which it is assimilated. But for Arendt, this is a misplaced aim with respect to how we assess and cope with the ramifications of totalitarianism and the conditions out of which it emerged:

> it seems we are on solid ground; for together with its evils we think we have inherited the wisdom of the past to guide us through them. But the trouble with the wisdom of the past is that it dies, so to speak, in our hands as soon as we try to apply it honestly to the central political experiences of our own time. (Arendt 1994: 309)

Arendt seeks to proceed in a manner appropriate to retaining a situated sense of the phenomenon at stake. The openness of her analysis allows us, again, to retain the sense of 'shock' engendered by the reality of totalitarianism and constitutes an attempt to think about a phenomenon that 'has brought to light the ruin of our categories of thought and standards of judgment' (Arendt 1994: 318).

It is true, of course, that reflecting theoretically upon phenomena is a linguistic engagement and, in seeking to reflect upon a novel phenomenon, we have only the language we have. As a result, established conceptual definitions and relations bear down upon what we have to say. It is all the more important, therefore, that we maintain here an approach that incorporates a formal amenability to continuing dialogue rather than stipulative definitional closure, preventing 'the ruin of the factual and the particular through the seemingly higher validity of general "meaning"' (Arendt 1977: 81). Accordingly, Arendt's analytical characterisation of totalitarianism comes only as a postscript to lengthy consideration of the historical phenomena that in no way exemplify totalitarianism itself but which prove pertinent to an understanding of the conditions that permitted its emergence.

In terms of this historical dimension to Arendt's investigation, she again adopts a theoretically mediated approach that resonates with the more abstract discussion of the themes explored in Chapter 3. We can point to phenomena that resonate with elements of totalitarianism and help us understand them, but these are not taken to provide an account that might render it thoroughly explicable (Arendt 1968a: 319). We have already noted that Arendt seeks to challenge and depart from much of what she takes to be inherent in modern historiography: where the emphasis is placed upon man-made processes which nevertheless can be seen as analogous to the processes of nature (Arendt 1977: 57–8). This reductive standpoint allows us to suppose, with the benefit of hindsight, that events were inevitable. In turn it has two related effects: first, to rob particular events of their individual significance by replacing the search for meaning with the assertion of explanatory closure; and second, to eradicate human responsibility, and the motif of freedom, from our history. In respect of a reflection upon totalitarianism, this approach threatens, once again, to marginalise our sense of its shocking and unprecendented novelty; in doing so, it may blind us to the meaning of the phenomenon, not only to the previously unrecognised dangers that accompany the power of human agency but also to the specific and potentially redemptive examples of the power to retain humanity and dignity in the darkest of times to which we might also attend.

In approaching the issue of totalitarianism, Arendt again takes her lead from the example provided by classical historiography, where it was assumed that 'the lesson of each event, deed, or occurrence is revealed in and by itself' (Arendt 1977: 64). This approach, Arendt argues, did not imply the exclusion of the contextual, or even of specific causal claims, 'but causality and context were seen in a light provided by the event itself, illuminating a specific segment of human affairs . . . [an event] disclosed its share of meaning within the confines of its individual shape' (Arendt 1977: 64). The narrative form, which lay at the root of the classical historiographical tradition, provides us with a model for a more appropriate and less reductive way of looking at the past. As we have also seen, for Arendt this also carries dangers: a smooth narrative completion may erode the sense of novelty and rupture that are written into human affairs, which are now permanently on our agenda in our attempts to understand the contemporary situation. The model that Arendt takes from the classical world which most resonates with her sense of her own theoretical engagement is that of Herodotus, whose narrative 'is sufficiently loose to leave room for many stories and no closed generality is relied upon to bestow meaning on the particular' (Arendt 1977: 64).

ORIGINS: RACISM, COLONIALISM, BUREAUCRACY

In the light of this, in *The Origins of Totalitarianism*, Arendt does not claim to offer a comprehensive historical account of the emergence of totalitarianism – still less a comprehensive explanation – instead, she takes up some historical themes that she believes may now look pertinent as a backdrop to its emergence: 'the event illuminates its own past but can never be deduced from it' (Arendt 1968a: 319). The emphasis here is upon themes which the experience of totalitarianism now points back to and which, in a symbiotic sense, may help us in our continuing attempt to understand. In terms of her more substantive exploration, I will begin by looking at what she has to say about these historical origins and then move, in turn, to her analytical model of the totalitarian regime before looking at the question of the nature of the evil that these regimes embodied. In appealing to the historical origins of totalitarianism, for Arendt 'there has been a tendency to simply equate totalitarianism with its elements and origins' and this is a mistake (Arendt 1968a: xv). Nowhere is her standpoint here more acutely demonstrated than in her comments upon the emergence of anti-Semitism as a key factor that provided fertile soil in which totalitarianism, particularly in its German variety, could grow.

One form of the 'normalisation' of totalitarianism, in the German case in particular, is prompted, for Arendt, by the very fact of the virulently anti-Semitic character of the Nazi regime. There has been a general tendency to see totalitarianism as the latest manifestation of the regime based upon violence and oppression, a phenomenon that has proved a persistent feature of our history – and, by implication, therefore, not special. In a similar but more specific vein, the Nazi regime could be seen as principally a regime of this kind propelled in particular by anti-Semitism, representing, therefore, the latest element in 'an unbroken continuity of persecutions and expulsions . . . down to our time' (Arendt 1968a: xi). The idea of the 'eternal' victimisation of Jews is, Arendt suggests, an 'easy' story that papers over the historical cracks and is reductive with respect to attempts to understand totalitarianism. It is also characteristic of what she refers to as 'escapist' theories: theories that admit a conception of permanent victimhood and which may equally allow an avoidance of responsibility. Arendt posed, in *The Origins of Totalitarianism* and elsewhere, hard and controversial questions about the general lack of resistance mounted by Jewish communities in Germany in the face of growing persecution. So a reductive assimilation of totalitarianism with more traditional forms of persecution and its absorption into a story that answers to this is not helpful, either in understanding the phenomenon, whether in its specifically anti-Semitic form or otherwise, or in understanding how people reacted to it.

None of this means that, in the German case, anti-Semitism was not central: it was certainly no mere adjunct to the Nazi standpoint. Stoking anti-Semitic feeling and promoting violence against Jews was not simply a useful 'scapegoating' device for the regime: it was central to the ideology (Arendt 1968a: 6). Gaining a sense of just how it was central to the ideology may tell us something. The emergence of anti-Semitism as a central feature of the ideology had two immediate effects. First, it aided the process of the identification of enemies (both external and internal) which was central to totalitarianism generally and which justified the implementation of a regime of terror in the context of constant struggle against the enemy. Second, it insinuated an anti-political form of political culture, again characteristic of totalitarianism generally, which eradicated customary juridical assumptions: the treatment of Jews was meted out 'regardless of what they had done or omitted to do, regardless of vice or virtue' (Arendt 1968a: 8).

The phenomenon of anti-Semitism in Europe, as it developed from the eighteenth century and through the nineteenth, can be seen in Arendt's terms as a distinctively social phenomenon and so as a feature of the private rather than the public sphere: 'social discrimination and not political anti-Semitism discovered the phenomenon of "the Jew"' (Arendt 1968a: 61). It was a phenomenon, then, that was limited in its range and was largely independent of public questions of guilt or punishment. It could even be understood, in relative terms, as benign: the sense of difference upon which it rested, ranging 'from innate strangeness to social alienation' amounted potentially to the basis for a social *modus vivendi* (Arendt 1968a: 67). But the politicisation of these distinctions changed things dramatically. Arendt had already explored the position of the Jew in society in her biographical study of the German Jewish salon hostess Rahel Varnhagen and the question that presented itself to Jews of being either a parvenu or a pariah (Arendt 1957). This discriminating social categorisation of the Jew as 'other', and the establishment of a social distinction by reference to 'a natural fact of birth', at the same time coincided with a broader sociopolitical development.

It coincided with the development of bourgeois society and the increasing colonisation of the political by the sociopolitical concerns and interests that constitute the principal driving forces of the culture of modernity. The period from the late nineteenth century to the early twentieth century was one where 'politics itself was becoming part of social life' (Arendt 1968a: 80). The collapse of the political into the social resulted, for Arendt, in the dissolving of the business of the public sphere into a series of social and economic questions and imperatives. This was a radical development which in general terms had profound consequences for the role of anti-Semitism, but it is feature often missed in the course of more conventional narratives that focus upon persistent outbreaks of anti-Semitic sentiment. Arendt finds a more acute account of this subtle shift in biographical and literary references. In Proust, she suggests, 'there is no better witness . . . of this period when society had emancipated itself completely from public concerns' (Arendt 1968a: 80). Proust's literary insight shows us equally the sense in which, during this period of the socialisation of the political, the category of crime becomes conflated with that of vice – including the vice of Judaism, which becomes a politicised category. To be Jewish is no longer viciously exotic but potentially culpable. She equally finds illumination in a biographical sketch of Benjamin Disraeli, who was of an entirely assimilated background but who sought to realise his social and political ambitions actually by emphasising his 'exotic' character and by implication the exceptional nature of the Jewish people. This carried an echo of current race theories:

> race theories finally served much more sinister and immediately political purposes . . . [but] it is still true that much of their plausibility and persuasiveness lay in the fact that they helped anybody feel himself an aristocrat who had been selected by birth on the strength of a 'racial' qualification. (Arendt 1968a: 73)

That his strategy proved a success for Disraeli was in general due to (and illuminates) a context where social categories, including race, were insidiously colonising the political.[2] The conflation which might, in his time, have allowed Disraeli to profit from the exotic 'vice' of Judaism, equally, and in the light of a decline in our political and juridical culture, allowed Jewishness to be construed, in due course, as a crime.[3]

The supplementation of political categories with inscribed social categories, and the increasing dominance of the latter over the former, made for the erosion of the public persona in its political and juridical forms, lodged in citizenship, leaving persons vulnerable to the imposition of categories and definitions which, when realised politically, proved anti-political. More specifically, anti-Semitic categories, when politicised, proved virulent. In this sense, for Arendt, there is no doubt that the 'deciding forces in the Jews' fateful journey to the storm-centre of events were . . . political' (Arendt 1968a: 89). The Jewish question, as a social issue, became a political catalyst 'until finally a disintegrated society recrystallised ideologically around a possible massacre of Jews' (Arendt 1968a: 53).

A second element amongst the conditions that now can be seen as pertinent to an understanding of the emergence of totalitarianism, and one which also made its contribution to the development of race thinking, was the phenomenon of imperialism. The imperative to expand into remote territories for purposes of imperial rule and exploitation constituted a movement that could draw readily upon race theories to provide a justification: colonial enterprises could, whatever their instrumental aims, be lent a respectability by reference to a narrative about bringing a measure of civilisation to the uncivilised, a narrative underwritten by assumptions as to the inherent inferiority of other races. Racism, in this way, developed as much more than an unreflective individual or collective response to the encounter with otherness and took its place as central to the ideology of imperialism (Arendt 1968a: 158). And to the extent that imperialist ventures provided in themselves a template for a prevalent political culture, racism too became a political category to which appeal could be made.

A further notable feature of the culture of imperialism concerns its 'depoliticising' mentality. The development of colonialism in the mid- to late-nineteenth century is reflective of the 'political emancipation of the bourgeoisie' (Arendt 1968a: 123). Colonialism unleashed the ambition of modern capitalism to expand and to increase profit through the opening up of new markets. It revealed, in this sense, the incipient global ambitions of capitalist enterprise and, by the same token, it marked the beginning of the release of this enterprise from the shackles of the nation state and the accompanying political constraints (Arendt 1968a: 124). To the extent that these forces were able to transcend conventional politics, they equally had the effect of transforming politics in their own image. Central to the imperialist ethos was 'expansion as a permanent feature and supreme aim of politics' (Arendt 1968a: 125). The theme of conquest rebounded upon the politics of the imperial nations in the form of what Arendt describes as 'pan-movements', regional, expansion-orientated movements that were fuelled by the imperialist spirit, downgrading domestic politics and presenting themselves as political parties standing above sectional political interests. They become, in image, 'parties above parties', introducing a tendency to turn parties into 'movements' with ambitions beyond the politically constrained context of the nation state (Arendt 1968a: 250).

The imperialist regimes were, for Arendt, ruthless enterprises geared to the maximisation of profit. They were, in this sense, highly instrumentalised and this had implications for their political character. These regimes, for instrumental purposes, bypassed familiar categories of political accountability, responsibility and citizenship. They represented 'political power without the foundation of a body politic' (Arendt 1968a: 135). The result, Arendt argues, was a 'ruthless imperial rule by decree', something shown in the use of the police and the military as the principal instruments of rule unconstrained by the usual limitations applied by a civil authority (Arendt 1968a: 131). The culture of imperialism allied politics to a military operation, so the corresponding political structure was essentially bureaucratic; and bureaucracies, when unconstrained by political structures assuring accountability to a body politic, are arbitrary. They may, of course, have their own logic governing their operation, and the colonial enterprises certainly did. But from the point of view of the political, and of the potential citizen, they remain arbitrary in the sense of lacking any enforceable constraint – and so what is done to those over whom they rule is utterly beyond their power.

It is worth noting again, here, that in exploring the resonances that imperialism may have for us, Arendt does not offer a comprehensive history of the phenomenon, concentrating specifically on European colonialism in Africa and Asia in the period from the 1880s to the First World War (Arendt 1968a: 123). Even within these parameters, it is not a traditionally complete historian's account: she takes up pertinent strands in this history and develops them through examples and specific narratives. These are combined with literary accounts, particularly in the work of Kipling, and biographical fragments focusing upon key imperialist figures such as Lord Cromer and Cecil Rhodes, which provide examples of the expansionist mentality – combining abstract principle with a commitment to the maximisation of material gain, forging the basis for a novel form of government that marked an unprecedented gulf between rulers and ruled (Arendt 1968a: 211–16).[4]

The purpose of this kind of account is not to provide a definitive overview of events but to create thematic resonances that might inform our intellectual encounter with totalitarianism and with the situation it has created for us. We can point to themes that made themselves felt in the imperialist form of rule which, through their inverse impact upon the political culture of the imperialist powers themselves, provided features that helped create a context conducive to the rise of totalitarianism: 'some of the fundamental aspects of this time appear so close to totalitarian phenomena of the twentieth century that it may be justifiable to consider the whole period a preparatory stage for coming catastrophes' (Arendt 1968a: 123). The principal motifs of bureaucracy, supranational expansionism and the politicisation of biological categories such as race, all made themselves felt in the domestic political culture. The colonial regimes were certainly not totalitarian, but for Arendt they represent emerging features prototypical of the kind of anti-politics that was realised to its full extent in the totalitarian regimes of the twentieth century. They provide, therefore, illuminating reference points when it comes to characterising these regimes.

THE PROFILE OF TOTALITARIAN REGIMES

Arendt, as we have seen, is committed to understanding totalitarianism in its complete novelty, as an unprecedented phenomenon. It is unprecedented in the strict sense that it does not just represent a novel variation with respect to the categories defining forms of government that we have long held. Our established thinking on this, inherited from the classical world, still, broadly speaking, recognises various forms of government, each internally differentiated in respect of their lawful or lawless (legitimate or illegitimate) manifestations: in Aristotelian terms, monarchy or tyranny; aristocracy or oligarchy; polity or democracy. Totalitarianism, however, eludes this classificatory system and any of its more contemporary reformulations. Again, to assimilate totalitarianism with more traditionally recognised political forms is to familiarise it and to evade the 'shock' that accompanies confrontation with the radically new – a confrontation that prompts us to think anew.

The particular temptation, in Arendt's view, is to equate totalitarianism with the more traditional category of tyranny, the lawless rule by fiat of an individual. There may be superficial reasons for making this equation: it is characteristic of totalitarian regimes that they incorporate a 'leader principle', whereby an individual becomes the personification of the regime and its ideology (Arendt 1968a: xxxiii). However, the analogy is a misleading one. The rule of the tyrant is lawless, but for Arendt the principle of totalitarian government is not lawlessness but terror. Totalitarianism indeed rejects established positive law but it is not strictly speaking arbitrary: it appeals instead to law as a product of 'suprahuman' forces, 'the law of History or the law of Nature' (Arendt 1968a: 461–2). An appeal of this sort draws our attention to the fundamentally ideological character of totalitarianism. Ideology replaces the 'principles of action' that characterised more traditionally conceived political formations. Arendt wants to offer here a definite account of ideology as we now encounter it. It is not, however, abstractly formulated and it is a conception that arises out of the experience of totalitarianism itself. It is a formulation equally, again, that resists the temptation to equate totalitarian ideology with modes of political thinking that have gone before and which might be thought to explain it. However, it may have a broader range of application in that it sheds some light on the germinal features of nineteenth-century ideological formations that were not in themselves totalitarian but which contained the seeds of the mentality that made totalitarianism possible: 'the real nature of all ideologies was revealed only in the role that ideology plays in totalitarian domination' (Arendt 1968a: 470).

Some related features make themselves felt, for Arendt, when we look at the role of ideology in totalitarian regimes. The ideology offers a 'total explanation of the past, total knowledge of the present and the reliable prediction of the future' (Arendt 1968a: 470). This total vision is in turn made available through an appeal to a 'scientific' mode of thinking that rests upon particular experiences or reference points, but raised to axiomatic status, from which can be deduced consequences that follow with an iron logic (Arendt 1968a: 471). This is aided by the tendency of the ideology to frame its account of historical process at the highest level of abstraction and with the broadest scope of ambition. In an acute resonance with the 'pan-movements' associated with the colonial era, the totalitarian party is literally a 'movement' with historical ambitions to which the structures of the nation state and its political apparatus may merely present obstacles.[5] The aims are 'millennial' and their reach universal, excluding awkward particularities that might reconnect people with reality, including traditional political structures associated with the modern state. This complete account, immune to any shocks of experience and to anything unprecedented, creates a hermetically sealed world-view, where we are 'emancipated from reality' (Arendt 1968a: 470).

The role of ideology, in view of these features, is not simply to provide a set of aims around which people can be mobilised but to bind people to an inexorable process, the ends of which are beyond their control and are independent of any sense of contingency. Reality has a habit of generating contingency and so the point is to avoid letting reality back in to experience. The ideal subject of totalitarianism is the person for whom 'the distinction between fact and fiction (i.e. the reality of experience) and the distinction between true and false (i.e. the standards of thought)

67

no longer exist' (Arendt 1968a: 474; see also Kateb 2002). The real aim, in this sense, is complete disempowerment; the human capacity to act depends upon a sense of reality to which one can respond and affect in spontaneous fashion, and this reality is what ideology seeks to replace.

This aim of creating a false universe within which people are trapped is further pursued though the operation of a general regime of terror designed to impose the twin conditions of isolation and conformity. Again, terror is a principle of the totalitarian regime and not simply a contingent tool to be deployed in the eventuality of dissent or opposition: it is 'an instrument to rule masses of people who are perfectly obedient' (Arendt 1968a: 6). In this sense, the system of terror accords with the principal aim of totalitarianism, which is to rob people of their human qualities, and particularly the disposition to act freely and to take responsibility for what one does. Its operation is directed to all members of society, regardless of where they may stand, whether they are disposed to support or oppose the regime: 'terror chooses its victims without reference to individual actions or thoughts' (Arendt 1968a: 467). The idea, in more traditional tyrannies, of the tracking down of 'suspects' gives way here to an emphasis upon the 'objective enemy', who is identifiable regardless of anything they have said and done and who, therefore, is whomever the regime chooses, and can be anyone. The severance of the question of guilt and responsibility from the judgments of individuals and the articulations of these in action amounts to the attempted negation of the moral and juridical personality of individuals: 'transforming the human personality into a mere thing' (Arendt 1968a: 438).

In a further resonance with the conditions out of which totalitarianism emerged, Arendt sees these key features as embodied in a bureaucratic structure capable of organising a whole society, or an empire, in the light of the millennial ideological commitments of the regime. We must again, however, avoid here the easy characterisation of this aspect of totalitarianism through assimilation with precedents; we should give the fullest attention to its surprising features rather than ironing them out by subsuming them under familiar categories. One notable feature of totalitarian bureaucracies, which challenges a familiar view that they are 'monolithic', is for Arendt their curiously 'shapeless' character. They are constructed around overlapping, duplicated and parallel functions, involving multiplication of offices. This results in an amorphous structure lacking reliable chains of command or clear divisions of responsibility (Arendt 1968a: 405). Arendt suggests that this feature answers to a paradox in respect of totalitarian rule: on the one hand, the movement must seize the apparatus of rule and infuse it with the informing ideology, but on the other, it must equally ensure that the apparatus does not stabilise. Stability is the enemy of the totalitarian form; it creates the possibility of identifiable forums, official and unofficial, within which recognisable terms of debate and forms of accountability can arise, and with these, something resembling politics. Stable regimes are easier targets for organised opposition (Arendt 1968a: 391). The chaotic totalitarian bureaucracy keeps everyone guessing and so keeps them, as it were, consistently on the 'back foot'.[6]

A related and equally striking feature of the totalitarian apparatus is what Arendt sees as its fundamentally non-utilitarian character, something which confirms it as marking a decisive departure from the expropriating structures that served the imperialist enterprise. This again dissuades us from normalising analogies: 'our bewilderment about the anti-utilitarian character of the totalitarian state structure springs from the mistaken notion that we are dealing with a normal state after all – a bureaucracy, a tyranny, a dictatorship' (Arendt 1968a: 411). Prosaic instrumentalities are never, for Arendt, constitutive of the overarching aim of the totalitarian regime: its true purpose is again the destruction of the personality, making it superfluous in the light of an abstract ideology. In the case of Nazi Germany, Arendt notes, even when the regime was losing the war, it nevertheless resisted recourse to more instrumentally orientated strategies. Indeed, it became even more urgent to make 'an all-out attempt to realise through ruthless totalitarian organisation the goals of totalitarian racial ideology' (Arendt 1968a: 410). For Arendt, one of the key features in the Nazi case that confirms the point is the fact that the camps, which never served instrumental purposes and into which a significant level of resource was placed, continued to operate even when the regime's resources were stretched to breaking point in a failing military enterprise.

And the camps themselves form a central theme for Arendt in characterising this manifestation of totalitarianism: they constitute 'one of the main reference points for the true understanding of totalitarian domination, which stands or falls with the existence of these concentration and extermination camps; for, unlikely as it may sound, these camps are the true central institution of totalitarian organisational power' (Arendt 1968a: 438). The existence of the camps, and more particularly in relation to the prosecution of the 'final solution' in the Nazi case, present for Arendt 'one of the main difficulties' in the understanding of the phenomenon of totalitarianism (Arendt 1968a: 438). It is also a key, however, to the unprecedented character of the phenomenon. The difficulty is presented by 'the peculiar unreality and lack of credibility that characterise all reports from the concentration camps' (Arendt 1968a: 483). The difficulty that Arendt identifies here is one that has persistently made itself felt and is evident in the peculiar susceptibility of the Nazi Holocaust to emasculation and denial. And although Holocaust deniers may be a small and ideologically motivated group, of broader concern is the extent to which denial of the Holocaust becomes a 'point of view' to be heard.[7] The Holocaust as an object of historical memory shows a 'fragility' that no amount of evidence or testimony has proved capable of wholly overcoming.

The sense of unreality here is one that reproduces itself, Arendt argues, in the memory of the victims of the camps themselves: the camp inmate, she suggests, was in a position where 'he had a story to tell of another planet', invoking 'remembered occurrences that must seem just as incredible to those who relate them as to their audience' (Arendt 1968a: 441, 464).[8] How do we account for these difficulties in remembering and recounting? For Arendt, they reflect the fact that the camps created conditions where the attempt at the destruction of the personality, the removal of the characteristics that make the humanity of human beings, was taken to its fullest extent. For the regime, the camps were 'laboratories to carry through its experiment in total domination' (Arendt 1968a: 392). In the camps, the severance between the capacities for agency and responsibility on the one hand and any question of the fate of the person on the other was rendered complete. The victim's presence in the camp and the fate suffered there were each, from this point of view, wholly arbitrary: nothing they did, or could do, mattered at all. Corresponding with this rendering of persons as non-persons was the fact that their deaths were unrecorded, as if they had never been born. For Arendt, this is unprecedented: historically, mankind 'even in its darkest periods, granted the slain enemy the right to be remembered, as a self-evident acknowledgment of the fact that we are all men' (Arendt 1968a: 452). What was attempted in the camps was neither punishment nor persecution but obliteration, such that even death was robbed of its meaning, 'making martyrdom, for the first time in history, impossible' (Arendt 1968a: 451).[9]

These features of the situation give us a sense of its resistance to recovery, a point which takes us back to the earlier theme of narrative.

Traditionally, we have expected that the recovery and preservation of our historical experience is achieved in narrative form. Meaningful narrative gains sense and coherence in virtue of a thematic unity, revealing intelligible human engagements that display an eligibility for judgment. For this to be realisable, the subjects animating the narrative need to solicit our recognition. In respect of the Holocaust, where the experiences of victims are those of persons experiencing a 'living death', turned into non-persons, narrative meaning must prove elusive. Although we can recognise as persons those who survived to testify, there is nevertheless a difficulty in knowing them and speaking about them *as* participants in an unspeakable context.

The phenomenon of the Holocaust, then, prompts us to reconsider the possibilities of narrative. The rupture in our experience that it has insinuated leads us to a permanent recognition of the limits to the cathartic experience of narrative remembrance. In respect of the Holocaust itself, the continuing attempt at remembrance is important but may always have a Sisyphean quality. It confronts us consistently with a break that throws us back on our own resources. We become aware, that is, of the limits to a reliance upon redemptive narratives and the historical guarantee of meaning that they may have been thought to promise. The challenge thus presented to traditional categories and assumptions would seem to lend a new contingency to our attempts to conceptualise our experience; a sense of contingency that, equally, henceforth becomes a permanent feature of experience itself. It is a challenge that Arendt seeks to meet throughout her work through the mediations she adopts, designed to incorporate and to acknowledge formally this new sense of contingency. As we have noted, these include a recognition of the limits to narrative plenitude and the adoption of her fragmented historical approach.

Totalitarianism and Evil

No account of Arendt's treatment of totalitarianism would be adequate without attention to her comments on the question of evil and, in particular, her controversial commentary on the case of Adolph Eichmann. In *The Origins of Totalitarianism* Arendt describes the evil embodied in totalitarianism in terms of the attempt to destroy our humanity – to create a world in which all persons are superfluous in the sense that it does not matter whether they are alive or dead. It is a 'radical evil' that transcends the familiar category of crime: we cannot capture, by the application of this category, 'a thing which as we all feel, no such category was ever intended to cover' (Arendt 1968a: 415).

However, Arendt modified her account in the light of her observations of the Eichmann trial in Jerusalem in 1961. It is worth noting that she did not repudiate the possibility of 'radical evil'. It is also worth noting that she did not offer the later account, summed up in the well-known reference to the 'banality of evil', as a comprehensive conceptualisation of evil per se (Arendt 1965: 252).[10] Nevertheless, she adapted her account of the character of the evil embodied in totalitarianism on the basis of her observations of Eichmann, observations that she felt tell us more about totalitarianism than any broad social scientific categorisation – a point that takes us back to the illumination gained and the challenge presented by a careful look at specific cases and persons, mediating theoretical findings. What Arendt saw in Eichmann was not what she had expected. The individual who had played such a key role in organising the transportation of victims to the death camps was not devilish, not evidently a beast in human form; and he was not, as the prosecution at the trial had described him, a 'perverted sadist' (Arendt 1965: 276). Nor did he appear to be driven by a deep commitment to racist ideology. He was, in fact a man of limited intelligence, and, more importantly, of limited imagination: he lacked 'demonic profundity' (Arendt 1965: 228). In this sense, he was not capable of appreciating, either at the time or afterwards, the moral enormity of his actions. His guiding principle was one of obedience to the law as it was and to the orders that he was given: during his participation in the prosecution of the 'final solution', Eichmann was, for the most part at least, untroubled by feelings of conscience and was entirely consumed by the practicalities of the tasks facing him. His narrowness, his inability to think and judge for himself outside of the rules that he encountered, did in a sense mean that in respect of what he had done, he could not tell right from wrong.[11]

Arendt's commentary on the Eichmann case was famously controversial.[12] She had a number of criticisms of the trial itself and the way in which it was conducted.[13] Amongst them was her complaint that the principal charge laid against Eichmann was that of crimes against the Jewish people. This, she argued, lent the proceedings a parochial character that underplayed the significance of the Holocaust as an event. Whilst it is true that the vast majority of victims of the 'final solution' were Jews and that anti-Semitism was a key element of Nazi ideology, the charge nevertheless potentially blinds us to the sense in which totalitarianism embodies the attempt to eradicate qualities of humanity more generally. For Arendt, the charge of crimes against humanity was more appropriate (Arendt 1965: 269). The more parochial indictment threatened to assimilate the Holocaust with other cases that together constituted a long history of anti-Semitism. But for Arendt, this reflected the more general sense in which the Eichmann trial 'never rose to the challenge of the unprecedented [and] buried the proceedings under a flood of precedents' (Arendt 1965: 263). By contrast, she suggests that 'the camps are the laboratories where changes in human nature are tested, and their shamefulness therefore is not just the business of their inmates and those who ran them according to strictly "scientific" standards; it is the concern of all men' (Arendt 1965: 458).

If this was a controversial point, other observations that Arendt made, again making reference to the peculiar kind of challenge that the case presented to our customary categories, proved even more so. The sense in which, for Arendt, Eichmann was not capable of appreciating the moral significance of what he did was a case in point. For some, there was a sense here that Arendt was letting Eichmann 'off the hook' in asserting that he did not really know the import of what he was doing. However, Arendt's account is resistant to this accusation. Eichmann, she reports, was certainly not incompetent and did not qualify for mitigation on the grounds of insanity – a number of psychiatrists examined him prior to his trial and pronounced him to be sane and in possession of his faculties (Arendt 1965: 25). Furthermore, the death sentence that Eichmann received was, for Arendt, wholly appropriate. Whatever the extent to which Eichmann lacked the imagination to see the moral significance of his actions, he was guilty of participation in an unprecedented crime and the punishment he received was commensurate.[14]

There were, however, further doubts concerning Arendt's account, doubts that focused upon her characterisation of Eichmann and its felicity with respect to our expectations as to the attribution of individual guilt. For Arendt, Eichmann was remarkable for his ordinariness: 'the trouble with Eichmann was precisely that so many were like him, and the many were neither perverted nor sadistic, that they were, and still are, terribly and terrifyingly normal' (Arendt 1965: 276). The implication that it is all too easy to take from this is that there is 'an Eichmann in all of us', or in other words, that any of us might have done what Eichmann did in the circumstances that he faced. Again, Arendt's account resists such a ready inference. The thought that we may all have done what Eichmann did (with the further conclusion that this mitigates his guilt) is perniciously false. It trades upon a sense of the interchangeability of persons; but the fact that, in the modern context and from a sociological point of view, this kind of behaviourally grounded interchangeability may have a certain currency, and is demonstrated in the high level of conformity upon which totalitarian systems proved able to prey, is not enough to determine our judgment with respect to questions of guilt.

There are two related points to be made here, the first of which addresses the sociological issue of conformity and the second draws the emphasis back to the question of moral judgment with respect to individual guilt. First, no matter how much sociological and psychological evidence may be available to measure and confirm social conformity, it cannot establish the interchangeability of persons: 'under conditions of terror most people will comply but *some people will not*, just as the lesson of the countries to which the Final Solution was proposed is that "it could happen" in most places but it did not happen everywhere' (Arendt 1965: 233). This fact challenges the subsuming of moral judgment under sociological categories. It also prompts us to focus upon what Arendt sees as a wholly spurious notion of 'collective guilt'. She notes the tendency particularly amongst German youth in the 1950s and 1960s to accept this notion, but it is not, she suggests, morally authentic: 'it is quite gratifying to feel guilty if you haven't done anything wrong' and the young Germans who took on the mantle of collective guilt were at the same time 'surrounded on all sides and in all walks of life, by men in positions of authority and in public affairs who are very guilty indeed but who feel nothing of the sort' (Arendt 1965: 251). Second, this draws our attention back to the question of individual guilt, assessed on the basis of what one has done, rather than on the basis of what many people might have done. Arendt notes that it was precisely a conflation of these two considerations – the sociological and the moral – that formed part of Eichmann's defence, but it could not possibly hold up:

> if the defendant excuses himself on the grounds that he acted not as a man but as a mere functionary whose functions could just as easily be carried out by anyone else, it is as if a criminal pointed to the statistics on crime . . . and declared that he only did what was statistically expected, that it was mere accident that he did it and not somebody else. (Arendt 1965: 289; cf. Culbert 2010: 148)

The fact is that it was Eichmann and not somebody else, and this remains central to our judgment as to his guilt and as to the punishment he deserved: to concede to mitigation on the grounds of sociological information, of what Arendt sees as behaviourist propositions, is to concede to assumptions that resonate with the conception of human nature characteristic of totalitarian ideology itself and its expectations as to the possibility of the manipulation of that nature.

At the same time, the apparently awkward consideration remains that Eichmann's thoughtlessness and his corresponding disposition to conform and obey meant that, whilst he was aware of what he was doing and whilst nobody put a gun to his head in order to force him to do it, he did not appreciate its moral significance; in the sense that we noted earlier, he did not appreciate the difference between right and wrong. Does this not provide grounds for mitigation? For Arendt, the answer is no; but it is equally an issue that alerts us to the sense in which the experience of totalitarianism challenges our established moral categories and the whole moral edifice that has been built upon these categories. Our moral tradition associates evil with acting upon base motives and dispositions but we have now confronted

> evil which could no longer be understood and explained by the evil motives of self-interest, greed, covetousness, resentment, lust for power and cowardice; and which therefore anger could not revenge, love could not endure, friendship could not forgive. Just as the victims in the death factories or the holes of oblivion are no longer 'human' in the eyes of their executioners, so this newest species of criminals is beyond the pale even of the solidarity of human sinfulness. (Arendt 1965: 437)

From this point of view, Arendt would have agreed with the characterisation of the Holocaust as 'an upside-down miracle' (Bauer 1978: 31). The point here, then, is that our moral tradition, which has provided us with a sense of the relation between wrongdoing and the propensity to act upon well-recognised malign dispositions or forms of moral weakness, has now been upset. The confidence in judgment, indexed against the reference points that our moral tradition supplied, is now no longer available to us; and we have again been thrown back upon our own resources with respect to the capacity for independent judgment. As we noted in Chapter 2, for Arendt, the fact that in Germany after the Second World War these traditional moral reference points were readopted as quickly and easily as they were discarded under totalitarian conditions is no comfort. The above sense of 'solidarity in human sinfulness' is no longer a form of solidarity that we can rely upon, and we are faced with a permanent requirement to think about this issue, as with others, without the crutch of tradition.

The implications of this for Arendt's account of the role of ethics and moral judgment will be explored later. For now, it is sufficient to note that the above considerations constitute one dimension to a broader set of challenges that the experience of totalitarianism, and the rupture that it revealed, presents to our sense of the pitfalls and potentialities associated with the capacities of human beings and, equally, the question of how we are to theorise them in a context that has been changed permanently by an unprecedented event.

THE IMPLICATIONS OF TOTALITARIANISM

For Arendt, the experience of totalitarianism presents the most severe challenge to our sense of ourselves, our capabilities and also to the traditional ways in which we reflect upon these capabilities. I will conclude this chapter by reviewing briefly the themes that this challenge places on the agenda from Arendt's point of view, in that the phenomenon of totalitarianism presents back to us, in extremis, aspects of our more conventional modern experience out of which it emerged.

The first feature of our experience that totalitarianism both embodies and exposes is our vulnerability to the initiation of processes that are beyond our control. It is, for Arendt, a central aim of totalitarianism to create conditions under which individuals are absorbed into, and define themselves by reference to, historical processes which transcend any and all capacities for autonomous thought and action. The totalitarian creed dictates that no one can ever make a difference. This creed equally, however, reflects a broader theme associated with modernity: 'the modern concept of process pervading history and nature alike separates the modern age from the past more profoundly than any other single idea' (Arendt 1977: 63). The corollary to this sense of subjection to process is the thought that historical and natural processes may be harnessed and directed. This was a central feature of totalitarian ideology, where 'nothing is meaningful in itself . . . [and] the process which alone makes meaningful whatever it happens to carry along, has thus acquired a monopoly of universality and significance' (Arendt 1977: 63–4). The sense of susceptibility to process, then, may become wedded to a purpose, to create a system where 'men are superfluous' and in which it is possible to allow 'the forces of nature or history to race freely through mankind, unhindered by any spontaneous action' (Arendt 1965: 465). This was evident in 'the totalitarian phenomenon, with its striking anti-utilitarian

76

traits and its strange disregard for factuality . . . based on the conviction that everything is possible' (Arendt 1968a: 87).

The motif of process is not, however, confined to its particular expression as it was operationalised in totalitarian ideology; its mark is more broadly impressed upon the culture of modernity. It is evident in the ambition of a complete and definitive mastery of things inscribed intellectually in the scientific attitude that seeks total understanding by grasping the underlying processes that govern phenomena, allowing us, thereby, to transcend all particularity and contingency. This hubristic inclination carries with it an extreme arbitrariness in that, in process thinking, 'every axiom seems to lead itself to consistent deductions . . . to such an extent that it is as though men were in a position to prove almost any hypothesis they may adopt' (Arendt 1968a: 86). The promise equally is of practical mastery through the application of scientific knowledge, to work on the world technologically in order to adapt it to what our preconceived theories of Man tell us we need. The results make themselves felt in modern societies where spontaneous action gives way to managed processes and exercises in social engineering. The price to be paid for these attempts at mastery of all phenomena, therefore, is a reconceptualisation of persons as subject to impersonal processes and to be acted upon as such.[15] None of this, of course, would justify intemperate claims that we now live in a totalitarian world, but it draws our attention to the dominance of the social over the political, with the concomitant threat to freedom that this may entail and which is a permanent concern.[16]

A further corresponding experience that we are drawn to consider here, with respect to the modern condition more generally, is that of what Arendt terms 'loneliness': 'what prepares men for totalitarian domination in the non-totalitarian world is the fact that loneliness, once a borderline experience usually suffered in certain marginal social conditions such as old age, has become an everyday experience of the ever-growing masses in the modern age' (Arendt 1968a: 478). What does Arendt really mean by loneliness here? There is a temptation, perhaps, to equate it with a condition of isolation; but whilst the two may be related, they are not the same.[17] The person who suffers isolation is not necessarily, in Arendt's sense, lonely. In the absence of the companionship of others, one can still enjoy one's own company, something which, as we saw in Chapter 2, is central to the experience of being able to think and judge for oneself. True loneliness comes with a condition where one no longer experiences one's own company in this sense.[18]

77

It is nevertheless the case, in Arendt's account, that conditions of isolation may leave one *vulnerable* to loneliness; of particular significance here is the sense of isolation, in which Arendt is particularly interested, as a political condition, where the companionship that one lacks is that of one's fellow citizens with whom one can interact publicly and exchange opinions. It is through the exchange of opinion with others that one can constitute oneself as an identity, articulated in the 'voice of one unexchangeable person' (Arendt 1968a: 476). The experience of isolated thinking is one where we remain in a state of equivocation – an inherently endless eternal dialogue that may readily become nugatory and lose any sense of reality – reflecting the point noted earlier that the always fraught relation between thinking and plural worldly experience is central to the integrity of each.

It is in the context of this that Arendt comes to see loneliness no longer as a contingent experience relating to particular isolating social circumstances but rather as a mainstream experience characteristic of modern mass societies. What underlies this experience is not the contingent isolation that comes with a lack of particular companions but the conditions under which persons may be far from isolated in the familiar sense but who, existing in a mass and subject to what appear as inexorable social and historical processes, encounter one another not as 'unexchangeable persons' capable of authentic dialogue, but as entirely 'exchangeable' persons subject to a common fate. These are the conditions under which mass loneliness is possible. So, what people significantly lack in these circumstances is not the simple presence of others with whom one can enter into personal relations but who are equally subject to fate; but rather, others who, in virtue of their differing standpoints, interests and experiences, can be genuine interlocutors, with whom one can both disagree and reach agreements:

> what makes loneliness so unbearable is the loss of one's own self which can be realised in solitude, but confirmed in its identity only by the trusting and trustworthy company of my equals. In this situation, man loses trust in himself as the partner of his thoughts and that elementary confidence in the world which is necessary to make experiences at all. Self and world, capacity for thought and experience are lost at the same time. (Arendt 1968a: 477)

This is an experience that Arendt associates with the broader conditions of 'world alienation', where individuals have a common fate but lack, by the same token, 'a common world which would at once relate and separate them' (Arendt 1968a: 89). The 'world' in this sense refers us to a mode of experience that constitutes just the opposite of that implied by the emphasis upon 'process' as the central category through which our self-understanding is focused. It marks instead a context of relative permanence, through the collective establishment of public institutions of the sort that were either compromised or destroyed under totalitarianism and which, more generally, look like potential obstacles to the realisation of ends deduced from process-thinking. And so, just in virtue of its relative stability, it can incorporate a defined public realm within which free human agency, in its novelty and contingency, can take place.[19]

These are some of the features, then, in view of which the experience of totalitarianism prompts us to think again about our own circumstances, as well as about *how* to think. They are themes that do not spring from a 'finished' account of totalitarianism. The 'abyss' that separates the world of the living from that of the 'living dead' presents a permanent obstacle to such a completion. This does not mean that dwelling on the horrors of totalitarianism is not a requirement and is not illuminating. But it does not lead to any fixed philosophical or ideological conclusion; it rather alerts the sensitive mind to the conditions in which we find ourselves and to the need, presented to us *by* those conditions, to think in a way that avoids final solutions of any variety.

This takes us back to the need for revision of our political theorising and the pursuit of non-traditional modes, suitable to taking into account the possibility of unprecedented experiences and their implications. For Arendt, to recognise the unprecedented in the shape, particularly, of the 'upside-down miracle' of totalitarianism, equally focuses our attention on the sense in which we can affirm the possibilities that the capacity for action, for the initiation of the unprecedented, can work *for* rather than *against* human freedom; on the spontaneity which 'can never be entirely eliminated' (Arendt 1968a: 438). An analysis of the theme of anti-politics in totalitarianism, incorporating a recognition that human capacities can be co-opted and used against humanity can actually *reveal* something of the nature and possibilities attaching to these capacities, inviting us to think about them in ways that we have avoided traditionally, paying only 'lip service to the estimate of action as the highest activity of man' (Arendt 1977: 84). This becomes a key preoccupation in Arendt's work and forms a central theoretical motif in her principal exploration of the character of the public realm, in *The Human Condition*.

NOTES

1. For a comparison between Arendt's analysis of totalitarianism and other contemporaneous accounts, see Söllner (2004).

2. It is worth noting that the real and specific socio-cultural basis of the distinctions that emerged and became politically pertinent in this period forms a basis for Arendt's disagreement with Sartre's analysis of the 'Jewish question', where the gaze of the anti-semite generates the category of Jewishness (Arendt 1968a: xv).

3. In this respect, Arendt also finds illumination by reference to the Dreyfuss affair in France (Arendt 1968a: 89–120).

4. Cecil Rhodes personified this particularly in his belief in his own functionality, his belief that he embodied a force that meant that he could do nothing wrong because anything *he* did became right (Arendt 1968a: 215).

5. It is for this reason that, for Arendt, whilst totalitarian ideology may make an appeal to nationalist sentiment, its characteristic scope transcends this. The nation is celebrated in so far as it has the capacity for world dominance. This is why she argues that Italian fascism, in its early form, whilst fiercely nationalistic, was not fully totalitarian (Arendt 1968a: 258–9).

6. On Arendt and the tendency of bureaucratic institutions to dehumanise, see May (1997).

7. See Lipstadt (1994) and also Vidal-Naquet (1992).

8. Arendt's point here is confirmed in the analyses of survivor testimonies undertaken by Lawrence Langer, who notes a sense of frustration on the part of many when attempting to tell their stories. Finding no ready way to make their experience answer to what is recognisable, they are susceptible to 'anguished memory', which, far from being redemptive, collapses into uncertainty: 'the seeds of anguished memory are sown in the barren belief that the very story you tell drives off the audience you seek to capture. Those seeds often shrivel in the further suspicion that the story you tell cannot precisely be the story as it happened' (Langer 1991: 61).

9. For more on this theme, see Levi (1989) and Rotenstreich (1981).

10. For discussions of this issue, see Bernstein (1997, 2010). See also Kateb (1983).

11. The question of thoughtlessness here is not to be confused with lack of intelligence; in Arendt's view, even highly intelligent people can be thoughtless. This is an issue that engages the question of Arendt's response to the fact that her mentor, Heidegger, involved himself in Nazism. She described this involvement as an 'error'. This was a comment that some have regarded as an unacceptable understatement. Although it is worth noting that, for Arendt, the issue goes deeper than a simple mistake: Heidegger's failure of judgment is related to the 'worldless' character of his philosophical enterprise which manifested its own kind of thoughtlessness. Villa argues that Heidegger displayed a similarity with the thoughtlessness of Eichmann (Villa 1997). For a sterner verdict upon Arendt's response to Heidegger, see Bernstein (2000: 288–91). See also Young-Bruehl (2006: 163).

12. Some of the exchanges in the 'Eichmann controversy' are collected in Arendt (1978). Some comments by Arendt on the debate are to be found in Arendt (1965: 280–98). Other overviews are in Benhabib (2000) and in Young-Bruehl (1982: 337–94).

13. For her detailed criticisms, see Arendt (1965: 253–79).

14. That it *was* an unprecedented crime prompts Arendt to proffer her own justification

for the death sentence, at variance with the more conventional verdict reached by the court – see Arendt (1965: 277–9).

15. Here, Arendt is close to some of the arguments associated with the early Frankfurt School concerning the self-defeating character of Enlightenment thinking, promising liberation through scientific mastery and delivering only disempowerment. See, for example, Horkheimer and Adorno (1979). Despite the similarities in this respect, however, Arendt was far from sympathetic to the Frankfurt theorists – see Baehr (2010: 3–4).

16. Some have nevertheless seen in Arendt an exaggerated sense of the 'rise of the social' – see Pitkin (1998).

17. To this extent, Arendt's illustration of loneliness by reference to the circumstances of old age may not be helpful, implying as it does a condition where one is robbed of the companionship of social contacts and colleagues – the condition of 'retirement'.

18. This also indicates the sense in which totalitarianism may erode the operation of conscience, which, as we saw previously, Arendt argues is related to the capacity to think (Arendt 1968a: 452–3).

19. A further concrete reflection of this loss of access to a realm of public engagement, for Arendt, is the widespread and increasingly common phenomenon of 'statelessness' in the modern world. The stateless represent, in stark manner, the broader experience of 'superfluousness' experienced by the mass of people in modern societies, 'the deprivation of a place in the world which makes opinion significant and acting effective' (Arendt 1968a: 296). Correspondingly, they lack the substantive rights that are conferred by a political community. And all talk of universal human rights proves meaningless in their case; something which shows up the hollowness of such talk. For Arendt, the concept of rights is a political one and thus meaningful rights can be established only within the context of a substantive community where they are institutionally guaranteed. In so far as they are 'forced to live outside the scope of all tangible law' the stateless are denied the only right that can genuinely be considered a universal demand – the 'right to have rights', that is, the right to belong to a political community (Arendt 1968a: 293, 297).

CHAPTER 5

Theorising Political Action: The Human Condition

The experience of totalitarianism leads Arendt to reproblematise our situation, our capacities and possibilities, with a renewed sense of their fragility and with a modified sense of the modalities through which we understand and re-present them to ourselves theoretically. What will not do here, she thinks, is another comprehensive theory of human nature. The ruptures and fragilities that recent experiences have brought to light undermine an enterprise of this sort; and commensurately, to persist in such an enterprise promises only to provide us with another reified self-conception that is likely to prove as inadequate in the face of the realities of our experience and the challenges it presents as previous formulations have proven to be. The vulnerabilities that our recent experiences have exposed were brought to light *in extremis*, by the way in which human powers have been organised and put into the service of rendering persons as 'material' to be worked upon with a view ultimately to eradicating human qualities. This indicates to us the susceptibility of persons to the conditions we make for ourselves: 'in addition to the conditions under which life is given to man on earth, and partly out of them, men constantly create and their own self-made conditions' (Arendt 1958: 9). The fact that we are able to formulate definitive accounts of natural phenomena is a function of the capacity for understanding which is itself related to our capacity for self-conditioning – and in this sense it provides the very reason why such definitions fail when we attempt to apply them to ourselves. The attempt at comprehensive self-definition in the form of theories of human nature is akin to the attempt at 'jumping over our own shadows' (Arendt 1958: 10). This is why, in Arendt's view, the philosophical tradition, which has sought definitions of human nature, resorted to a standpoint beyond that of human beings themselves, appealing to the divine or the eternal – to the 'god of the philosophers' (Arendt 1958: 11). This appeal inevitably turns out only to underwrite the assertion of questionable claims as to the 'true' nature of mankind, and there is nothing to be gained by the 'complacent repetition of "truths" which have become trivial or empty' (Arendt 1958: 5).

So, despite the ambition that is implied in the title *The Human Condition*, it is hardly surprising that Arendt does not offer a comprehensive and definitive theoretical account of human nature; the formal and substantive characteristics of the work reflect this. Arendt focuses upon key experiences that we can associate with the *vita activa* – with 'human life in so far as it is actively engaged in doing something' (Arendt 1958: 22). This focus quite deliberately leaves out of the account other significant facets of human life: in particular the contemplative and the affective. The categories that she explores, she says, 'do not explain what we are or answer to the question of who we are' (Arendt 1958: 11). The reason for her focus on these particular categories of experience is, again, that these are the experiences that a reflection upon totalitarianism draws to our attention as standing in need of re-examination. In view of this, her exploration of the conditions of our conduct is a situated one, in the light of what has become apparent to us: 'a reconsideration of the human condition from the vantage point of our newest experiences and our most recent fears' (Arendt 1958: 5). In particular, totalitarianism, and the conditions out of which it emerged, draws our attention to the question of freedom and its newly revealed fragility in the light of a decline in our understanding of, and capacity for, authentic action, as the fullest expression of our freedom. Along with this comes an appreciation of the contingency of the public realm. The discussion in *The Human Condition* pays attention to this atrophied category of experience, together with other dimensions to the *vita activa* with which it may have become confused or to which it may have conceded.[1] The point of the discussion is not simply to define freedom as a facet of human existence but rather to revive it as a preoccupation. The thrust of the work is in this sense dialogic, reflecting again the kind of epistemological mediation discussed in Chapter 3: it prompts continuing reflection upon, and discussion of, the experience of freedom, through which we might yet, as it were, talk it back into existence, within the horizon of what we take to be our potentialities.

This sense of the recovery of lapsed potential lends a historical aspect to the discussion, particularly with respect to past construals and embodiments of action. Again, however, Arendt's approach is a mediated one. It is not a task to be undertaken through the application of the techniques of traditional historiography. As we have seen, the totalitarian experience, in Arendt's view, signalled a rupture with the past that simultaneously showed us the wholly contingent character of the realm of freedom. This has a dual impact upon the manner in which we can now relate to the past. We now find ourselves in circumstances where the past no longer delivers traditions that might anchor our understanding of ourselves and the meaning of our experience. Equally, and more specifically, the need to make the contingent realm of freedom our object is no longer met by the finality and closure that historical narrative might once have promised. In our political thought now, a central emphasis needs to be placed upon spontaneity, upon that which is unconditioned by the past; a theme that is missed to the extent that 'the historical sciences have been permitted to supply the field of politics with their methods and categories' (Arendt 1994: 321). In the light of this, Arendt refers to examples principally from the ancient world, not as sources of traditional wisdom nor to provide the basis for a sense of narrative continuity that would allow them an unmediated applicability to the present. In the spirit of the 'pearl diver' analogy discussed in Chapter 3, Arendt 'raids' the past for images that may remind us of lost experiences and atrophied capacities that might help us to think with originality about our current condition.

Thinking about the *Vita Activa*

In the context of these methodological concerns, Arendt thematises the *vita activa*. From a historical point of view, she suggests it has become 'overloaded with tradition' (Arendt 1958: 12). We can see its origins in ancient Greece, developing, as we have noted before, out of the perceived distinction between the 'noisy' life of activity on the one hand, and the 'quiet' contemplative life, personified by the philosopher, on the other. It was a distinction central to the birth of our tradition of political philosophy and its assertion of the superiority of the *vita contemplative* over the *vita activa*: the unquiet life was an inhibition upon the contemplative search for truth, since 'eternity discloses itself to mortal eyes only when all human movements and activities are at perfect rest' (Arendt 1958: 15). This standpoint was nowhere more completely expressed than in Plato 'where the whole utopian reorganisation of *polis* life is not only directed by the superior insight of the philosopher but has no aim other than to make possible the philosopher's way of life' (Arendt 1958: 14).

We noted in Chapter 2 the sense in which, for Arendt, the prejudicial elevation of thinking over acting has proved consistently problematic and damaging to each of the terms in the hierarchy. Equally, the unpolitical culture that the tradition insinuated, combined with concrete social and economic developments, can be thought to count amongst the conditions that rendered us vulnerable to the emergence of a thoroughgoing anti-politics. In these respects, a refocusing on the character and significance of the *vita activa* not only presents a challenge to the vestiges of the tradition but also, and by the same token, may prove particularly pertinent to a reflection upon the challenges presented by our current situation. This refocusing depends, for Arendt, upon the intellectual effort, informed by historical examples, to retrieve experiences associated with the public realm that have been emasculated, or whose significance has been obscured, by traditional theoretical assumptions. They are experiences, Arendt wants to suggest, that resonate when we discover a vocabulary in which to talk about them that is resistant to the clouding effects of traditional discourse:

> the curious discrepancy between language and theory . . . [is] a discrepancy between the world-orientated 'objective' language we speak and the man-orientated, subjective theories we use in our attempts at understanding. It is language, and the fundamental human experiences underlying it, rather than theory, that teaches us that the things of the world, among which the *vita activa* spends itself, are of a very different nature and produced by different kinds of activities. (Arendt 1958: 94)

The point here is not that we can seek a vocabulary that 'cuts through' our theoretically informed perspectives toward a knowledge grounded upon a fundamental sub-stratum. Rather, it is a matter of developing a phenomenal awareness, recovering a sense of phenomenal reality though the ability to speak in non-reductive, dialogic terms about our experience, informed by appropriate exemplifications that gain relevance by answering to our situation as we find it.

What this approach allows, in Arendt's view, is a renewed sense of the internal differentiations within the *vita activa* which the tradition, in asserting the priority of the contemplative, regarded as all equally noisy and inferior, to be subject to external legislation. The differentiations that Arendt wishes to identify here – between the categories of labour, work and action – represent 'the most elementary articulations of the human condition . . . [constituting] permanent features of life in that they cannot be irretrievably lost so long as the human condition itself is not changed' (Arendt 1958: 6). This does not mean, however, that they cannot be neglected, cannot decline or that one cannot subsume another. And indeed, it is the decline and 'colonisation' of the capacity for action, the capacity that the discussion in *The Human Condition* is aimed at drawing to our attention, that is of principal concern for Arendt. And it is of concern to us in the wake of totalitarianism; in view of the decline of the capacity for action and the attempt of totalitarianism to emasculate that capacity entirely so changing the human condition. The categories of labour, work and action are 'schematic definitions' against which we recognise 'the world we have come to live in'; and see that the capacity for action is 'the centre of all other human capabilities' (Arendt 1977: 63). As Arendt sees it, 'considerations like these are not at all meant to offer solutions or to give advice'. At best, they might encourage sustained and closer reflection on the nature and the intrinsic potentialities of action, 'which never before has revealed its greatness and its dangers so openly' (Arendt 1977: 63).

Labour, Work and Action

The categories by which Arendt characterises the *vita activa* are ways of making sense of key aspects of our experience without providing an exhaustive or definitive taxonomy of human activity.[2] Each of the categories has its own character and implies a distinctive mode of association between persons engaged in that activity. It is worth now reviewing briefly the categorical distinctions that Arendt draws as a basis for assessing their significance not just as phenomenological descriptions but with respect to how they illuminate current social and political conditions. Each of the categories in the hierarchy of activities to which she refers prepares for the characterisation of the next by revealing its limitations; and again, the ultimate purpose here is to focus our attention upon the category of action.[3]

The category of labour refers to activity geared to the maintenance of life, meeting the requirements of biological necessity. As such, it is a sphere of activity in which we are closest to nature, and its character mirrors that of natural processes, being cyclical in form. Our biological needs are constant features of life and so the activity of meeting them is constantly reproduced. Further, labour leaves nothing lasting behind it, producing for the purposes of consumption, and its products disappear rapidly either through consumption or decay. So labour mirrors the 'changeless, deathless repetition' of the cycles of nature. It requires little in the way of ingenuity or intelligence – nature dictates – and in this sphere, human beings are characterised principally by their sameness. Accordingly, interaction is at its least sophisticated. Significant interaction comes with plurality or difference between persons in respect of their activities, aims and perspectives; the sameness of our biological needs precludes this. At the level of labour, our existence is 'worldless and herd-like' (Arendt 1958: 100). In Arendt's view, then, labour, the sphere of *animal laborans*, is both the least interesting and the least dignified in the *vita activa*.

Given that, historically, many have lived lives largely given over to the activity of labour, Arendt's account here could create the impression of disdain, reproducing the disdain in which the ancient world held those in a condition of slavery. However, her concern is with the activity itself rather than with those who engage in it. In any case, she suggests, the idea that labour was despised in the ancient world because of the inferiority of those engaged in it is a prejudice of modern historians: 'the ancients reasoned the other way round and felt it necessary to possess slaves because of the slavish nature of all occupations that served the needs for the maintenance of life' (Arendt 1958: 83). To the extent that labour says anything about those most engaged in it, it says something about us all – that we are subject to intrinsic natural necessities, and the only way of at least partially relieving the burden that this creates for us is forcibly to place the burden upon others (Arendt 1958: 119). But what makes this use of force so unacceptable is that the greater the burden of labour placed upon us, the less the opportunity for escape into regions where our higher and more distinctively human faculties are engaged. Here, the characterisation of labour begins to illuminate the contours of a conception of freedom, Arendt's principal concern, by thematising in an initial way a sense of freedom as the escape from the realm of necessity: '[one's] freedom is always won in his never wholly successful attempts to liberate himself from necessity' (Arendt 1958: 121). This is a theme that also allows her to identify ways in which the enslavement of persons to the demands of nature have been reproduced socially, and which draw our attention to the ongoing need to preoccupy ourselves with, and talk about, freedom.

Labour's perceived disadvantages both make available and can be measured against the more sophisticated category of work, the manufacture of durable objects. Unlike labour, where products are consumed or rapidly decay, work generates lasting products that are not for consumption but for use. This contrast lends a significance to work that labour does not have. The products of work have a relative durability that makes them the 'furniture' of a common, lasting and stable context. Work, then, equally provides us with a sense of space and location, promising to mitigate the sense of utter sameness associated with the sphere of labour: persons located in a durable worldly space furnished by the products of work become distinguishable from one another and so capable of interacting in the light of differing perspectives. Work itself has intrinsic features that mark it out from labour. It involves invention in working upon the material of nature to fashion it into something that escapes natural decay; and as such, it requires an instrumental intelligence. Work, as Arendt sees it, involves the formulation of blueprints for the production of fashioned objects, formed in the imagination, and the development of suitable techniques for their realisation. It therefore engages more sophisticated faculties than labour. That this superiority of work is achieved through an interference with nature and a halting of natural processes means that work contains an intrinsic element of 'violence'. The appropriation of the 'raw materials' of nature and their refashioning into a worldly object is to kill a life-process: work is a 'destroyer of nature' (Arendt 1958: 139). The satisfaction that comes as a reward for work, in part at least, stems from the exercise of strength and the realised ability to dominate nature. By the same token, it encompasses, as an activity, differences between persons who may engage in different work activities and bring to bear different competences. We have seen that difference creates conditions for interaction: in the context of work, we stand as producers of objects that have use-value. As such, our principal mode of interaction is as producers of things that have exchange value; and so the principal interactive motif of this sphere is that of the market (Arendt 1958: 160).

So, in the movement from labour to work, we take a step away from the homogenising imperatives of necessity and assert ourselves as distinct and intelligent beings: *homo faber* steps out of the condition of isolation given by the sameness of *animal laborans* and moves into a worldly interactive realm. At the same time, for Arendt, there is a sense of limitation here. In the sphere of work, we confront one another as distinct; but we do so in a manner mediated by the instrumental dynamics of exchange. We become distinct beings, but this distinctness is subject to the reductive effects of exchangeability and so we do not appear as unique persons: uniqueness is precluded by definition under the conditions of market exchange.

This sense of limitation draws us toward, and is measured against, Arendt's third category in the *vita activa*, the category of action. She seeks to reaffirm the experience of action, now marginalised, and bring it back to our attention, again mainly through reference to exemplifications from the ancient world. In contrast with the spheres of labour and work, which together constitute the private realm, action constitutes a public realm. Action, in contrast with labour or work, is unconditioned by considerations of necessity or instrumentality; public action takes the form of words and deeds, according to principle, and embodies thereby the capacity to bring something new to the world: 'the fact that man is capable of action means that the unexpected can be expected from him' (Arendt 1958: 178). In this sense, action answers to the condition of 'natality', that each person enters the world as a unique presence. It constitutes, therefore, the disclosure of persons in their uniqueness, a disclosure of 'who' one is rather than simply 'what' one is. It embodies the 'agonal' spirit of self-disclosure and the desire for 'glory', inspiring persons to show themselves in their uniqueness, as unexchangeable (Arendt 1958: 41).[4] The sense of disclosure here, of making one's unique mark on the world, renders action the most dignified dimension to the *vita activa*, where we are furthest from the homogenising category of nature and expressive of our fullest freedom.[5] For Arendt, 'the greatest that man can achieve is his own appearance and actualisation' (Arendt 1958: 208).

The sphere of action is therefore equally a sphere of plurality, where we disclose ourselves to others and interact in our full difference as persons: 'plurality is the condition of human action because we are all the same, that is human, in such a way that nobody is ever the same as anyone else who ever lived, lives or will live' (Arendt 1958: 8). And the opportunity for disclosure indicates that action is an undertaking that cannot be realised successfully either anonymously or surreptitiously. Nor is the disclosure of the self in action reducible to specific motives or ends – these are factors that play a part in the formation of individual intentions that can nevertheless be assimilated and categorised, revealing the 'what' rather than the 'who'. One's distinctive identity can only be displayed in the specifics of a 'performance'. It is a display, in turn, that stimulates the operation of reflective judgment in others; a form of judgment, as we have seen, that passes a verdict on the basis of the particular case rather than through the imposition of general categories.[6] The judgmental gaze of others is what confers meaning upon action and which provides a sense of the persona of the agent: 'only my equals can say who I am and tell me'

(Arendt 1958: 145). The gaze of others, then, far from undermining our freedom, confers upon disclosure the sense of meaning that is its hallmark: 'being seen and being heard by others derive their significance from the fact that everybody sees and hears from a different perspective' (Arendt 1958: 67). By the same token, the equality afforded by the public realm is not reducible to a sense of the sameness of persons: quite the contrary, it is the difference between them, animating the condition of plurality that makes for the possibility of interaction and judgment on the part of persons considered not with respect to their personal concerns or circumstances but as citizens. The public realm, in this way, secures 'an equality of unequals that stand in need of being "equalised" in certain respects and for specific purposes' (Arendt 1958: 215). This secures a sense of equality that is authentically political in that it is in no way reducible to any categories derivable from nature.

The visibility of action and its exposure to the judgmental gaze equally makes possible its preservation from the ravages of time through memorialisation and remembrance, which rescues agency from the futility that threatens all the engagements of mortal beings; the danger of being gone and forgotten and of having made no mark. The original model from which we gain a sense of this, for Arendt, is associated with early antiquity in the form of the poetic narration of heroic deeds, exemplified in Homer, 'a shining example of the poet's political function' (Arendt 1958: 197). But his model now resonates with a broader sense of remembrance and its forms: 'the written page or the printed book . . . paintings or sculpture . . . all sorts of records, documents and monuments' (Arendt 1958: 95). These forms of recording and remembering preserve the disclosure involved in action and permit the preservation of the biographical identity of the agent and the story into which they have inserted themselves, exemplified originally in Achilles, whose exploits attained their true meaning through the story of his life and those who judged him (Arendt 1958: 194).

The model from early antiquity stands in need of adaptation however. It centred upon the exploits of heroic 'adventurers' whose unbounded actions were the stuff of poetic immortalisation. We now understand the circumstances of action in a modified way: we think of action taking place in a bounded context, where interactions take place in the context of accepted terms of engagement, established by institutional and legal arrangements. These create, as it were, relatively familiar terrain upon which persons can interact and equally make for a more accessible sense of meaning attaching to what is enacted by those with whom we interact.

The result is a transposal in the terms of action such that the requirement for immediate and urgent physical confrontation with otherness, characteristic of the tales of early antiquity, gives way to a context in which our principal mode of interaction is through speech: 'the actor, the doer of deeds, is possible only if he is at the same time a speaker of words'. Through the spoken word, the actor announces 'what he does, has done and intends to do' (Arendt 1958: 178–9).

The image that answers to and informs this more bounded sense of the context of action comes with the idea of the polis, the characteristic political focus of the city state. The polis provided, within its system of laws and institutions, the context in which free action could take place. Again, the terms established in this political context are not to be seen as an 'external' constraint upon the capacity for action; and this is so in two senses. First, the terms of interaction make coherent action possible – they establish common terms of reference such that action becomes comprehensible, and thereby susceptible to the attribution of meaning and the possibility of memorialisation and remembrance. Without them, action runs the risk of incomprehensibility and forgetting. The irreducibly plural context of action – where actions prompt responses from other perspectives, also themselves actions – lends it always a potentially 'boundless' quality, such that chains of interactions can constitute processes that run out of control. As a result, boundaries become important. Second, the terms established in the polis are themselves answerable to the capacity for action. The boundlessness of action 'is only the other side of its tremendous capacity for establishing relationships' (Arendt 1958: 191). It is the very spontaneous and creative aspects to action that make it simultaneously capable of forming freely made, institutional agreements, whilst constantly carrying the potential to dismantle the resultant arrangements and recreate things anew (a point to which I shall return in Chapter 6). In this sense, 'the frailty of human institutions and laws generally, of all matters pertaining to men's living together, arises from the human condition of natality and is quite independent of the frailty of human nature' (Arendt 1958: 191).

We can say, in this sense, that the intrinsic tension between free human conduct and the institutional and legal limitations that constrain it and provide a context is ultimately a constitutive tension internal to the capacity for action itself. In affirming these features of human action and the intrinsic contingency that it embodies, Arendt wishes, again, to challenge to traditional 'solutions' to the questions posed by the realm of public affairs. As we have seen, in our tradition, the disturbing contingency of the public realm has prompted the search for something more permanent and more reliable. This is a theme illustrated in the consistent preoccupation historically with the regulative image of a 'lawgiver' – a ruler rather than an actor – who provides us with a recipe on the basis of an appeal to something 'higher'. Plato's 'god of the philosophers' provides a template for this that is reproduced historically in the form of 'Providence, the "invisible hand", Nature, the "world spirit", class interest' (Arendt 1958: 185). The susceptibility of the public realm to emasculation, to which our recent experience testifies, suggests equally that it only exists substantially to the extent that it is continually animated in and through action.

Recognition of these features, for Arendt, constitutes recognition of the possibility of human freedom, enacted in circumstances where, released from constraining concerns, we can interact under conditions of equality in citizenship. This image equally draws out, for Arendt, the sense of freedom as *empowerment*, as the generation of power through action and interaction, making a memorable mark on the world: 'without a people or a group, there is no power . . . when we speak of a "powerful man" or a "powerful personality", we already use the work "power" metaphorically; what we refer to without metaphor is "strength"' (Arendt 1972: 113). Power, in this sense, should be distinguished from the exercise of force or strength, which are, as we have seen, characteristic of the sphere of work and which engage means that depend upon violence. In Arendt's view, force and violence are antithetical to action, short-circuiting the empowering interactions that make an authentic public realm. The combination of impotence and use of force, for Arendt, is characteristic of tyrannical regimes; and their lack of potency is shown, she suggests, in the fact that such regimes leave behind them no meaningful story of public interaction. They engage, again, the sense of dark times, periods of relative anonymity, that we now recognise all the more acutely because the tendencies embodied in tyranny were again pressed to a qualitatively new level in totalitarianism, the ultimate rule of 'nobodies', attempting to make nobodies of us all.

THE PUBLIC, THE PRIVATE AND THE SOCIAL

The distinctions between labour, work and action mark, then, a hierarchy that incorporates the progression away from constraint toward freedom;

and it is a progression that is coeval, in Arendt's view, with the movement away from isolation toward interaction and away from conformity toward plurality. They are also distinctions that allow Arendt to impress upon us a sense of a distinctive public realm, brought out by a contrast within the *vita activa* between public action and the spheres of labour and work, characteristic of the private realm. This sense is illuminated by reference back to that ancient distinction between the polis and the household – although not thereby reducible to this as a 'model' for us – and it releases in turn a sense of the characteristics of the public realm, characteristics that can be explored in relation to two connected phenomena.

First, the public realm can be understood in terms of what Arendt calls a 'space of appearances', a context in which 'everything that appears in public can be seen and heard by everybody and has the widest possible publicity' (Arendt 1958: 50). It can be understood as a phenomenal realm in which visible conduct provides our common reference point and confirms our common sense of reality; a reality that is not, contra the tradition, reducible to or resolvable in terms of some deeper metaphysical touchstone. It is equally, therefore, a sphere in which how one appears to others constitutes the reality of one's persona qua citizen. In comparison with this sense of reality, for Arendt, 'even the greatest forces of intimate life – the passions of the heart, the thoughts of the mind, the delights of the senses – lead an uncertain, shadowy kind of existence' (Arendt 1958: 50). This does not mean that Arendt denies the importance of such personal experiences. It is simply that such experiences do not bring the assurance, the confidence in their reality and meaning, that public disclosure brings: 'the secrets of the human heart necessarily remain secrets and may retain an ineffability even for the self' (Arendt 1958: 50–1).[7] Second, the idea of the public realm implies the image of a 'world' – that is, of a humanly constructed common context, a shared world of things that locate us spatially, such that located interactions are possible. In a significant metaphor, Arendt refers to the things of the world as located 'as a table is located between those who sit around it; the world, like every in-between, relates and separates men at the same time' (Arendt 1958: 52). The separation between persons, that allows them to adopt their own distinctive perspectives and so to establish difference, at one and the same time makes possible coherent interaction between plural beings: 'the world provides a context that gathers us together and yet prevents us falling over each other' (Arendt 1958: 52). We noted earlier that in terms of Arendt's categories that characterise the *vita activa*, the shared world that we inhabit can be seen as a product of work, of the activity of *homo faber*. What it makes possible, in the form of public interaction, however, is distinct from the instrumental logic governing work; and it is equally distinct, as we have seen, from the condition of labour. It is vital, for Arendt, that these often and increasingly blurred distinctions are reaffirmed, even if their practical and institutional expression cannot be predetermined theoretically.

The central point here is that action as a distinctive phenomenon and an encapsulation of freedom is not resolved, theoretically or practically, into terms that answer to the constraints of the private dimension of the *vita activa* – the requirements of biological necessity under which we exist as *animal laborans*, or the instrumental constraints under which, as *homo faber*, we work. Action as authentic self-disclosure is unconstrained by anything other than 'inspiring principles' that, as free agents, we choose to enact. This aspect to her account of the public realm has led to a question as to whether Arendt's conception of action can deliver enough of substance to be persuasive: the question of what, beyond the reference to self-disclosure, action is actually *about*.[8] However, Arendt is quite clear that public words and deeds are always *about* something, in addition to being a disclosure of the agent, and these are in no way incompatible: they are disclosures, 'even if their content is "exclusively" objective, concerned with the matters of the world of things in which men move . . . and out of which arise the specific, objective worldly interests' (Arendt 1958: 182).[9] Action, then, arises in a 'web of relationships where many and opposing ends are pursued' (Arendt 1977: 84). And the pursuit of ends and goals are 'elements in every political action' (Arendt 2005: 194). The point, then, is not that political action must neglect all considerations that pertain to necessity or interest but rather that the logic of action, and the context that gives it coherence, are not reducible simply to these comparatively banal factors. The point is to retrieve something in terms of meaning for the category of actions that escapes the constraints supplied by estimates on the basis simply of how far they are instrumentally effective and their ends desirable. The urgency of a distinction of this sort, for Arendt, is only now fully apparent and has become so in view of events that, crystallising and casting a light back upon the conditions of their emergence, show that this distinction, in theory and practice, has been undermined.

The compromising of the autonomy of political action and the public realm, as we have already noted, can be traced back to the origins of our tradition of political philosophy, promising a blueprint that, if applied, could eradicate the 'boundlessness and uncertainty of outcome' associated with action and so could provide a remedy to the 'frailty' of human affairs. The application of remedies of this kind, however, threatens to modify the character of the political, assimilating it with the practice of rule. This in turn reduces the realm of action to the level of work, reconceiving it as an instrumental undertaking geared to the realisation of the blueprint. In terms of the original distinction between the polis and the household, this amounts to the subjection of the former to the character and con-cerns of the latter, where hierarchical arrangements pertained for the purpose of organising the efficient meeting of private needs and interests. The freedom promised originally by the polis – precisely freedom from all privately given constraints and from all hierarchies – is undermined and the meaning of public conduct as memorable disclosure is compro-mised by its answerability to instrumental considerations. The 'in order to' that governs work replaces, through the practice of rule, the 'for the sake of' that was the motif of free action according to inspiring princi-ples. The distinction between acting and making was emasculated in the philosophical tradition that held the distinctive and autonomous arts of politics in low esteem (Arendt 1958: 19). Those who animated the early tradition never doubted the distinction between the household and the polis, even though they sought ways to be free from the burdens presented by the uncertainties of political life and so to secure what they took to be the superior life of quiet contemplation. In seeking these, however, they insinuated into the political culture a reductive appeal to instrumental considerations that has proved a persistent feature of our conception of the political, and one which has taken on a greater significance in the modern age.

The instrumental practice of rule has, in combination with the exten-sive economic and technological developments that have characterised the modern age, acquired a commensurately greater role and scope with respect to the meeting of needs and interests on a mass scale. The result is 'gigantic, nationwide administration' geared to the organisation of a society where production and consumption are most efficient, secured by the bureaucratic rule of the state. Modern mass society becomes 'the facsimile of the one super-human family' (Arendt 1958: 29). The social realm, as we now encounter it, is neither public nor private, in terms of the original distinction. Our sense of this distinction is thoroughly blurred in the wake of these developments, which are ultimately detrimental to both realms. The dominance of questions to do with the management

95

of need and interest eradicates the promise of free self-disclosure in the light of the public gaze; but it equally undermines the role of the private in providing a haven from the light of the public (in which no one would wish to exist permanently), a place of one's own where one is concerned with private requirements in companionship with those who share those requirements and the space in which they are met.[10] The sense of belonging provided by private space is increasingly replaced by a sense of inescapable belonging only to society.[11]

For Arendt, recent experiences point us toward a sense of the consummation of the principle of society in that the subsuming of the public realm under instrumental auspices is supplemented by an increasing assimilation of the instrumental category of work itself with the sphere of labour. In a sense, technological developments in the modern period – mechanisation and the development of sophisticated tools – have helped ease the burden of labour but they have not changed the basic character of that burden, in terms of the routine meeting of changeless needs. However, the very same technological developments have equally had a significant impact upon the sphere of work. The increasing division of labour consistent with technologically refined processes have created circumstances where the manufacture of durable objects, once characterised by the skill and intelligence of the craftsman, now resembles the routine and cyclical process of labour. The process of automation, in particular, has created a context in which the work of the manufacturer increasingly reproduces the absorption of the labourer into a process that is given, endless and de-skilled, independent of one's own capacity to formulate blueprints and to find suitable means for realising them. At the same time, the vast increase in productivity that has come with these developments now means that the very abundance of the products of work renders them more than ever objects of consumption, making durability an obsolete quality.[12]

These modified technological conditions accord with and intensify the 'social' viewpoint characteristic of modern mass society. The motif of the sphere of labour becomes the dominant one: the life-process becomes the central concern and the principle of our mode of relating, such that 'all things become objects of consumption' (Arendt 1958: 89). We lose, in this sense, the experience of objective reality that comes with a common, durable world. Correspondingly, even the limited difference between persons embodied in the sphere of work lapses in favour of the principle of sameness that governs the life of socialised man, the 'unitedness of many into one' in a society of jobholders and labourers (Arendt 1958: 214). Politics gives way to social management, where the worldly perspectives that relate and separate us, and the free interactions that these make possible, are redundant. In the light of these considerations, for Arendt, 'it is quite conceivable that the modern age – which began with such an unprecedented and promising outburst of human activity – may end in the deadliest, most sterile passivity history has ever known' (Arendt 1958: 322).

ARENDT'S ACCOUNT OF THE PUBLIC REALM: SOME QUESTIONS

So a concern with the retrieval of the experiences of the *vita activa* and the distinctions and relations between them, arises out of, and may help shed light upon, the remarkable experiences of the recent period. Arendt's emphasis in *The Human Condition* is upon the search for illumination rather than comprehensive explanations of those experiences. The promise of completion in terms of the explanation of our condition is, in Arendt's view, a prominent preoccupation but one that she treats with suspicion. In large measure, the social scientific techniques that are the favoured means by which to come to a potentially complete social self-understanding reproduce and naturalise the experiential limitations and compromised self-image that infuse the life of 'socialised man'. As we saw in Chapter 1, for Arendt, 'behaviourist' social science presupposes and legitimates the sense of the sameness of persons that underlies mass society: it is a measure of the 'victory' of society that we have substituted the category of behaviour for that of action (Arendt 1958: 45). Much of our conduct may indeed have a routine character but this is not where the potential meaningfulness of life is revealed: 'the meaningfulness of everyday relationships is not disclosed in everyday life but in rare deeds, just as the significance of a historical period shows itself only in the few events that illuminate it' (Arendt 1958: 42). The essentially statistical impulse underlying behaviourist social science has the effect of 'flattening out' conduct, marginalising the surprising or the novel; and in doing so, it threatens to obliterate the sense of meaning that is created by unexpected acts and events, reasserting the 'exchangeability' of persons and contexts.

So, as well as writing against the tradition of political philosophy, she also opposes the contemporary promise of intellectual completion in the form of this behavioural picture answering to a socialised culture and

97

offering engineering solutions to social problems. In seeking to resist these ways of thinking, each of which in their own way anticipate homogenised conditions of conduct, Arendt simultaneously seeks to retrieve and thematise an image of action answering to the 'pre-philosophical' commitment to the polis, which embodied the aim of making 'the extraordinary an ordinary occurrence' (Arendt 1958: 197).

This leads Arendt to seek a distinctive and non-complacent way of thinking and speaking. She adopts a voice that is appropriate to a recognition both of the extraordinary element that lies at the heart of the human capacity for freedom and the equally extraordinary manner in which the capacity for action has, lately, been turned against humanity itself; something we appreciate as long as we remain sensitive to the 'shock of experience'. A reconsideration of these two related phenomena requires a manner of thinking that answers to contingency and which, accordingly, resists conclusive statements that would insinuate a sense either of the possibility of eternal redemption or of the certainty of loss. The fact that the problem we now face concerns a highly contingent dimension to our experience, and the fact that it has come to light now, in a manner that it has not appeared before, combine to prompt a theoretical voice that captures the epistemological and temporal circumspection that we have already noted. The realisation of this in *The Human Condition* may be brought out through a consideration of three related criticisms that may be directed at Arendt's discussion.

The first criticism that can be levelled at Arendt's treatment of the *vita activa* is that it is partial and orientated to her own particular preoccupations (cf. Villa 1999: 204). But this is a judgment that would seem to measure Arendt's account against a yardstick supplied by reference to a putative comprehensive and objective account of human experience of a sort that she is not seeking to supply. Her account is certainly partial in the sense of lacking an appeal to traditional forms of theoretical and historical objectivity. But the resultant partiality, if understood in this traditional sense, is mitigated by the appeal that Arendt makes to our collective sense of experiences that have been thrown into relief in view of threats that we may now see have been posed to them, and which stand in need of reconsideration. Her account, therefore, is orientated toward a continuing debate concerning our condition in conscious recognition that events have led us to reconsider the categories through which we articulate a self-understanding. The theoretical implication here, which answers to the idea of an epistemological mediation to theory accords, equally, with the experiential sense in which complete collective self-knowledge is a questionable ambition given that others, to whose gaze one is subject, may have something to say about it. It thus embodies a *formal* partisanship with respect to the political, the basis of which is discursive.

A second related criticism that can be made of *The Human Condition* is that the distinctions drawn by Arendt between the categories she uses are overstated. This relates to the point we noted earlier that, for some, Arendt's urgent concern to distinguish the public and the private in the *vita activa* leave us with a conception of the political bereft of substance. We noted in relation to this point that Arendt does think that political action is about something other than simply, as it were, itself: it engages practical concerns. It is only that the phenomenological significance and intrinsic meaning of action transcends this. The current point, however, puts the matter more broadly, raising the question of whether Arendt's categorical distinctions are anyway too sharply drawn. There is no doubt that the distinctions that Arendt draws within the *vita activa* are sharp ones; and there is equally no doubt that, at least in the context of modern experience, they can look overdrawn. We see this in that the distinction between the conduct of the labourer and the engagement of the 'craftsman' that provides Arendt's model for the sphere of work no longer looks any more than an idealised contrast. However, as we have noted, the phenomenological distinctions by means of which she characterises the *vita activa* are designed to highlight what we might see to be a certain homogenisation with respect to our forms of conduct. The sharpness of the distinctions she draws therefore has heuristic value in allowing us to draw out the nature of the 'socialisation' of modern mass societies. The validity of the categories that Arendt identifies lies not in general foundational claims concerning human nature but in the specific, historically derived experiential images upon which she draws, the power of which derives from the light they potentially throw on our recent experiences of mass, socialised contexts and the basis that this provides for meaningful and sustained discussion about the circumstances that made for the possible emergence of totalitarianism.[13] She makes historical references in a mediated sense in order 'to trace back modern world alienation . . . to arrive at an understanding of the nature of society as it has developed and presented itself at the very moment when it was overcome by a new and yet unknown age' (Arendt 1958: 6). Equally, the distinctions that Arendt draws invoke images that liberate our sense of the public and of the capacity for free action that we have become unacquainted with in the modern context and about which we are less in the habit of thinking and speaking: 'we are now in a much better position to see the consequences when both the public and private spheres of life are gone, the public because it has become a function and the private because it has become the only common concern left' (Arendt 1958: 69). Arendt establishes in *The Human Condition* an understanding of successive attempts to escape from 'the calamities of politics', an understanding made available by reference to a newly recovered sense of the public realm.

This relates to a third question about Arendt's discussion: it is arguable that in talking about the character of freedom, Arendt refers back to an idealised model derived from a reading of ancient city state politics that is contestable and in any case hardly applicable in the modern context. But this point also requires qualification. Arendt's invocation of city state politics is not based upon a comprehensive account of the sociopolitical structure of the ancient city, and is developed rather on the basis of particular experiential themes and reference points. By the same token, it is not presented as a model to be recreated or a blueprint to be followed; a claim which, as we have seen, would be very much contrary to the form and substance of Arendt's political thought. Rather, the image of non-instrumental agonal freedom is designed to inform a discussion of the possibilities of freedom in our contemporary circumstances, of the extent to which our modern social concerns may be thought to carry a cost with respect to freedom and how far particular modern examples of political action may show how it persists as a capacity, although now with a sharper awareness of its fragility. Again, Arendt offers no substantive formula as to how freedom can be accommodated in the modern world: her mediated approach instead seeks to thematise it in relation to our contemporary self-understanding, and to heighten our sense that ultimately any 'solution' to the problem of the decline in the ability or opportunity to enact freedom lies in action itself. This, for Arendt, is the contribution that theory can make in circumstances of a threadbare political culture, rather than providing recipes that substitute for action and so may only contribute to the decline.

To conclude, Arendt is drawn to the phenomenon of action because it is doubly implicated in the light of modern experience. On the one hand, this experience has shown us the fragility of action and the costs of disempowerment that may be incurred by its neglect. This, she wants to suggest, derives from its inherently spontaneous character and the fact, therefore, that it cannot be sustained by factors extraneous to it, material or metaphysical. On the other hand, its unconditioned character and its propensity for the unprecedented also shows its self-destructive potential – the sense in which it can be harnessed and turned against humanity, in the light of the principle that 'everything is possible'. These considerations, which thematise action as a central consideration of our time, thematise equally, for Arendt, its redemptive potential. The unconditioned and spontaneous nature of action is the source of its fragile value as an expression of freedom and also of its self-destructive possibilities, features that have never before been so apparent to us.[14]

The above considerations take us back to Arendt's view that the potential 'boundlessness' of action, its potentially uncontrollable character, is only the other side of its capacity to create relationships. The principal examples here to which she points are the capacity to make and keep promises and the capacity for forgiveness. These are capacities to which I shall return in more detail later; but it is relevant to note here that they have the potential to be public enactments which, once made, henceforth change the landscape. They may draw a line and establish new and stable terms of interaction; and in this way, they constitute authentic, unconditioned forms of action that are self-limiting and so establish new limits upon the otherwise unlimited chains of consequences that action can unleash. These are examples of action which show that its very vulnerability, in its contingency, can also be its strength. So we are drawn to the sense in which the capacity for action may promise the possibility of a sustainable context for the exercise of freedom: 'the experience of totalitarianism demonstrates that human dignity needs a new guarantee which can be found only in a new political principle . . . whose validity must comprehend the whole of humanity while its power must remain strictly limited' (Arendt 1973: ix). In respect of our experience in the modern world, the phenomenon of drawing a line and effecting a 'new start' is something that we can reflect upon in relation to the experience of revolution.

NOTES

1. As Canovan notes, one can only fully understand the discussion in *The Human Condition* in the light of that in *The Origins of Totalitarianism* (Canovan 1992: 100). See also Dietz (2000).
2. As Tsao notes, it is a failure to appreciate this point that leads to the mistaken conclusion that her category of action is designed to provide an (underdeveloped) image

of what politics should be about; whereas, in fact, she is drawing our attention to the neglected capacity for acting in public on matters of principle in the company of others – see Tsao (2002).

3. There is undoubtedly something of a rhetorical element in Arendt's account here, and in the decisiveness of the distinctions that she draws between labour, work and action. Whether they are quite as distinct as she implies could be questioned, as she occasionally recognises; but her treatment serves to highlight the category of action in particular and the key issues that press upon us in the light of our contemporary circumstances. Equally, as we shall see, the fact that her categories may appear to us, in the light of modern experience, somewhat blurred, is a fact of some significance and one which Arendt wishes to explore.

4. The scope of the 'agonal' in Arendt's account of action has been a matter of debate. Bonnie Honig, for example, sees it as a central feature, emphasising action as a virtuoso performance, disclosing a unique identity, driven by the 'the self's agonal passion for distinction and outstanding achievement (Honig 1991: 80). Disch, however, sees this interpretation of Arendtian action as unduly 'narcissistic', driven by a highly individualist desire for glory; it is an interpretation, she suggests, that loses a sense of plurality through an emphasis upon 'excellence in competition' (Disch 1994: 83). There is no doubt, however, that the ancient examples that Arendt refers to as models (although by no means as blueprints) do, as she offers them, contain strong agonal elements. At the same time, she does not suggest that agonal politics is at odds with plurality. Disch notes Honig's view that the virtuosity that is central to agonal self-disclosure is never merely a solo performance, needing for disclosure of meaning and identity the presence of others with whom one acts. However, she remains concerned that, understood in this way, the model of action does not leave us an adequate basis for understanding how action can be integrated into a stable and just polity. Disch's own solution here is to assert a procedural political ethics, grounded in discursive decision-making and subject to publicity in a context of the critical recognition of difference. I would question this formulation in terms of its fidelity to Arendt and would see the issue of the ethical integration of action in different terms; but I will return to this issue in Chapter 7.

5. Arendt finds an indication of this in monuments erected to the 'unknown soldier' after the First World War, intended to memorialise those who had been 'robbed, not of their achievement but of their human dignity'. It is a theme expressed with particular clarity in William Faulkner's story A Fable, the hero of which is the unknown soldier (Arendt 1958: 181).

6. Arendt finds an image here in Sophocles' Oedipus Rex, where the diamon of the person appears to others and takes on the character of an example (Arendt 1958: 193).

7. This also indicates a lack of transferability between the public and the intimate: 'because of its inherent worldlessness, love can only become false and perverted when it is used for political purposes such as the change or salvation of the world' (Arendt 1958: 52).

8. For discussions of this point, see Kateb (1983: 16–22) and Pitkin (1998: 177–202).

9. In referring to the example of the polis, Arendt sees the activities of the citizen in terms of 'jurisdiction, defence and the administration of human affairs' (Arendt 1958: 41). Knauer notes that worldly actions will have concrete motives and goals attached to them aside from the principles harboured by the agent that indicate 'what one stands for' (Knauer 1980: 725).

10. Privacy, then, is far from unimportant in Arendt's view. It is a form of experience that is represented most powerfully in artistic terms: poetically in Goethe and visually in Rembrandt and Leonardo (Arendt 1958: 51).

11. In Arendt's view, this accounts for the revision, in the modern period, of our sense of the private sphere into terms of the altogether narrower and less robust category of the 'intimate'.

12. The decrease in the expenditure of labour power and the concomitant increase in consumption still does not involve a liberation from necessity; it creates, for Arendt, 'the serious problem of leisure ... of how to provide enough opportunity for daily exhaustion to keep the capacity for consumption intact' (Arendt 1958: 131).

13. That Arendt is not holding up the ancient understandings of the *vita activa* as an authoritative standard by which to judge more recent accounts is evident in the fact that she notes the general tendency in the classical world to neglect the distinction between labour and work (Arendt 1958: 85).

14. Arendt finds an articulation of this in Kafka: 'he found the Archimedean point, but he used it against himself, it seems that he was permitted to find it only under this condition' (Arendt 1958: 248).

CHAPTER 6

Theorising New Beginnings: On Revolution

Our recent realisation of the vulnerability to domination inherent in our depoliticised society prompts, for Arendt, a search for examples, albeit fleeting ones, where the modern age has seen a re-emergence of freedom. In a context where we do not appear to be able to generate a reliable forum in which freedom can be enacted, where the extraordinary can arise consistently in the ordinary course of things, we need to look to the rare events that mark an upsurge of the authentic capacity for action. We may find these, she thinks, in the distinctively modern phenomenon of revolution: revolutions are 'amongst the most recent of all political data' (Arendt 1973: 12). This suggests that a study of revolution will be of value in shedding light on our current situation; and its more particular relevance, for Arendt, lies in the fact that it illuminates a problem which has never revealed its pertinence more acutely than it has now – the problem, politically speaking, of enacting something entirely new, of creating something out of nothing. This is the problem that has turned out to be at the heart of the political.

The approach that Arendt takes to this study is historical and comparative; but, in keeping with the tendency that we have noted consistently, it is hardly conventional. The historical dimension to *On Revolution* is mediated by a concern with the novel experience of the present:

> we are not here concerned with the history of revolutions as such, with their past, origins and course of development. If we want to learn [about] . . . its political significance for the world we live in . . . we must turn to those moments when revolution made its full appearance, assumed a kind of definite shape and began to cast its spell over the minds of men. (Arendt 1973: 43–4)

104

So rather than providing historical explanations, Arendt's account aims to extract from revolutionary experience a sense of the authentic enactment of freedom, where the coincidence of freedom and the idea of new beginnings is evident. Correspondingly, she does not seek through her analysis to provide a definitive and therefore timeless conceptual account of revolution, an aim that would potentially undermine its particular experiential significance for our political self-understanding in the contemporary period. The point is to gain illumination from some of the most prominent revolutionary experiences of the modern period rather than re-presenting these experiences as cases that can be deployed for purposes of explanatory or conceptual closure. This equally introduces a corresponding epistemological mediation: the analysis of revolutions provides us with reference points for reflection and dialogue concerning the question of beginnings. By the same token, for Arendt, the problem of political beginning is insoluble, at least when posed in traditional theoretical terms. It is a problem that is internal to action itself and from a theoretical point of view needs to be recognised as such. This recognition is demonstrated by a concession in theory to the ground of action itself; by theorising the internal structure of foundational action and the problems that it contains, rather than seeking to solve those problems. The resultant voice, again dialogic, promises a continuing discussion of action, with its possibilities and problems, rather than attempting finally, in theory, to stipulate its possibilities and render it unproblematic.

In the light of these aims, Arendt approaches her principal reference points, the French Revolution of 1789 and the American Revolution of 1776, not in terms of comprehensive historical accounts but as unfolding dramas, capturing their most illuminating elements. In turn, the political resonance of these key elements are conveyed, appropriately, in speech; in the words of the central *dramatis personae*, the words of the 'men of the revolution', impressing upon us how they saw and understood the enterprise in which they were engaged, and the words of the revolutionary theorists who inspired them both in philosophical and literary modes. The point, for Arendt, is to encapsulate for purposes of reflection the character of a novel experience rather than to render it prosaic through the application of a more abstract theoretical framework.

LIBERATION, FREEDOM AND FOUNDATION

Arendt is in no doubt that revolution, as it now appears to us, is a modern phenomenon. The origins of the term, she argues, lay in the developments in scientific thinking in the early modern period, and particularly in astronomy, with reference to the observable revolving motion of heavenly bodies. When imported into the political realm, this carried metaphysical significance in terms of the cyclical character of human affairs, and so thematised a sense of consistent periodic return or restoration. This, she suggests, was the sense attached to the idea as it was initially applied – to the restoration of the British monarchy in 1660 and to the Glorious Revolution of 1688, when an enforced change of monarch effected a restoration of the authority of monarchical rule (Arendt 1973: 42–3). When carried over later into the context of the French and American revolutions, each could appeal to this conception, in terms of the restoration of freedom in the face of despotic rule of a monarch or a colonial power. But in order to achieve such a restoration in these contexts, it proved necessary not to return to a previous order, creating instead something new; and this gives us our more recent sense of the revolutionary experience and the spirit of novelty that it appears to contain (Arendt 1973: 45).

This establishes for us a new and highly pertinent problematic in terms of the distinction and relation between the phenomena of liberation and freedom. Liberation equates with the escape from oppression, which, in the modern world, has most often been understood in terms of the demand for basic negative freedoms – life, liberty and property. But these, as we can now see, do not equate with the living of a free life and certainly do not secure the conditions for resisting domination even of quite obvious and unmediated sorts. They in no way guarantee, that is, 'freedom as the political way of life' (Arendt 1973: 33). In terms of the inspiring principles that might inform action, the hatred of oppression, which 'is as old as recorded history', is not in and of itself a political passion; it is, in fact, 'politically sterile' (Arendt 1973: 125). It does not capture the more politically grounded passion for establishing the conditions perpetuating the enactment of freedom. We are alerted to this in the 'foundation legends' that pose the problem of new beginnings in the light of this preoccupation: the biblical story of the exodus of Israel's tribes from Egypt; Virgil's tale of Aenaes after his escape from Troy and the foundation of Rome. These are tales of liberation but equally incorporate the theme of the future promise of freedom (Arendt 1973: 205). In the modern setting, for Arendt, we seem to have lost sight of this issue. We think of the 'radical' act of liberation and the 'conservative' act of creating a stable and lasting arrangement for the enactment of freedom as standing in opposition, in that these two terms have solidified into contrasting ideological positions: one of the 'symptoms of our loss' in terms of modern political thinking (Arendt 1973: 223).

When thinking about modern revolutions, the distinction between, and the equal importance of, liberation and freedom has also been difficult to recognise in that the actions of the revolutionaries in achieving liberation – 'the speechmaking and decision taking, the oratory and the business, the thinking and the persuading and the actual doing' – are characteristic political engagements which themselves constitute enactments of freedom (Arendt 1973: 34). This very fact can blind us to the importance of realising, as a result of revolutionary action, the conditions for the continuing enactment of freedom, to the need for 'the foundation of a body politic which guarantees the space where freedom can appear' (Arendt 1973: 125). This limitation in the understanding of the revolutionary undertaking was one that sometimes afflicted revolutionaries themselves, and can be detected also in the accounts of those historians who have placed their emphasis upon 'the first and violent stage of rebellion and liberation . . . to the detriment of the quieter second stage of revolution and constitution' – a temptation that befalls the historian in so far as he is only, or conceives himself only to be, 'a storyteller' (Arendt 1973: 142). We have noted that narrative plays a part in Arendt's general approach, and it does so in *On Revolution*. But again, it is a narrative input that serves to prompt and inform concerns that have arisen in view of our recent experience. In Arendt's view, as we have seen, the closure that narrative completion might promise may curtail our sense of the problematic that may linger for us in light of the revolutionary experience, not simply in the form of a narrative lesson, even of a tragic form, but in terms of the unresolved issue of freedom as it presents itself to us. The point, then, is to resist catharsis and to leave a remainder.

We can understand this in terms of the further challenge that is presented to us in a context of revolutionary action, when we recognise that the achievement of liberation, an act of destruction, stands in an acute *tension* with the attempt to achieve a new and stable realm of freedom; when it seems that 'nothing threatens the very achievements of revolution more than the spirit which has brought them about' (Arendt 1973: 232).

107

This is a problem that makes itself felt in the experience of modern revolutions and is specifically reflected in the fact that revolutionary liberation is, more often than not, brought about by violence; and violence is antithetical to politics, being 'speechless', a means of bypassing all the elements of intelligent interaction that make politics and which allow for the enactment of freedom. But it equally indicates a more general point. If revolution is to create the conditions for freedom, it does so as a result of actions which, although embodying the spirit of free action, appear pre-political, 'a beginning that is separated from everything following it as though by an unbridgeable chasm' (Arendt 1973: 20). They seem to constitute that which, from the point of view of any subsequently stable public realm, looks arbitrary and resistant to judgment or justification.

It is this, for Arendt, that seems to underlie a tendency that we can see in modern revolutions to search for some 'higher' law or principle that justifies the act and by which revolutionaries were able to measure, at least in principle, the success of their enterprise. The early modern revolutionaries were sensitive to the problem of a shortfall with respect to the justification for their destructive acts and, by the same token, a deficit with respect to what their enterprise promised. In response, they tended to seek 'a new absolute to replace the absolute of divine power', but this is intrinsically problematic. As we have seen, for Arendt the imposition of transcendent laws or principles upon the intrinsically relative realm of human affairs is an inclination that threatens politics and the possibility of plural enactments of freedom: 'power under conditions of plurality can never amount to omnipotence, and laws residing on human power can never be absolute' (Arendt 1973: 39). It also, and correspondingly, assimilates political action to the (violent) engagement of 'making', of working upon human material in order to realise a blueprint. To see more of this issue as it is associated with the revolutionary act of foundation it is useful to review Arendt's account of her two principal cases.

FRANCE AND AMERICA

For Arendt, as the drama of the French Revolution unfolded, it appears that the original concerns with liberation from a tyrannical monarchy were combined with, and ultimately supplanted by, a new inspiring principle: a concern with the suffering of the poor. This was a phenomenon that, in the context of an emergent mass society, was no longer hidden in the obscurity of rural existence and was newly visible as the experience of the poor on the streets of Paris. The condition of the poor presented a visceral and emotive image and in turn, a powerful revolutionary motive. The revolutionaries became driven by the 'passion of compassion' (Arendt 1973: 71). Compassion had already been thematised in political theory in the work of Rousseau, where it played the part of a disposition to respond to the suffering of another, a natural, unmediated disposition that formed part of the moral bedrock against which Rousseau was able to gauge the corrupting effects of the mediated set of relations associated with an alienating sophisticated society. It was then introduced into the revolutionary context by Robespierre, who 'brought it into the market-place with the vehemence of his great revolutionary oratory' (Arendt 1973: 81).

This central dimension to the motivation for revolutionary action played an equally central part in the prosecution of the revolution and helped seal its fate, leading us again to reflect on the appropriateness of this motive in politics. Compassion is an immediate and emotionally charged disposition that implies an urgent response to a situation. For Arendt, this renders it a doubtful basis for political action, where more mediated responses are required, reflecting a plural distance between persons related and separated in a public realm: 'compassion abolishes the distance, the worldly space between men where political matters, the whole realm of human affairs, are located' (Arendt 1973: 86). The visceral immediacy of compassion for the other closes down the reciprocal relations of mutual visibility that underlie the phenomena of action, public appearance and judgment. Its immediacy is underwritten by the fact that the passion of compassion depends upon the immediate apprehension of suffering of a single fellow human being – a feature that would seem to render it untranslatable into any political terms. However, the revolutionary experience in France showed the sense in which it could gain at least pseudo-political relevance through the translation of compassion into the corresponding sentiment of pity – a generalised sentiment preserving the immediacy of compassion in the form of a generalised, emotive response to the suffering of a mass of people. Pity 'socialises' compassion and brings it into the public realm as a boundless sentiment. This transcends the terms of the public realm defined as a realm of mutual visibility: in the French context, the appearance that the poor in mass society made was not in the guise of plural citizens but rather as an abstract and undifferentiated mass whose condition stood in need of relief by all means necessary. For Arendt, there is a legacy here:

since the days of the French Revolution, it has been the boundlessness of their sentiments that made revolutionaries so curiously insensitive to reality in general and to the reality of persons in particular, whom they felt no compunctions in sacrificing to their 'principles', or to the course of history, or the cause of the revolution as such. (Arendt 1973: 90)

These features of the 'social question', as they made themselves felt in the conduct of the French Revolution had two related consequences. The first was that, in serving the interests of an undifferentiated mass of suffering people, the revolutionaries found their absolute justification, raising their enterprise beyond the level of political opinion and supplying it with a transcendent principle, again deriving from Rousseau, in the form of an appeal to the idea of the 'general will'. This appeal, which corresponded with the 'capacity to lose oneself in the sufferings of others', provided a reference point for the enterprise of representing the general mass of the people under a principle of unanimity (Arendt 1973: 81). As Robespierre emphasised, revolutionary legislation was made in the name of 'the people' rather than in the sense of 'the republic' (Arendt 1973: 75). The second consequence, in the light of this theoretically transcendent and practically urgent requirement to represent the general will, was that the revolution bypassed the apparently more prosaic elements of political interaction. Carried forward by the 'intoxicating' sense of embodying the will of the crowd, the revolutionaries sought to short-circuit the less immediate processes of discussion, deliberation and compromise that are characteristic of politics. For Arendt, the authority of the new regime was built upon the will of the people taken to be a unity, and a system built on an abstraction of this sort 'is built on quicksand'; the only thing that saved the regime was the power to manipulate this will, construed as a 'national will' under circumstances of dictatorship (Arendt 1973: 163).

The combination of the sense of an overarching principle with a commensurate sense of the urgent need to bypass conditions of plurality goes a long way, in Arendt's view, to explaining the systematic violence to which the revolution resorted. Revolutionary violence appears justified in general, rather than only in particular, where one has an overriding reference point that renders dissent 'objectively' a fault and so 'counter-revolutionary' by definition. Robespierre saw himself as an architect, building something new out of human material, according to the principle of the general will, which justified the 'aboriginal crime' that so often has been associated with the foundation of new political formations (Arendt 1973: 208). In light of this, the liberation from tyranny that the revolution effected was accompanied not by the establishment of the conditions for freedom but rather by the attempt at liberation from necessity, an aim that justified oppressive and violent measures under an absolute legitimating principle. The need of the people 'was violent, and as it were, pre-political; it seemed that only violence could be strong and swift enough to help them'; and the revolutionaries pursued this aim with 'an emotion-laden insensitivity' (Arendt 1973: 91). For Arendt, the French revolutionaries sacrificed the possibility, that their revolution had made available, of building 'artificial' laws adequate to defining a free polity, in favour of articulating 'natural' laws which the masses obeyed, 'the force of elemental necessity'; it became a matter of 'liberating the suffering masses instead of emancipating the people' (Arendt 1973: 110–11). The difficulty of resolving this social question meant that the violent work in which Robespierre and his colleagues were engaged was pushed to an extreme, and the revolution into terror, giving us an intimation that the social question may not be resolvable by authentically political means.

Arendt's account of the drama of the French Revolution thematises three related features that are generalised from the particular example. First, it illuminates further the character of the problems that, as we saw in Chapter 5, Arendt suggests arise from a conflation of the political and the social. The revolutionaries' concern with the existence of poverty and its dehumanising effects was of course morally legitimate and comprehensible, but problematic in becoming the guiding principle of the revolution. Material want is dehumanising because it puts people 'under the absolute dictates of their bodies' (Arendt 1973: 60). However, rendering this question as a political one subjects the political itself to the urgent question of need, requiring, it seems, a closure of what makes politics, 'shunning the drawn out, wearisome process of persuasion, negotiation, and compromise, which are the processes of law and politics' replacing them with 'swift and direct action . . . that is . . . action with the means of violence' (Arendt 1973: 87). This underlines for us the difficulties associated with the appropriation of politics in the service of a concern with what the ancient world regarded as 'the cares and worries that actually belonged in the sphere of the household', concerns that had no place, then, in the public realm but which, in the conditions of modern mass societies, are difficult to keep out of it.

The second, related, feature highlighted in this drama is the issue of the passions and dispositions that may be regarded as appropriate to politics. We have seen that the concern with the social question was grounded in compassion, raised in the French Revolution to the highest political virtue. It is a passion entirely appropriate to the experience of human suffering but is alien to a 'talkative and argumentative interest in the world' (Arendt 1973: 86). We have noted that compassion relates to public suffering but when politicised through its translation into pity for 'the poor' becomes problematic. For Arendt, this is wholly related to the fact that it is an unmediated disposition that cannot unproblematically be applied to the mediated public realm. This has more general implications with respect to the purity of moral dispositions bearing comparison, again, with the earlier discussion of conscience in Chapter 2. The contrast between immediate sentiment of this kind and the mediated interactions defining politics are illustrated, for Arendt, in literary terms, in works such as Melville's *Billy Budd, Sailor* and Dostoyevsky's *The Grand Inquisitor*, where unmediated goodness is presented as inarticulate or mute, revealing its close connection, in a worldly context, with violence. So the pathos of goodness supervenes upon the public world as a depoliticising and violent force, showing us how, in politics at least, 'absolute goodness is hardly any less dangerous than absolute evil' (Arendt 1973: 82).[1] I shall return to the question of moral dispositions in politics in the next chapter, but we can note that the above theme implies a third feature that arises from Arendt's account here: the invocation of a pre-political absolute.

We have seen that the appeal to the general will that was essential to the French revolutionaries' attempt to resolve the social question invoked a sense of a unitary moral purpose that accorded with their pity for the poor en masse. In the course of the revolution, the perceived need to justify the work they were doing on the human material at their disposal, which transcended all dissident opinions or alternative perspectives, led to increasingly querulous appeals to an 'immortal legislator', to 'natural law' and ultimately to the attempt at creating a cult of the 'supreme being'. This aspect in the discourse of the revolution testifies to its failure to recognise theoretically the possibility of freedom, sacrificing it practically in the light of a blueprint justified in non-relative and pre-political terms.[2]

The conditions that pertained in the context of the American Revolution were significantly different from those in France, and certainly had an effect in modifying the Americans' understanding of their own revolutionary task. As in the French case, the American drama was propelled initially by the desire for liberation from oppression; but in America, the concern with political freedom remained an inspiring principle of the revolutionary action taken and informed the way in which it was played out. Of central significance in this respect was the fact that concentrated abject poverty was not the pressing issue in America in the way it was in the mass societies of Europe.[3] Poverty of course existed in America but not in the concentrated mass form that became so visible in the French context. And this permitted the American Revolution to retain an orientation to the political question of freedom rather than conceding it to a social concern. Arendt notes that a key figure amongst the men of the American Revolution, John Adams, recognised the problem of poverty but framed it in a manner radically different from the way in which it had been framed by Robespierre and his colleagues in the French case. Instead of seeing the poor as a collectivised mass, whose suffering was the object of pity, Adams saw the problem in terms of the 'obscurity' to which poverty condemned the poor: their lack of time and resources effectively negated their ability to participate in public affairs. This meant that the act of liberation from oppression required and implied the establishing of conditions of citizenship such that all, regardless of material status, could have the opportunity to participate in public life. This entailed a recognition that something more than the capitulation to immediate 'intoxication' of the act of liberation was needed; a recognition of the relation between 'foundation, augmentation and conservation' (Arendt 1973: 201).

It was this recognition that established a central place for the task of constitution-building in the aftermath of the act of liberation; the success of which in America can be measured against its conspicuous failure in France.[4] The constitutional concern of the American revolutionaries was made evident, for Arendt, in the fact that they appeared to recognise the central distinction between power and authority in a polity and also the relation between them. If the act of liberation unleashed the possibility of collective self-empowerment, authoritative institutions were equally required in order to stabilise the context in which that empowerment could be realised. If power was to be expressed through the democratic structures that were organs representing the popular will, the judiciary, most prominently although not exclusively embodied in the Supreme Court, represented the inspiring principle of authority, stemming back to the revolutionary act of foundation, providing a set of limitations to the collective experience of power that were nevertheless responsive to that exercise, engaging in 'a kind of continuous constitution-making' (Arendt 1973: 200).

There was, in this way, an authentically and recognisably political spirit informing the American enterprise which meant that the principal concerns that shaped that enterprise were geared, in the wake of the act of liberation from oppression, toward freedom. Accordingly, in the American case, the revolutionary project, as an act of liberation, incorporated the experience of 'public happiness', which directed the revolution toward the instantiation of freedom by means of the establishment, through agreements, of lasting institutions: 'the Americans knew that public freedom consisted in having a share in public business, and that the activities connected with this business . . . gave those who discharged them in public a feeling of happiness they could acquire nowhere else' (Arendt 1973: 119). The passion for freedom was in this way the informing spirit of the American Revolution. And to the extent that this passion incorporates an authentic sense of political freedom, it is a passion mediated by the more 'distanced' preoccupation with the freedom of the other, as fellow citizen, rather than with an overriding identification with the other as another self. In America 'the word "people" retained . . . the meaning of manyness' (Arendt 1973: 93). Correspondingly, the passion of compassion and its homogenising expression in the form of pity for the masses played no part in the moral architecture of the revolution.

These features mark the sharp distinction between the political concerns of the American revolutionaries and the social concerns of their French counterparts. But although the distinction is marked, it is not wholly categorical. Although the difference remains 'profound', it was nevertheless the case, for Arendt, that the social question 'interfered with the course of the American Revolution no less sharply, but far less dramatically, than it did with the course of the French Revolution' (Arendt 1973: 137). The tendency to replace public aspirations with private ones, and to see this in characteristic modern terms of the privileging of private consumption, was well enough established in early liberal thinking and was influential in the American case. Despite the awareness of Jefferson and others as to the importance of participatory freedom, the revolution sacrificed this to a construal of freedom in private terms. This neglect of political freedom is evident, for Arendt, in the wording of the Declaration of Independence, with its emphasis upon life, liberty and the pursuit of happiness. In the context of the cultural markers that had already been laid down, where freedom was understood in negative terms, the ambiguous phrase 'the pursuit of happiness' could carry correspondingly private rather than public connotations. The Declaration blurred the distinction between public and private, between freedom and personal well-being, and as a result, the concern with the former receded. This was borne out, for Arendt, in the developing political culture in the United States, where a system of representation and rights was understood to secure protection for the individual to achieve a condition of private well-being. Correspondingly, increasing prosperity created leisure, seen not as an opportunity for public participation but for consumption. Conspicuous consumption became a replacement for public visibility.

This is not to say that the distinction between the French and American revolutions does not remain illuminating: measured against the index of public freedom, the American Revolution was a relative success in comparison with the French. It is true that they took the freedom that they experienced as revolutionaries somewhat for granted and gave insufficient attention to means of preserving the possibility of that experience; but their awareness of it, and of its importance, allowed the pressing desire for private well-being to be 'held in abeyance at least long enough to throw the foundations and erect the new building – although not long enough to change the minds of those who were to inhabit it' (Arendt 1973: 138).

The other related feature of the American Revolution that prevents us from accounting it wholly a success with respect to the question of freedom is that its prosecutors could not avoid the appeal to an absolute principle as justification and guidance for their enterprise. The liberal principles that informed their thinking and introduced the central element of private freedom, the freedom to secure well-being, into their political discourse introduced equally the idea of 'natural law', familiar from early liberal thinking, into their lexicon. The revolution could claim its rationale and secure its direction not simply from the political requirement of establishing the conditions for freedom in plurality but also, and more fundamentally, with respect to a claim about natural, universal negative rights possessed by all persons in virtue not of their difference but rather of their sameness. References to natural law, as they supervene upon the public realm, have the appearance of being absolute and therefore 'superhuman' – that is, transcendent of and immune to negotiation. This aspect of the foundational discourse of the American revolutionaries accounts equally for its theological dimension, with its references to future rewards and punishments as a basis for its authority (Arendt 1973: 191).

What could be considered here, from the point of view of freedom, something of a failure of nerve is expressed again, for Arendt, in the Declaration of Independence. The phrase 'we hold these truths to be self-evident' demonstrates precisely the difficulty presented by the clash between the relative condition of the political and the search for an absolute that has concerned revolutionaries in the act of establishing and justifying a new arrangement. The statement that 'we hold these truths' is authentically political, marking a commitment to 'an agreement necessarily relative because related to those who enter it' (Arendt 1973: 193). However, the accompanying statement that they are truths held to be 'self-evident' provides us with a pronounced and significant modal contrast. The invocation of 'self-evidence' introduces an appeal to an absolute, carrying the sense of compulsion that comes from reference to a proposition that is beyond opinion. The 'we' that hold the truths concerned is thereby transcended and they lose their status as a contingently formed body of persons constituting themselves as a polity. As Arendt notes, the truth asserted in the Declaration, that 'all men are created equal', is hardly a proposition that could carry with it the self-evidence of, for example, a mathematical proposition; but the formulation that is given hints at a comparable level of authority. And in turn, the authority of self-evidence is not quite equivalent to that of an invocation of the divine, but 'bears the signs of divine origin' (Arendt 1973: 194). In Arendt's account, then, the American revolutionaries resorted to the invocation of an absolute; and this compromised their ability to establish lasting conditions for the enactment of freedom unencumbered by the sense of compulsion that authority in the form of an appeal to the absolute brings to the public realm.

Again here, a measure of circumspection is called for. The American revolutionaries were, at least partially, able 'to transcend the narrow and tradition-based framework of their general concepts' in the light of the requirements and the experience of foundation (Arendt 1973: 229). In their own limited way, therefore, they mounted resistance to the 'severe blows' that our long tradition of political philosophy has dealt to the concept of opinion, denigrated as the opposite of truth (Arendt 1973: 229). To this extent, despite the resort to an absolute principle, what made the American Revolution a relative success was the establishment of a new and lasting constitution with an, albeit compromised, commitment to freedom at its centre. Again, it managed to institutionalise to an extent, a combination of power and authority: it was an institutional arrangement that bore comparison with the 'Roman principle' of 'the

116

organised multitude whose power was exerted in accordance with laws and limited by them' (Arendt 1973: 199). So the question that arises here in the American case is how far the sense of ambiguity and of compromise that it involved really reaches. For Arendt

> one is tempted to conclude that it was the authority which the act of foundation carried within itself, rather than the belief in an immortal legislator, or the promises of reward and the threats of punishment in a 'future state' or even the doubtful self-evidence of the truths enumerated in the preamble to the Declaration of Independence, that assured the stability of the new republic. (Arendt 1973: 199)

Why, in Arendt's view, are we 'tempted' to draw this conclusion? The (deliberate) uncertainty of tone here may be explained in that the partial comparison that Arendt makes between the French and American cases is resistant to assimilation and instead seeks to create space for the problematisation of key issues. The partial parallel that she draws is suggestive of the fact that the intrusion of the social into the political is pervasive, leaving us with a sense that it may not be subject to mitigation. At the same time, it problematises the wholly related question of new beginnings, suggesting that it is an issue that we do not have to see simply as paradox, and which may be a political question, to be resolved politically rather than in theory.

The Americans' search for an absolute, does supply us with a partial parallel in terms of the social aspect of their mission – an element that involved transcending the relative and plural condition of the political in favour of a unifying socio-economic goal, albeit based upon a rather different construal of the concept of equality. But there is a further issue here as to whether this partial parallel reflects a more general point; a deeper philosophical issue that might pertain to revolutions per se in so far as we cannot accept the idea of something being created spontaneously between persons without prior guidance or a conditioning principle beyond opinion: the creation of something out of nothing.

From a philosophical point of view, the stabilising justification for a new beginning would seem to require something beyond the arbitrary confluence of opinion that appears to have brought it about, an ethical reference beyond the realm of appearances, if it is not to appear wholly arbitrary (and so, in a sense, under-theorised). It would equally look insoluble in the context of more recent historical explanatory perspectives (the traditional alternative to the tradition). In the light of this, spontaneous foundational agency would seem akin to lifting ourselves up by our own bootstraps. Spontaneity remains the central problem and an absolute must be found somewhere, whether in the form of the general will, natural law, or, later, the logic of history.[5]

This is an issue that draws our thinking back to the political itself. For Arendt, the question of revolutionary novelty may be insoluble from a philosophical point of view, but she does not see it as a philosophical question; it is rather wholly a political one.

In the light of this, Arendt wants to thematise discursively, and in the light of ongoing political experience, what she takes to be clues in the American case, particularly in comparison with the French: the possibilities of entertaining spontaneity in the enactment of new beginnings, once viewed in non-traditional terms, may have theoretical purchase and can inform our considerations concerning political freedom in our time. The contrast between the thoroughly social mission of the French revolutionaries and their resort to dictatorship and terror, and the politically aware American revolutionaries, with their more modest social ambition, reveals the way in which the act of liberation requires, if it is to secure freedom, an act of constitutional foundation that we can understand as a spontaneous new beginning.

CONSTITUTIONAL FOUNDATION

The search for an absolute in the context of political action was, for Arendt, closely related to the terms of occidental religion reproduced in the early modern reference to natural law. It was assumed that man-made laws took the form of commandments which applied independently of mutual agreements and did so because they could claim a higher authority. This tradition exercised a powerful intellectual influence at the time of the eighteenth-century revolutions. One exception to this, however, amongst the pre-revolutionary theorists was Montesquieu. He found no reason to resort to an appeal to the absolute because he understood law in the Roman fashion as a 'rapport' between persons or entities, and therefore as relative by definition. The question of absolute validity therefore did not apply (Arendt 1973: 188–9).

This way of thinking implies that foundational acts are *sui generis*, and so, if they are to be successful in creating a new republic, must be self-sustaining. An element of this is evident, for Arendt, in the American case where rights were proclaimed as rights of citizenship in the context of a newly formed site of power where persons participated and so maintained it, something enshrined in a constitutional arrangement that incorporated a separation of powers. The authority of the constitution correspondingly derives from its capacity to be amended and augmented. Although this strain was not the only one in the thinking of the American revolutionaries, it gives us insight into the possibility of foundational action liberated from the dependence upon an absolute. This 'Roman' element suggests the sense in which 'the act of foundation ... develops its own stability and permanence and provides a context for augmentation by all the subsequent innovations and changes that are possible on the basis of the foundational act' (Arendt 1973: 202). This illuminates the sense of revolution as a genuine 'interruption' with respect to given conditions and processes, creating something that 'was brought into being by no "historical necessity" and no organic development, but by a deliberate act', an act that draws upon, and incorporates the principle of 'the combined power of the many' (Arendt 1973: 214, 216).

In spite of the intrusion of a particular form of the social question into the American Revolution, the political concern with freedom was strong enough to shed light on the idea of an authentically political revolution, allowing us to consider the possibility 'that men are equipped for the logically paradoxical task of making a new beginning' in that they could create, between them, a new space where the passion for public freedom could be consummated in a sustained way. In other words, they could act so as to ensure the survival of the principle that informed the revolutionary act itself:

> there exists a solution for the perplexities of beginning which needs no absolute to break the vicious circle in which all first things seem to be caught. What saves the act of beginning from its own arbitrariness is that it carries its own principle within itself, or, to be more precise, that beginning and its principle ... are not only related to each other but are coeval. (Arendt 1973: 212)

This provides us with a sense in which the foundational act can, as it were, continue to resonate over time by making visible a principle of freedom 'which inspires the deeds that are to follow' (Arendt 1973: 213). What is striking with respect to the 'solution' to the perplexity of new beginnings here is that it lies within the realm of action itself: the answer to the problem of spontaneity lies in spontaneity. It is the foundational act itself that discloses and makes visible the principle that it contains, rather than being answerable to and conditioned by a prior axiom; and it is this that allows the act to create the conditions for its own reproduction 'in spirit' through the arrangements that it creates. It may well be that as long as it is posed in more traditional philosophical terms, foundation always retains the element of paradox. But we find here reasons to resist the traditional demand that action must be made answerable to theory; and the reasons here come from the illumination that we gain from the examples available to us.

In more specific terms, the study of modern revolutions provides illumination in that the problem of action in the modern context reasserts itself in the guise of the social question. We have seen that, in Arendt's view, whilst the French Revolution wholly sacrificed political concerns to social ones, the American Revolution retained a sense of freedom, but nevertheless a sense that was mediated by the question of private prosperity, the legacy of which has had a significant corrosive effect upon the ability of the American constitutional settlement to preserve the spirit of public freedom. This testifies to the fact that the social question is a persistent political problem in the modern world; one that will not disappear in the foreseeable future and which continually problematises the issue of the instantiation of freedom: we face the prospect, for now, and possibly permanently, that 'liberation from necessity, because of its urgency, will always take precedence over the building of freedom' (Arendt 1973: 112). However, from an analysis of the contrast between the key elements of the French and American cases and their aftermath, we can thematise an idea of political freedom and of foundation that provide us with resources to question the dominance of the social question in modern politics and the effect that it has had on the conduct and organisation of the public realm.

In the light of questioning of this sort, we have reason consistently to interrogate modern democratic systems in terms of the ability to incorporate freedom. It is arguable that these systems, for Arendt, struggle to achieve more than the incorporation of a measure of control of the rulers by the ruled. And this qualification does not necessarily do much to undermine the dominance of the principle of rule itself. Equally, the system of electoral representation tends to rest upon the representation of interests rather than publicly formed opinions, according with an emphasis upon private well-being rather than upon public happiness. The political sense informing the American Revolution, at least in its early stage, crystallised in a rather different political form, and one which provides us with an example that brings into focus problems raised by the rise of the social and the form of governance that we have seen to arise along with this phenomenon – the 'council system', which germinally constituted a means of preserving the spirit made visible in the revolutionary act itself.

The Council System

In contrast with the centralising appeal to a general will in France, in America the state constitutions were drawn from the views of local bodies – districts, counties, townships – which in turn fed into federal arrangements (Arendt 1973: 165). This provides us with an example of power enacted from below, and a system designed to preserve that power. The example reveals, in Arendt's view, 'the intimate connection between the spirit of freedom and the principle of federation' (Arendt 1973: 266).

The council system, as Arendt characterises it, embodies a recognition of this connection. It stems, in Arendt's work, from the example of localised and dispersed bodies that can be seen to have sprung up in circumstances of revolutionary upheaval: the revolutionary societies and municipal councils in France; the localised assemblies and meetings in America; and later, the system of soviets in Russia. In the American context, where the influence of these localised bodies was most long-lived and influential, Arendt notes Jefferson's plan of 'elementary republics' – the building of the republic on the basis of these combined subdivisions, which he thought could secure 'the salvation of the revolutionary spirit' (Arendt 1973: 251). This 'ward system', as Jefferson called it, 'was not meant to strengthen the power of the many but the power of "every one"' and these localised bodies were not to be 'a mere supplement to the existing institutions [but rather] a new form of government' creating a political context where an emphasis could realistically be placed on the value of participation itself, on one's share of public happiness (Arendt 1973: 254). These dispersed and diverse bodies represented the 'formation of a new power structure which owed its existence to nothing but the organisational impulses of the people themselves' (Arendt 1973: 257). The councils, in Arendt's view, did not see their mission in purely instrumental terms, in terms of a determinate task to be performed the completion of which would mark the lapse of their *raison d'être*. For Arendt, 'they invariably refused to regard themselves as temporary' and thus constituted themselves as potentially lasting 'spaces of freedom' (Arendt 1973: 264). The residual institutionalisation of this in the form of a federal system and the separation of powers that it implies are sometimes seen as a recipe for impotence; but for Arendt, this is far from the case. As long as we understand power, again as empowerment generated by the mutual exchange of opinions, a diversity of forums in which such exchanges can take place only augments power and stabilises it through mutual agreements. The council formation corresponds with and embodies the concept of action: it 'arises out of the elementary conditions of action itself' such that the 'central power' of the polity does not 'deprive the constituent bodies of their original power to constitute' (Arendt 1973: 267). In the process of agreement, opinions need sifting and mediating; and this can only be achieved by 'passing them through a body of men, chosen for the purpose' (Arendt 1973: 227). But the proliferation of these bodies in a system where representation at one level answers to previous levels provides for decision-making that carries the confidence of persons as opinion-holders and judges of the process. So it is only if we see power in the non-political guise of rule (in the name of imposing a set of absolute principles or, in more recent form, the furthering of the collective interest) that a disaggregated system looks inefficient.

A further, and related, aspect to the contrast that the image of the council system sets up with modern democratic politics concerns the role of the political party. Hierarchical party organisations provide mechanisms for the mobilisation of popular support where representation effectively replaces and transcends the free exchange of opinions. The councils embodied in themselves a challenge to the party system per se, to a system where party programmes take the place of freely formed consensus. It is no accident that, in the context of modern revolutions, it has been common to see party organisations emasculating the role of localised council organisations. The reason that this usurping of the role of the 'real organs of revolution' was not, in Arendt's view, explicable in terms of 'bad faith' or 'the drive for power' is that revolutionary parties have a culture of, and commitment to, representation in common with all other parties, something that finds its basis not in the contingent opinions of plural persons but in relation to an aggregative principle that always potentially transcends *actual* expressions of opinion in favour of a presupposed collective aim or interest (Arendt 1973: 273). The revolutionary societies that sprung up across France were crushed in the name of the general will; in the course of the Russian Revolution, the system of soviets was emasculated by the Bolshevik party, acting in the name of a collective historical interest (Arendt 1973: 246–7). And as we have seen, the American case was a much more mediated one; but even here a more centralised representative model developed according with the emergent political culture that emphasised the representation and furthering of private interests.

These points again generate illuminating contrasts between the image of the council system and, in the modern context, a construal of politics geared to the pursuit of a blueprint and the management of interests; but it does not, as Arendt sees it, represent a contrast between two blueprints justified in terms of a specific sense of purpose. We noted earlier Jefferson's proposal for a system of subdivisions or wards suitable to the dispersal of sites of power. Arendt observes a certain 'vagueness of purpose' in his proposed system. She regards this sense of indeterminacy as deliberate and as testament to the fact that Jefferson did not wish to attach to his system a set of specific functions on the basis of any predetermined model. In a similar spirit, and in accordance with the mediated approach that Arendt takes, she invokes the image of the council system as a reference point for a continuing discussion concerning the possibilities of the political in the context of what she takes to be the major problems that we face, and in particular, of the ongoing problem of the relation between the political and the social as it makes itself felt to us now. One of the points that emerge from the study of revolutions, Arendt puts thus:

> if it is true that the revolutionary parties never understood to what extent the council system was identical with the emergence of a new form of government, it is no less true that the councils were incapable of understanding to what enormous extent the government machinery in modern societies must indeed perform the functions of administration. (Arendt 1973: 273)

In this sense, the council system does not provide, in and of itself, a recipe for solving the question of the political and the social. The sense it conveys, however, allows us to problematise that question in a manner that gives due consideration to the character of public freedom and to the generative power of the political itself: 'it would be tempting', Arendt says, 'to spin out further the potentialities of the councils, but it is certainly wiser to say with Jefferson "Begin them only for a single purpose; they will soon show for what others they are the best instruments"' (Arendt 1973: 279).[6] The council system deals in the exchange of opinion. We noted earlier that diverse opinions need 'sifting' and forming into a (contestable) public view; the council system, in this form, answers to the maintenance of contestability here, reflecting the idea that 'no single individual – neither the wise man of the philosophers, nor . . . divinely informed reason . . . can ever be equal to the task of sifting opinions, of passing them through the sieve of intelligence . . . and thus purify them into a public view' (Arendt 1973: 227). In this sense, the formal character of the council system as Arendt characterises it delivers no blueprint and, quite to the contrary, answers to the resistance she seeks to mount in theory to the traditional search for a univocal resolution to the 'problem' of the political.

Arendt's comparative study of revolutions, and the themes of action, foundation and the establishment of new political arrangements that arise from it, all, then, have the circumspect character that we have associated with a non-traditional, mediated approach to political theory. As we have also noted, central to this is a resistance to the inclination to search for a morally authoritative ideal that might appear in a political context as a blueprint for the best polity. This clearly raises a question as to the ethical component in Arendt's political thought.

Notes

1. The conversion of private passion into public commitment in France, as Arendt notes, made itself equally evident in the revolutionary regime's constant emphasis upon moral purity as a public standard. It was this, she suggests, that rendered the experience of hypocrisy a central theme, short-circuiting the mediating effects of public disclosure and displacing questions of legal and political criteria for judgment. This emphasis prefigured later concerns, in totalitarian settings, with confessional purging, the institutionalising of admissions of 'inner' guilt.
2. The origin of this inclination can and must be understood in context; but as we have noted, it is not a feature exclusive to the French case: more generally, for Arendt, 'theoretically the most far-reaching consequence of the French Revolution was the birth of the modern concept of history in Hegel's philosophy', reintroducing the philosopher's absolute into human affairs, such that 'everything that had been political – acts and words and events – become historical', falling under the category of necessity (Arendt 1973: 51–2).
3. As Arendt recognises, the exception to this was the institution of slavery, 'the primordial crime upon which the fabric of American society rested' (Arendt 1973: 71). This was, of course, a phenomenon that was to become a highly visible and significant issue in the political history of the American polity, but was at the time hidden from view.
4. In the French case, the constitution of 1791 'remained a piece of paper' and its lack of effect was shown in the subsequent 'avalanche of constitutions' (Arendt 1973: 125).
5. The Russian revolutionaries, for Arendt, put their faith not in action but in historical necessity and, as a result, became 'the fools of history' (Arendt 1973: 58).

6. Although she cannot resist the temptation of adding that they might be 'the best instruments, for example, for breaking up the modern mass society, with its dangerous tendency toward the formation of pseudo-political mass movements, or rather, the best, most natural way for interspersing it at the grass roots with an elite that is chosen by no-one but constitutes itself' (Arendt 1973: 279).

CHAPTER 7

Political Theory and Political Ethics

The approach that we have seen Arendt taking in her major engagements in political theory, an approach which, at least from the point of view of the tradition that she seeks to oppose, is novel in the mediations that it displays, generates a question central to an understanding of her thought: the question of political ethics.[1] The key issue here is whether and in what sense Arendt's political theory can incorporate an ethical component. It is commensurate with her anti-traditional approach that she does not appear to offer a political ethics of a conventional sort: she does not offer, that is, a set of precepts that can be applied to politics such as to guide the conduct and organisation of political life in the light of an image of the best kind of polity. We have seen that, for Arendt, the formulation and application of precepts like this reflects an inclination to legislate for politics from a vantage point outside it, seeking thereby an escape from, and the emasculation of, the inherently plural and conflictual sphere of politics. The aim of the tradition was to supply 'standards and rules, yardsticks and measurements' by which to resolve the contingency that, for Arendt, is the chief characteristic of the public realm (Arendt 1958: 102).

The prospect of resolving the argumentative and potentially anarchic business of politics by the application of moral principles, thought to be authoritative because they were beyond argument, has proved a false promise. The experience of totalitarianism shows us how readily such precepts may be jettisoned in the light of the belief that 'everything is possible'. The anti-political character of this conviction is evident in that, as we noted in Chapter 4, political action requires a stable context in which to take place: the public stage needs defining by reference to

126

constraints, including ethical ones. But we now see that traditional moral precepts cannot necessarily supply stability in this context: the capacity for action can always outrun them. For just this reason, the application of abstract precepts to politics begins to look inappropriate with respect to the internal integrity of politics itself. These considerations re-invoke the references that we have seen Arendt making back to what she takes to be a pre-traditional classical image of politics as an agonal engagement, understood in terms of self-disclosure in a plural setting propelled by the desire for glory. Action in a context of this kind differs from the more prosaic forms of human conduct that may be judged by 'moral standards': by contrast, 'political action can be judged only by the standards of greatness' (Arendt 1958: 205). This clearly prompts a question as to whether any ethical constraints we might seek to associate with politics can be anything other than obstacles to self-disclosure; an issue that has led to doubts concerning the possibility of Arendt's thought accommodating any sense of ethical constraint.[2]

The model to which Arendt refers, on the face of it, opens up a gulf between the political and the moral that looks hard to bridge. And to an extent, this thought is reinforced if we think back again to Arendt's treatment of the question of conscience discussed in Chapter 2. We noted there that conscience figures as a product of the ability to think, to engage in a dialogue with oneself, and that it is effective in that it presents obstacles to action that would, on reflection, make one incapable of living with oneself. But it remains of marginal political significance. Conscience arises as a phenomenon that is both internalised and absolute; and in both of these senses, it transcends the plural conditions of the public realm, where opinion and the exchange of opinion is the informing motif. It may become relevant in 'emergencies', where, politically, one is in danger of colluding with evil (a phenomenon which equally, from a political point of view, appears as an absolute borne of transcendence of the circumstances of plurality). But the modal distance between politics and the operation of conscience would seem to reinforce the gulf between the political and the moral in Arendt's account. I will refer back to the issue of conscience later, but for now it is worth reviewing, in light of the above considerations, how Arendt's political theory stands in relation to the more established contemporary ways of theorising a political ethics.

Arendt and Modern Political Ethics

Putting it in broad terms, we can refer to two particularly influential ways of grounding political ethics. The first is in terms of a set of procedural principles, more or less independent of substantive conceptions of the 'good', that establish fair and reasonable terms of co-operation in a polity and which provide criteria for just institutional arrangements. The second is in terms of a set of shared, culturally inscribed conventions that imply arrangements which, at the public level, answer to our common image of the good life. It is hard to see how Arendt's political theory can be made to answer to either of these formulations. Initially, given Arendt's resistance to foundational principles that transcend the plural conditions of the public realm, we might think that a political ethics consistent with her approach would be informed by reference to a contingent, culturally grounded set of values that might form the basis of an ethically well-ordered polity; an ethics of the sort we might associate with 'communitarian' thinking. This would, in a prima facie sense at least, seem to answer to the idea of contingent agreement that is of the essence with respect to Arendt's conception of the political. However, it is difficult to see how Arendt's approach can be assimilated with the proposals for a framework for political ethics that appeals to cultural convention. They *do* appear to move the ethical focus away from the 'coercive' injunctions that Arendt associates with the philosophical tradition. But equally, they represent a standpoint that is undesirable from an Arendtian point of view because they depend upon a kind of solidarity in belief that sits uneasily with the emphasis upon plurality that she takes to be central to the experience of the political. The point here is not that shared cultural beliefs lack, from a theoretical point of view, sociological significance; it is rather that, from the point of view of political plurality, injunctions derived from a shared cultural perspective still have a supervenient and constricting character. In Arendt's view, it is in the nature of political action 'to break through the commonly accepted and reach into the extraordinary, where whatever is true in common and everyday life no longer applies because everything is unique and *sui generis*' (Arendt 1958: 205). A communitarian grounding for political ethics would seem, in this sense, to threaten spontaneity and so neglect the political in favour of the imposition of a given set of ethical prescriptions.[3] In general, in Arendt's view, standpoints that would place stress upon criteria that apply as a result of shared cultural understandings or reference points are depoliticising.

If Arendt's political theory does not sit easily with an ethical appeal to shared cultural convention, can it be made consistent, despite the reservations noted above, with an appeal to more foundational principles if, perhaps, these are conceived of 'thinly', in procedural form? The most obvious reference point for the assimilation of Arendt's thinking with this kind of approach is in terms of the discursive element that is central to her conception of the political and, in turn, the concept of reflective judgment. We noted in Chapter 2 that reflective judgment, as a product of the capacity to think, consists in the ability to pass a general verdict upon a particular which can claim intersubjective communicative validity in so far as the judgment is made in the light of the putative standpoints of others, answering to the operation of the 'enlarged mentality'. Judgment, thus understood, is the mental operation most proximate to the realm of action and has a pertinence to the public realm where agents and action appear in their specificity and invite the assignment of meaning.

What work can the concept of judgment do with respect to the possibility of a political ethics? It would certainly seem that, in Arendt's account, the *verdicts* of reflective judgment cannot be the source of any foundational ethical principles, because they do not have a claim to universality. For Arendt, '[judgment consists in] the ability to see things not only from one's own point of view but in the perspective of all who happen to be present . . . judgment is endowed with a certain specific validity but is never universally valid' (Arendt 1977: 221).[4] In this sense, the operation of judgment is tied to the particularities of appearance and reception, to performance in its particular setting.

Of course, it could still be argued that the formal operation of judgment itself, regardless of the particular contextual verdicts that it delivers, has a universal character, grounded in the condition of plurality, which may itself establish a set of principles that carry substantive ethical authority and which would legitimate, for example, a procedural conception of justice. It is a formulation of this sort that Seyla Benhabib has in mind in seeking to reconstruct from Arendt's work a communicative ethics in the form of a 'procedural model of enlarged thought' (Benhabib 1988: 29–51). On this kind of account, the communicability of judgment, its discursive currency, points us back to formally grounded principles: the character of judgment may retroactively legitimate substantive procedural principles that supervene upon the practice of politics. The appeal here is not to formal logic but to the universal conditions of reflective judgment; but it is not likely that the reference to judgment can do the work expected of it in this interpretation: judgment, in Arendt's account, is too deeply rooted in the phenomenal conditions of appearance (cf. Villa 1999: 151–2). The suitability of a theory of judgment to underwrite retroactively a supervening political ethics depends upon its capacity to make an appeal to universal conditions that are of direct and substantial procedural significance. Arendt does not, and could not, draw this kind of implication from her conception of judgment: whilst her conception does answer to, and presuppose, a general image of the public realm as a self-sustaining sphere of communicative interaction, it is an image that incorporates too much contingency both in content and form to provide a basis for fixed and substantive principles of political ethics. The contingent and phenomenal character of the public realm, as Arendt sees it, places it at one remove from foundational ethical claims, even of a procedural sort.

However, it is just this phenomenal account (implying terms of reference internal to what we have created *as* a public realm) that may provide a basis for political ethics, not because it *presupposes* substantive constraints but because it implies an understanding of how constraints might *arise* in the context of the public realm itself. In order to take this further, it is useful to look at those capacities that form features of the public realm and which, in Arendt's account, are of some moral significance.

Promising and Forgiveness

The capacities for making promises and for forgiveness to which we referred in Chapter 5 as central to the possibility of a coherent public realm, mark out, for Arendt, 'the only strictly moral duty of the citizen . . . the condition of all other, specifically political, virtues' (Arendt 1972: 75). Their importance lies in the fact that they are capacities which supply 'control mechanisms' built into the very faculty of action itself (Arendt 1958: 246). Their effect is to prevent action running out of control, creating endless processes of enactment and response that may become destructive. They limit, in this sense, the potentially problematic ramifications of the unpredictability and irreversibility that are intrinsic to action.

How far reference to these capacities takes us in terms of a substantive political ethics, however, is questionable. Arguably, promising and forgiveness appear only to mitigate these particular problematic aspects of action; and so they are, whilst significant, insufficient to underwrite a general framework for a political ethics (cf. Kateb 2000). Arendt recognises this, noting that offering capacities that help provide a stable context *for* political action as the basis of an ethics operating *in* the political realm is a confusion (Arendt 1958: 246). Nevertheless, even if they cannot underwrite a substantive political ethics, the significance that Arendt affords to promising and forgiveness is suggestive. The pertinence of these capacities to the public realm lies in the fact that their character answers to the nature of public action: they are enactments that have the properties of being unconditioned and revelatory or self-disclosing, features that we have already seen to be hallmarks of public agency. Furthermore, as enactments the significance of which comes from their character as utterances, they find a place in the linguistic fabric of the public realm. If we consider these enactments specifically from a linguistic point of view, we can see them from the perspective of the Austinian theory of linguistic performatives; as speech-acts. In this light, and in terms of linguistic theory, it is their illocutionary character, their nature as doing something in speaking, that gives promising and forgiveness their significance: contractual in the former case and declaratory in the latter (Austin 1975: 183). They constitute, when understood in these terms, linguistic enactments that provide a degree of stability in the sphere of action.

The significance of this can be drawn out further by a comparison between the engagements of promising and forgiveness as public enactments on the one hand, and the more abstract, supervening injunctions associated with more traditional formulations of political ethics on the other. In Arendt's terms, injunctions of the latter sort have, at least when viewed in relation to the linguistic fabric of the political, a transcendent and univocal character. At the same time, and just for this reason, their claim to authority depends upon the fact that they are notionally articulated in an originary voice that is not, and cannot be, attached to anyone in the plural setting of the public realm. They cannot, in this sense, be afforded performative status in the way that promising and forgiveness can; and their linguistic status remains constative, articulating that which was the case prior to the articulation. Performative status can only be attached, as it were, to an agent.[5]

If these considerations provide us with a sense of why abstract moral injunctions may lack purchase from the point of view of the public realm, then our attention is pointed back again to the issue of the performative conditions of speech in politics. We noted earlier that Arendt's conception of the political places the act of disclosure, and therefore

131

the phenomenon of visibility, at the centre of its ontological field. The more specific redemption of these concepts, in the context of the present discussion, lies in a consideration of linguistic performatives in a rhetorical context. With respect to 'control mechanisms', where self-binding speech-acts can interrupt and limit chains of enactments and responses, it is the illocutionary character of speech that appears decisive. Where we are concerned with more substantive forms of ethical constraint or guidance, applying to persons acting into the web of relations constituting the public realm, it is the perlocutionary, the sense of doing something *by* speaking, that may matter most in terms of the effects of speech-acts upon others and the response prompted. Self-binding illocutionary enactments may have important boundary significance, establishing constitutive constraints in the public realm; but within this, in the setting of substantive political interaction, performative dynamics that define the effects of linguistic enactments in terms of the response of others may prove central.[6] We have seen that the political arena, as Arendt conceives of it, is one where no one is entirely the author of their own story, where actors are dependent upon others for the attribution, through judgment, of meaning. The perlocutionary conditions that pertain in a context of this sort are arguably crucial to forms of ethical constraint. In order to pursue this theme further, it is worth drawing out a comparison between Arendt's conception of the political and that of Machiavelli, also associated with a 'non-traditional' treatment of political ethics, to whom she refers back on occasions and with whom (limited) parallels can be drawn.

ARENDT AND MACHIAVELLI I: A COMPARISON

The initial parallel to be drawn here refers back to the point noted earlier: that the moral injunctions supplied by the voice of conscience have at best only marginal significance with respect to the public realm. The concern with the moral integrity of the self bypasses and so, from a moral point of view, transcends the worldly concerns characteristic of the condition of the political, where the question of the opinions and responses of others become crucial to the meanings of acts: the injunctions of conscience are largely irrelevant to a condition characterised by the 'moral irresponsibility inherent in a plurality of agents' (Arendt 1958: 220). Echoing this (and more generally, the broader contrast between the political and absolute goodness that we noted Arendt drawing in Chapter 6), we can refer to Machiavelli's view that good people come to grief in politics because politics is an engagement that requires priority to be given to the fate of the many rather than the moral wholeness of the self and so engages the disposition to favour the health of the city over that of one's own soul. In this sense, Arendt and Machiavelli share a recognition that the contrast between the private and the public has moral ramifications. A context where plurality is the principal experiential motif is one where unpredictability is guaranteed, where actions prompt reactions and 'reaction, apart from being a response, is always a new action that strikes out on its own and affects others' (Arendt 1958: 190). This is an unavoidable characteristic of the sphere of freedom; and the unpredictability that it involves pertains in a moral respect as well as in others (a characteristic that finds expression in the Machiavellian concept of fortune). In light of this, the move from the relative predictability and security of the private, where the moral wholeness of the self may be more reliably preserved, into the exposed and uncertain conditions of the public, requires courage (again in a moral sense as well as others). For Arendt, 'the only post-classical political theorist who, in an extraordinary effort to restore its old dignity to politics, perceived this gulf and understood something of the courage needed to cross it was Machiavelli' (Arendt 1958: 35). This initial comparison between Arendt and Machiavelli suggests two further concepts that their respective understandings of politics imply and which are pertinent to the question of political ethics.

First, the challenge presented by entry into the unpredictable public realm is to bring to bear a form of political virtue that is called upon by, and answers to, a plural and circumstantial context.[7] By contrast with a purely moral conception of virtue, its political formulation invokes the concept of virtuosity: the application of particular competences in relation to specific contexts and practices. In respect of the political agent, this sets up a requirement to act resourcefully in a context of unpredictable plurality (Machiavelli 1970: 369).[8] Arendt shares with Machiavelli here a reference back to the Homeric theme of virtuoso performance, revealing ability and commensurate aspects of character in the light of contingency.

Second, this sense of virtuosity carries with it the connotation of display, corresponding with the condition of visibility that we have seen to be central to Arendt's conception of the public realm, where, in acting and speaking, persons display a unique identity. The comparison here is with Machiavelli's emphasis upon the idea of 'reputation' as a central concern for the political agent: considerations of reputation are intrinsic to the practice of political virtue and help define both its nature and its limits (see Machiavelli 1981: 121; Arendt 1981/I: 131). Here again, we find a factor that serves to mediate the application of pure moral virtue in politics. Machiavelli argues, for example, that a political actor must seek to acquire a reputation for *compassion*, regarded as a desirable moral virtue; but in order to secure a reputation of this sort, it may be necessary to be less than wholly compassionate, less compassionate, perhaps, than one might be disposed to be in private life. The moral virtue of compassion pursued, as it were to the full or in an unmediated fashion in politics, may lead to circumstances where one is then required to act in ways that destroy one's reputation in this regard (Machiavelli 1981: 93). Arendt would agree with this. We saw in Chapter 6 that in the course of her analysis of the French Revolution, Arendt takes the view that the recourse to terror in that case was directly related to the fact that the revolutionaries were guided by sentiments, admirable perhaps in a different context, of compassion for the poor; sentiments which, when viewed from the point of view of the political, are non-negotiable and so potentially pathological.

Aside from the parallels we have drawn between Arendt and Machiavelli, there are equally sharp and important differences. I shall return to these, but for the time being it is worth noting that the themes of ambition, glory and appearance before an audience can help us shed light upon the implications to be drawn out of Arendt's political thought for the question of political ethics.

POLITICAL ETHICS AND JUDGMENT

We have seen that Arendt's conception of judgment is not susceptible to redemption in the form of a foundational political ethics, even of a purely procedural sort. However, given the centrality of visibility and appearance to political action, judgment may nevertheless play an important role with respect to the ethical considerations that make themselves felt in the public realm. We have seen that the conception of reflective judgment involves an appeal to 'common sense', which in Arendt's usage (owing a debt to Kant) is not simply a sense common to us all that could be unpacked and codified but is rather a sense expressed *in* judgments made with respect to the appropriateness of what we see before us in its particularity. It is a sense that, through its communicability (ensured, again, by taking into account the putative standpoints of others) fits us in

134

to a community of judges: the validity of my judgments 'will reach as far as the community of which my common sense makes me a member' (Arendt 2003: 140). Judgment, in Arendt's account, depends for its validity upon the range of 'people's standpoints I have in mind when I am pondering a given issue and the better I can imagine how I would feel and think if I were in their place, the stronger will be my capacity for representative thinking and the more valid my final conclusions, my opinion' (Arendt 1977: 241). Judgments appealing to the common sense solicit but cannot command, or otherwise guarantee, universal assent. The communicative solicitations of reflective judgment put us, as it were, on common discursive terrain, but do not carry the authority of a transcendent injunction.

What might this deliver in terms of possible ethical constraint and guidance applicable to political action? The judgments we make are circumstantial and are tied to the particulars of what is seen; and, in virtue of this, they answer to the condition of plural visibility characterising the public realm. However, it is precisely this susceptibility to judgment entailed in public exposure that implies a form of ethical constraint. This is so in that if the exposure to judgment forms an intrinsic and not just a contingent feature of action, then the question of judgment provides the basis of significant imperatives for those acting politically, springing from and internal to the engagement of action itself. This provides us with an understanding of political ethics contrasting with more traditional formulations that would require political actors to conduct themselves in accordance with a supervening ethical code, whether thickly or thinly conceived. The imperative that is introduced in Arendt's conception of the public realm is to act in the light of exposure to the circumstantial judgments and verdicts of spectators.

This is implied in the classical model that we have seen Arendt taking as her inspiring and corrective reference point. Here, the desire for disclosure and the achievement of glory 'did not know any "moral" considerations but only . . . the unceasing effort to be best' (Arendt 1977: 154).[9] So it is of the essence, in the context of action thus conceived, to submit to the public gaze and render oneself eligible for judgment. This point re-engages the issue of the perlocutionary circumstances that pertain to the public realm and the concern, for the agent, with what responses action may prompt. Of course, the question of response will always be of *practical* concern for the political actor in that political aims and projects need others to help carry them through: the actor seeks agreement in this sense. But part of this solicitation must refer to the judgment of others, not just in terms of practical consensus but also in terms of judgment, which, as we have seen, is sensitive to the particular act and to the particular 'who' that is disclosed in the act. This consideration is congruent with a central motivation for acting in an agonal context, in terms, again, of the ambition for glory. In common with Machiavelli, Arendt emphasises this ambition as central to the desire to move from private to public and it pertains aside from the more specific public ends and purposes that agents may harbour.

The passion for acting is internally related to the circumstances of being seen and of placing oneself in a context where one is subject to the judgmental view of spectator. It is this, as we learn from the classical model, which 'assures the actor that his passing existence and fleeting greatness will never lack the reality that comes from being seen, being heard and generally appearing before an audience of fellow men' (Arendt 1958: 198). This may provide us with an appropriate sense of ethical constraint. In subjecting themselves to the public gaze, agents equally subject themselves, Arendt argues (in terms cognate with those of 'greatness' or 'glory' but with a more familiar inflection), to the 'approbation' or 'disapprobation' that results from reflective judgment. Judgment passes a verdict on a particular that reflects, in its appeal to common sense, a view about 'what manner of action is to be taken in [the public realm] . . . as well as to how it is to look henceforth and what kinds of things are to appear in it' (Arendt 1977: 223).[10] The judgment of spectators therefore creates an imperative upon actors seeking approbation with respect to the disclosures they make. The imperative entailed here is not indexed against a prior moral precept but is generated in the anticipation of a verdict upon public conduct that implicates the agent – the 'who' that is disclosed. It is a verdict, in this sense, as to who deserves or does not deserve to inhabit the public realm: judgments, for Arendt, amount to 'choosing our company' and those seeking approbation seek, as it were, to be chosen (Arendt 1982: 270).

We have seen that the reflective judgment that spectators bring to bear upon action is circumstantial and resists formulaic codification. In view of this, it is for political actors to exercise their own judgment, taking into account the standpoints of others, in assessing what might be acceptable in the light of publicity and what might not. There is no blueprint for this, which is one reason (amongst others) why politics can be considered a risky business. So the faculty of judgment is important to the actor as well as the spectator. As a member of the same community of judges, the actor can appeal to the common sense to make a judgment as to the anticipated reception of potential disclosures: 'the critic and spectator sits in every actor' (Arendt 1982: 63).[11] The capacity for the exercise of judgment here is necessary if action is to constitute an achievement commensurate with the reward that comes with the confirmation and approval of one's public identity:

> by his manner of judging, the person discloses to an extent also himself, what kind of person he is . . . it is precisely the realm of acting and speaking, that is, the political domain in terms of activities, in which this personal quality comes to the fore in public, in which the 'who one is' becomes manifest. (Arendt 1977: 223)

And the ability to anticipate responses here is already implied in knowing how to act, how to insert oneself successfully into the web of public interactions.[12] The internal relation between action and judgment implied here parallels the relation that Kant posited, in the context of his own formulation of reflective judgment in application to the sphere of aesthetics, between artistic genius and taste: art is the product of genius but it needs the mediating influence of taste, which 'clips its wings . . . [and] gives guidance' (Arendt 1982: 62). The public actor is concerned with fame, and this 'comes about through the opinion of others . . . [the actor] does not conduct himself according to the innate voice of reason but in accordance with what spectators would expect of him. The standard is the spectator' (Arendt 1982: 55).[13]

A related aspect to the issue of what political ethics may be drawn from Arendt's account of the political concerns the motives and aims that draw persons into the public realm and the dispositions which are displayed once they enter it. We have seen that the classical model from which Arendt takes inspiration suggests that, aside from the principles and ends that come to the actor from outside, are the motives that provide, so to speak, the inner drive toward the public realm; and in this respect, the passion for appearance, for self-disclosure, and the 'ambition that strives for excellence' is a central factor (Arendt 1973: 276). It is this passion that provides the mainspring for a desire to enter the public realm, whatever the more concrete aims, and it is the passion that is consummated in the 'joy and gratification that arise out of . . . appearing in public . . . thus acquiring and sustaining identity' (Arendt 1977: 263). So it is in anticipation of the response prompted in spectators by action that the agent finds guidance and encounters constraints. Political actors desiring approbation need spectators to provide it; and there is no other more covert way of achieving 'glory'.

The emphasis that Arendt places upon the intrinsic value of public appearance, which has sometimes been taken to indicate that her theory of politics is lacking in a sense of substantive content, by no means excludes or seeks to marginalise the more concrete considerations that we recognise as informing political agency. As we have already noted, a number of elements may go to make up action: there will be specific, classifiable ends in view, there will be broader goals at stake and there will be inspiring principles. All of these are specific factors informing action. They are all circumstantial factors that inform practical judgments made by political agents – but none on its own provides the meaning of the act to which reflective judgment is directed. In terms of the perlocutionary dynamic, the dynamic of enactment and reaction, reflective judgment on the part of spectators is central as a response that has the effect of tying together the disparate elements that figure in public action.[14] Reflective judgment seeks a verdict on the 'complete' act, where these elements come together in a performance, potentially displaying virtuosity. It is in this sense, again, that acts disclose agents, and it is the 'who' not just the 'what' that is judged. It is just because of this, however, that exposure to judgment answers directly to the ambition for glory.

So, the point is that the resultant act, when it makes its appearance in the public realm, is more than simply an aggregate of the specific aims and goals that informed it; it becomes a complete performance, showing the agent-specific dispositions that disclose the 'who'; and this is the case 'even when they wholly concentrate on reaching an altogether worldly object' (Arendt 1958: 183).[15] But the dispositions disclosed in a complete act, inviting judgment, remain central to the issue of response and so to the desire for public approbation. In the light of this, the susceptibility to judgment that public exposure brings creates a further requirement for the political actor (and one that equally calls upon the capacity for exercising political virtue, as a public rather than a private achievement) – to judge *which* dispositions to consummate in public and which, as it were, to leave at home (see Arendt 1973: 98). The perlocutionary dynamics intrinsic to public appearance – of exposure and reception – provide the basis for an anticipatory judgment concerning the dispositions that are revealed in action and which are made visible in the acts observed, acts that may be disaggregated in terms of the patterns of motive, intention, aims and goals that they incorporate and which come together in a performance that reflects back upon the agent. Once again, there is no blueprint here, and so a principal requirement for the political actor is flexibility with respect to the dispositions that are brought to bear publicly. It is in the nature of appearance, for Arendt, that it 'has the double function of concealing some interior and revealing some "surface" – for instance of concealing fear and revealing courage, that is, hiding the fear by showing courage' (Arendt 1981/I: 37).

In ethical terms, this provides further confirmation that neither pure goodness nor evil are ways of life appropriate to politics. The purely good person, in public, will not leave any dispositions at home, and cannot if they are to live the complete life of goodness. But this does not commit us to the view that the political realm is simply venal. Arendt is resistant to the continuing 'prejudice' (stemming from the ethical expectations established by the tradition, measured against which politics appears constantly to disappoint) that politics is 'an unethical business' and 'a fabric of lies and deception woven by shady interests and even shadier ideologies' (Arendt 1990: 102, 2005: 98). Putting it in terms that answer to an experiential field constituted by appearances, Arendt (echoing Machiavelli) condemns acts that bring power but not glory: 'badness that comes out of hiding . . . directly destroys the common world . . . badness can no more shine in glory than goodness' (Arendt 1958: 77; see also Machiavelli 1981: 63). Power (understood as strength) may be achieved by covert methods, but glory is an irreducibly public phenomenon and can only be realised in and through the public gaze. So whilst unmediated goodness does not answer to the ethical terrain of politics, nor does evil: each is pathological with respect to the public realm. Constraints with respect to public action arise not as a result of a dispositional archetype but through exposure to the contingent and circumstantial judgments that may bring the approbation that the political actor seeks.

Arendt and Machiavelli II: A Contrast

We have seen the sense in which a certain parallel can be drawn between Arendt and Machiavelli that has value in shedding light on what is implied ethically in Arendt's conception of the political and the circumstances of visibility and contingency. We can also say, more broadly, that Arendt and Machiavelli share an 'anti-traditional' approach to theorising politics. Each rejects an appeal to transcendent principles, displaying a common fidelity to the terrain of the political, which shows itself methodologically in terms of their preference for the use of concrete cases and for learning from examples: Machiavelli was famously concerned to apply the imagination in order to learn from the great examples of the past with respect to how to think and act in contemporary circumstances; and Arendt was similarly inclined to invoke exemplars, both historically, in terms of the intellectual guidance or stimulation to be found in past events, and in more contemporary terms, with respect to the biographies of recent exemplary figures (Arendt 1968b; Machiavelli 1970: 68). I shall return to what might be the suggestive limits to the methodological parallel here. Before this, however, it is worth looking at a more immediately evident contrast to be made between Arendt and Machiavelli in terms of the departure Arendt makes on the question of the phenomena of violence and lying as potential features of politics.

Violence and lying are phenomena about which Machiavelli is famously sanguine but which Arendt regards as at least potentially problematic from a political point of view. For Arendt, they each represent potentially self-destructive forms of agency, as they are corrosive with respect to the conditions of public action itself. Significantly, in this sense, the reservations we might have here are not grounded in prior, supervening injunctions and are rather implied in a sense of the nature of the political realm itself. Violence is problematic in this respect because, as we have already noted, it is mute, whereas the principal characteristic of the public realm is speech. Violence always threatens to bypass, and so undermine, the communicative conditions that underwrite the possibility of collective empowerment through contingent agreements in action that is the promise of politics (Arendt 1972: 87). Arendt's rejection of violence as a political means, then, is not derived from a universal precept, and she is certainly no pacifist. It stems instead from the fact that violence is intrinsically antithetical to politics; a theme again established in classical thinking (Arendt 1973: 12).[16]

With respect to lying, the case is comparable but not identical. The issue that arises with lying in the context of politics is also not to be seen as grounded in a universal prohibition. This becomes apparent in that Arendt does not see all instances of lying in the public realm in the same way. The problem here is less with what she terms the 'traditional' lie, understood in terms, for example, of state secrecy or the diplomatic concealment of intentions. These she describes as 'mostly harmless' (Arendt 1977: 52). So the criterion of damage done to the fabric of the public realm does not disclose any absolute injunction to be truthful: 'truthfulness has never been counted among the political virtues and lies have always been regarded as justifiable tools in political dealings . . . the lie did not

140

creep into politics by some accident of human sinfulness' (Arendt 1972: 11). And lying may be considered in a political context as itself a form of action: the liar may 'stick to his lies with great courage where legitimate political issues are at stake'; lies potentially share the characteristic with action that they can be corrected *by* action. The more acute difficulty comes when lying in politics transcends specific expediency and becomes systematic, where it concerns the consistent manipulation of public perceptions and the rewriting of history. The problem concerns, then, factual truth being 'manoeuvred out of the world' (Arendt 1977: 231). This is a characteristic of the 'modern lie', in that it destroys our reference points in a common world where coherent judgment and action is possible.[17] The distinction between these instances of lying is not measured against a precept but is established instead by reference, again, to the damage that might be done to the public realm. This realm, although it is constituted by the exchange of opinion, is nevertheless and of its essence, a realm that we have already seen depends upon the common acknowledgment of factual truths, supplying a context without which the exchange of opinion lacks parameters and so loses its sense; a circumstance where domination can take up the space vacated by common empowerment, and where, as we have learned, mendacity and the denial of the factual record becomes an institutionalised norm.[18] Nevertheless, the contention that systematic lying destroys the public realm 'must not be confused with the protests of "idealists" . . . against lying as bad in principle' (Arendt 1977: 225).

In general, those forms of conduct that are to be regarded as undesirable in politics are so regarded not because they offend a prior principle but because we have good experiential grounds for seeing them as damaging to the dynamics of appearance that may itself be a source of constraints: they do not offend against constraints so much as destroy the conditions of their emergence. So Arendt's concerns about violence and lying in politics are framed in terms that confirm the anti-traditional standpoint that she adopts. At the same time, they begin to establish a distinction between her position and Machiavelli's. It is a distinction that can be elaborated by reference to a series of thematic contrasts: first, in terms of their respective models of politics; second, in terms of their understanding of the distinction between public and private; and third, in the light of these differences, in terms of their contrasting methodological approaches to political theory and what these deliver in an ethical sense. These are interrelated points but it is useful to disaggregate them and examine each in brief, as they reflect back upon Arendt's methodological position.

On the first issue, Machiavelli's preoccupation with politics is shaped by his related concern with the idea of necessity and with the problem of disorder in the polity. His conception of necessity plays a central role in establishing the relation between political virtue and fortune. The practice of political virtue, or virtuosity, in the face of contingent patterns of events, involves the ability to act in the light of necessity, a concept which, in contrast with later usages, refers in Machiavelli to characteristic means-ends relationships that make themselves apparent in our historical experience. So the ability to recognise means-ends patterns becomes central to the conception of political virtue; and the invocation of necessity, thus understood, therefore instrumentalises the model of political action. A closely related theme here is the emphasis placed upon the achievement of order. Whilst it is true that Machiavelli, in what Arendt would see as 'post-traditional' vein, saw a value to the polity in 'tumults' – in disagreements and debates mapped principally on to class divisions – the maintenance of order remains central and is a key aim associated with the practice of rule (Machiavelli 1970: 114).[19] Arendt departs from Machiavelli on these points. For Arendt, the concern with the practice of rule as instrumental to the achievement of order is a concern, as we have seen, insinuated by the tradition. It would be wrong to say that Machiavelli seeks the traditional kind of 'quietening' of the public realm; however, he does retain (albeit in a form that sheds the metaphysical grounding sought by the tradition) an image of politics as rule for the purpose of securing order, even if he does not think that the order secured can be permanent. He shares, to this extent, what Arendt sees as the traditional conflation of politics with making, conflating, in more strictly Arendtian terms, action with work. As a result, in Machiavelli's thinking, the themes of political ambition, the desire for glory and the realisation of public happiness are all susceptible to rendition in overarching terms that are instrumental. This contrasts with Arendt's emphasis upon 'inspiring principles' that inform public action, even where there is a specific end in view (Arendt 1958: 182, 1977: 84).

Second, and in turn, this establishes a difference of perspective between Arendt and Machiavelli on the question of how we frame the distinction between the public and the private. In the light of his instrumentalised conception of the political, Machiavelli theorises the distinction in a manner that introduces a commensurate distinction between the dispositions appropriate to each that appeals to the question of authenticity. In the instrumental conditions of the political, 'men in general judge by their eyes . . . everyone sees what you appear to be, few experience what you really are' (Machiavelli 1981: 101). Whilst Arendt and Machiavelli share an emphasis upon the constitutive character of appearances with respect to public action, Arendt departs from Machiavelli's framing of the distinction here in terms of a difference between public appearance, on the one hand, and 'what you really are' on the other; by reference to a duality between authenticity and inauthenticity. Arendt rejects this duality as a way of mapping the public/private distinction, whether the reference to private authenticity is framed in terms of the recognition of moral truths or, in more modern guise, in terms of a personal identity whose field of disclosure is the sphere of the 'intimate'. It is certainly true that for Arendt the private realm can be understood as a place of escape from the public; but this is not to be seen as an escape into a refuge of 'deep' authenticity: there may be senses in which I can be more 'myself' in public. Arendt refers back here to what she takes to be the Roman conception of the *persona*, referring to a mask that had a two-fold function: not only to replace the actor's face given by nature but also to replace it in a way that, in the dramatic context, 'would make it possible for the voice to sound through' (Arendt 1973: 106).[20] In this way, participation in the public realm underwrites the idea of an authentic public persona that will disclose dispositions that will never wholly map on to the characteristics that define one's private persona, but which answer to the public context of judgment in which one appears as what one *is* publicly and (in contrast with Machiavelli's view) no less authentically. This is a view that Arendt consciously advances in the context of an awareness, dawning upon us in the light of the recent experience of totalitarianism, that the private persona is every bit as negotiable (and so potentially manipulable) as the public can be.

Third, these differences between Arendt and Machiavelli, pertinent to a conceptualisation of politics and of the public realm, imply commensurate distinctions with respect to how to theorise politically. The contrast here, and its significance, can be brought out more fully by reference to what we noted earlier to be a shared methodological impulse: the theoretical inclination to seek concrete examples from which we can learn and, more specifically, figures whom we might wish to emulate in respect of political thought and action. We have seen this to be a suggestive point of comparison but it might nevertheless, at the same time, carry with it limits that it now pays to consider. Machiavelli's principal concern was with seeking cases and figures that were to be treated as objects of *imitation*; whereas Arendt's concern is with *emulation* proper. Whilst these two terms may sometimes be used synonymously, their respective cognates imply a difference. Imitation carries the connotation of mimicry whereas emulation implies an ambition to equal or to surpass the examples invoked, with the further implication, intrinsic to the concept of 'surpassing', that one brings to bear resources associated with the application of political virtue, or virtuosity, that go beyond mere imitation. In this sense, Machiavelli seeks instruction in historical examples, while Arendt seeks inspiration.

These distinctions help establish the novelty of Arendt's standpoint. Machiavelli's image of the public realm incorporates a dimension of predictability that makes relevant, as we have seen, an understanding of political agency as instrumental, such that reliable and historically validated means-ends relations can be modelled and used as a basis for conduct geared to the securing of the (temporarily) ordered polity. Whilst fortune throws up specific situations and corresponding practical challenges that are unexpected and unpredictable, Machiavelli maintains that, in general terms, 'the world has always been in the same condition' (Machiavelli 1970: 499). This is the conviction that underlies Machiavelli's search for maxims which, supported by appropriate historical examples, help us judge the appropriate deployment of means to ends in different political situations.[21] There is a contrast here with Arendt's position. Arendt thinks consciously, again in the light of our most recent experiences and so in the context of what she takes to be a changed world, both intellectually and practically. In this light, Machiavelli appears to display a confidence in the regenerative power of political action which, if accepted, would lead us to be more sanguine than we should be.

This confidence is supported by a cyclical model that Machiavelli uses to present a 'natural history' of the polity – a dramatic structuring that involves the act of foundation, the manufacture of civic virtue and the onset of corruption, where private interests take precedent over public ones, leading to civic decline and signalling the need for re-foundation, at which point, in Machiavelli's terms, the prince finds his moment. For Arendt, from a more contemporary point of view, this position begins to look complacent: experience has shown us that we have to contemplate the possibility of a deterioration of the political culture that goes beyond corruption. What Machiavelli could think of as disengagement resulting from a decline in civic virtue, Arendt describes in terms of a radical loss of power, engendered by a decline in public interaction and in the mutual confidence that comes with it; a decline that makes possible the active destruction of the public realm. We now know that the worst thing that can happen is worse than Machiavelli thought. The instrumental conception of the political that Machiavelli's thinking implies is one that we now have to treat with suspicion: 'we are perhaps the first generation which has become fully aware of the murderous consequences inherent in a line of thought that forces one to admit that all means . . . are permissible' (Arendt 1958: 229). And simply attempting to moderate this standpoint by ruling out *some* means is an ineffectual (and indeed inconsistent) response. The experience we now have to refer to must lead us instead to revise our understanding of political agency and the models that we employ to inform that understanding. The concepts of foundation and political empowerment remain, as we have seen, central to Arendt, but the stakes she thinks are now revealed to be high and implicate the possibility of politics itself. In this light, the prince, in fact, appears as a figure beyond the political realm of appearances and so represents, in vestigial form, the promise that politics can be rescued and sustained by a force outside it: a worldly version of the unworldly standpoint by reference to which the tradition sought to resolve the 'problem' of politics. For this reason, we have to attend to the culture of the political itself, no matter how threadbare this culture may be, as we experience it in the modern setting. Nothing outside it can be a substitute for this by giving a guarantee, either of a philosophical or a princely sort, as to its continuing integrity.

This consideration, in turn, takes us back to the terrain of politics itself as a source of internally generated constraints rather than making an appeal to supervening ethical formulae. Accordingly, Arendt builds the dynamics of appearance that supply an ethical component back into the conception of the political itself: the anticipated judgment of spectators, rather than being, as it were, an external brake upon the results of practical reasoning (a brake, we might say, upon what aims the political agent can 'get away with' on the basis on instrumental considerations) instead enters into practical political reasoning itself, into the formation of aims in the light of inspiring principles and in view of the desire for approbation.

POLITICAL ETHICS AND POLITICS

This sense of the ethical in the context of politics is one which, again, accords with the mediated approach that we have traced in Arendt's thinking. Her conception of the distinctive autonomous experience of the political is framed, ethically, in terms that answer to that autonomy and do so in light of our most recent experiences. This temporal mediation is matched, again, by a commensurate sense in which theorising political ethics, in light of this new awareness, involves a rejection of the traditional search for a prescriptive ethical formula, whether conceived in transcendental or instrumental terms, in favour of a recognition of an ethical dynamic internal to politics. From a traditional point of view, then, it is an account that concedes the substance of political ethics to the realm of appearances itself.

So what does Arendt's account of politics imply for an ethical approach to contemporary politics? The reference to contingent dynamics of disclosure means that Arendt delivers no substantive image of the best political order, the nearest she gets to this is in her account of the 'council system' that we examined in Chapter 6. We saw there that Arendt alights upon this image not by implication from a more abstract moral principle but in light of the, albeit fleeting, experiences of devolved popular participation associated with immediate post-revolutionary periods in modern times, experiences that carry resonances with the ancient model that is also a pre-traditional reference point. It is a general image of a hierarchy of open democratic forums, structured by a system of delegation: through discussion and debate in one forum, 'it will become clear which one of us is best suited to present our view before the next higher council' (Arendt 1972: 190). There is a contrast here with the more familiar form of representative democracy where the relation between representatives and their constituency comes to mirror that between ruler and ruled; a relation that party-based electoral systems do little to qualify. Arendt's picture here is taken from diverse experiences and, as we have already noted, is (deliberately) too broad brush to do service as a substantive recipe. But it is nevertheless suggestive with respect to how we might relate Arendt's account of political ethics to modern politics.

Arendt is well-known as a sceptic when it comes to modern politics; and her scepticism is derived, once again, from what we have learned from recent experience concerning the susceptibility of the modern 'managerial' version of liberal democracy to capitulate to mass domination and to relinquish the concept of freedom. This concern is reflected in Arendt's sense of the compromised nature of modern politics, where the capacity for judgment is attenuated on all sides and where action is compromised by its reductive answerability to considerations associated with

146

socioeconomic needs, interests and institutions. This is tied equally to the aim that we saw associated with the early modern revolutions, 'to conquer the seemingly sempiternal misery of mankind', an achievement which, in so far as it has been a success in affluent societies, 'is certainly one of the greatest achievements of western history and the history of mankind' (Arendt 1973: 138). But it is nevertheless an achievement whose means of realisation is to be problematised in view of the accompanying loss of freedom that has attended sociopolitical developments in the modern age, presenting us with a permanent question as to how we are to think and act politically. The ancient image from which Arendt draws inspiration is one to which these modern experiences draw our attention; but it is by no means an ideal applicable to our times. In modern, large-scale democracies, the image of universal direct participation is clearly unrealisable. This is not to say, however, that Arendt simply gives up upon contemporary politics, something evident in that she devoted considerable time and energy to commenting upon contemporary political events in terms that were critical and concerned but could not be described as despairing.

By way of exemplification here, we can think of Arendt's critical engagements with contemporary American politics; with, for example, the Vietnam War and attendant events. Certainly Arendt was critical of the US Government over this issue and argued that it was redolent of broader tendencies in modern American politics; especially of the 'quicksand of lying statements of all sorts' that had been engaged in (Arendt 1972: 9).[22] And how the case was handled and presented equally illustrated, for Arendt, damaging elements of self-deception on the part of those in power, reflecting an assimilation between political discourse and the techniques of Madison Avenue, the techniques of manipulation that rest upon the conflation of fact and fantasy. The resonances here with the systematic lying and emasculation of the truth that were characteristics of totalitarian regimes are, for Arendt, all too obvious and disturbing. They are not sufficient to prompt the drawing of reckless parallels with totalitarian regimes but are suggestive nonetheless, especially given that the terms of the manipulation involved were not aimed at deceiving the enemy but were formulated for domestic consumption. In spite of these severe critical judgments, however, Arendt finds positive tendencies with respect to the assertion of authentic political judgment. Those who seek to advance dubious and potentially illegal policies through sales techniques are likely to find that 'the same people who can be "manipulated" to buy a certain kind of soap cannot be manipulated . . . to "buy" opinions and political views' (Arendt 1972: 13). We can find, then, occasional and qualified grounds for optimism: 'attempts of the government to circum-vent constitutional guarantees and to intimidate those who have made up their mind not to be intimidated . . . are not enough, and probably will not be enough to destroy the republic' (Arendt 1972: 42).

This combining of a critical and sceptical view of contemporary politics with an appreciation of the sporadic expressions of authentic politics is typical of Arendt's analysis. The rise, in various forms, of civil disobedi-ence in the United States in the 1960s was unquestionably a sign of the failure of the political system and of the disintegration of the legitimate political authority which had been promised in the original political set-tlement that established the republic. At the same time, the emergence of civil disobedience itself promised a good deal in that it embodied an authentically political movement; a movement, that is, which was genuine in not being based upon the 'subjective' motivation associated with con-scientious objection but rather upon a political principle of agreement in opinion. The political form and content of these movements answer, for Arendt, a properly political spirit, and take their inspiration from political principles. This equally made them a force for change in that they dem-onstrated a capability to establish new or amended forms of agreement, in keeping, as Arendt sees it, with the American tradition of voluntary convergence in opinion as the basis of a political structure (Arendt 1972: 81).

Political virtues may now be 'out of the ordinary' but they are 'not as rare as we are inclined to think' (Arendt 1973: 276). And if vestiges of the authentically political remain in large-scale modern democracies, then the broad image of the council system carries implications that resonate and which retain the thematic emphasis upon an immanent and non-prescriptive political ethics. It would seem to be a requirement in large societies where citizenship is (almost) universal, for self-selecting political elites, consisting of those 'who have a taste for public freedom and cannot be happy without it' (Arendt 1973: 279).[23] It would also seem, by the same token, that it is essential to a large democratic polity that there are some who wish to be more prominent and to take a greater role publicly, because there are very many for whom the prospect of public appearance is distasteful, as it was for Arendt herself: 'the political way of life has never been and will never be the way of life of the many, even though politi-cal business, by definition, concerns more than the many' (Arendt 1973:

275). The experience of the council system points us toward a situation where 'those who organised themselves were those who cared and took the initiative . . . their title rested upon the confidence of their equals . . . authority [was] generated on each of the pyramid's layers' (Arendt 1973: 278). This equally reflects a situation where 'if those who belong are self-chosen, those who do not belong are self-excluded' (Arendt 1973: 280). A political elite, in Arendt's sense, is therefore in no way equivalent to a social, economic or cultural elite and is consistent with political freedom. We tend to resist this idea because we have become used to the idea, implied in the tradition, that elites imply the rule of the few over the many; but we can rather see it in terms of the protection of public space by the few that care about it. The idea of self-exclusion also answers to what Arendt takes to be the most important negative liberty established in the modern world: freedom from politics (Arendt 1973: 280).[24] We need, therefore, those who are driven, amongst other things (some of which may *otherwise* be realisable covertly), by the desire to appear; a desire that directly implies an acknowledgment of the power of judgment exercised by a community of spectators.[25] The public happiness sought by those who have a passion for political engagement depends upon the approbation of judging spectators. It is in this context that actors will seek, in pursuing their passion, to make judgments of their own as to what practical engagements and personal dispositions they should bring to bear and make visible. Again, it is in this sense that politics contains, within its own dynamics, the capacity to be a self-regulating sphere; which is why, for Arendt, the remedies against abuses of authority 'lie in the public realm itself . . . in the very visibility to which it exposes all those who enter it' (Arendt 1973: 223).[26]

None of this means that institutions, the rules that they may establish and the principles that they may embody are unimportant in terms of the constraints that they supply in relation to the public realm, and we have seen the significance that Arendt attached to constitutional arrangements and their importance to the modern experience of foundation. So, legal and institutional arrangements are central to a public realm in Arendt's account (see Waldron 2000). However, this does not settle the ethical question: politics entails spontaneous enactments, and the identification of a settled institutional arrangement within which these can take place does not exhaust the ethical questions we might ask with respect to these enactments. Institutional arrangements, in the context of an authentic political culture, as Arendt thinks of it, have to be seen as contingent products of free political action and agreement; as such, they can neither wholly capture nor wholly contain political action itself. The contingent judgments and verdicts that may have created an institutional settlement have a continuing part to play with respect to the ethical estimate of action taken within the (always modifiable) terms of that settlement.

The view that politics can incorporate the kind of ethical self-regulation implied here clearly departs from the traditional demand for a prior ethical grounding. But this demand, essentially a demand for commensurability between the political and the moral, has always been one that moral philosophy has found difficult to meet whilst at the same time giving due credence to the reality of the political, a reality that experience tells us is ineradicable: the argument that if moral theory cannot produce a pre-political code adequate to 'reforming' the realm of politics, then it must be *politics* that is lost, is uncomfortably nugatory. Arendt presents a potent challenge to this way of thinking.

Notes

1. Some of the ideas in this chapter were formulated initially for a paper delivered at a symposium on Hannah Arendt at the Centre for Citizenship and Public Policy, University of Western Sydney in 2009 and to be published in a forthcoming collection. I am grateful to the Centre and to participants in the symposium for helpful comments on the earlier paper.
2. See Jay (1978), Benhabib (1988) and Kateb (2000).
3. As Canovan notes, the appeal of the 'warmth' of community is not one to be found in Arendt, for whom 'warmth and light are often mutually exclusive' in politics (Canovan 1997: 13).
4. For contrasting interpretation on this issue, see Taylor (2002: 151–69) and Zerilli (2005: 151–88).
5. Supervening injunctions could only acquire such status if they were taken to be attached to a transcendental agent; but this would still not put them in a ready relation to the public realm. Transcendental agencies lack the principal qualification for recognition in the public realm: that of visibility.
6. Particular speech acts may of course have both illocutionary and perlocutionary effects; and in respect of politics, as Arendt sees it, these may combine in terms of the performative significance of the act; this would seem to be the case with foundational acts, the most creative of all in terms of political agency (Arendt 1977: 246–7). I am most interested here, however, in the forms of substantial ethical constraint that may pertain to the ongoing dynamics of political agency within an established polity, where the perlocutionary dimension would seem to be the most significant.
7. I have chosen to use the term 'political virtue' here as a translation of Machiavelli's *virtu*. As Crick (1970) notes, the simple term 'virtue' can answer to Machiavelli's

usage if taken in its archaic meaning of ability in relation to a particular practice, but in a modern context it carries connotations that take it sufficiently away from Machiavelli's meaning as to render it misleading.

8. For a useful commentary on this, see Ball (1995: 73–5).

9. For an exploration of the 'theatrical' dimension to politics on Arendt's view, see Villa (1999: 128–54) and also Curtis (1997).

10. Machiavelli points to the example of the Roman general Fabius, who was given an unusually free hand in his activities on the basis of the assumption that 'his actions would be . . . restrained and regulated by his love of glory' (Machiavelli 1970: 382).

11. This bears comparison with Machiavelli's view that a successful politician is one who is 'in accord with the times' and is able to assess the temper of the populace (Machiavelli 1970: 428). Ferrara correctly suggests that a central aspect of judgment, as Arendt conceives of it, lies in extracting oneself from contingent limitations of vision, and most notably, from ones own self interest. But he infers from this that the impartiality thus achieved equally means extricating oneself from 'a concern for his or her own good standing before the other actors' eyes' (Ferrara 1998: 117). It is not clear, however, that this follows with respect to judgments made by agents. There is a distinction between the pursuit of self-interest and the desire for glory that makes the verdicts of others on the agent so important: after all, the former can often be pursued covertly whilst the latter cannot.

12. Some commentators have argued that Arendt, in her later work, sees judgment as entirely separate from action, as a feature of the *vita contemplativa* that is brought to bear only with the passage of time. In this view, judgment is a capacity more appropriately associated with the engagement of the historian rather than with that of the political actor (see Beiner 1994: 382). Whilst it is undeniable that the historian has a significant part to play here – and it is not uncommon that public reputations are modified over time – this does not mean that the judgments made by spectators then and there is not significant, or that the anticipation of judgment on the part of actors is not central to their enterprise. There is a further point to be made here with respect to political theory. I suggested earlier that some commentators, such as Disch, have placed too great an emphasis upon the narrative mode in explaining Arendt's approach to political theory. This said, it is a mode that is undoubtedly relevant as an element in political thinking and Disch is right, I think, in resisting Beiner's claim that Arendt's account of judgment in her later work marks a shift of emphasis from judgment exercised by political agents to that exercised by the disengaged storyteller looking back. Disch's account of the role of judgment in political theory retains its proximity to reflective judgment in the practical context when she says that it is a matter of 'a critic who tells the story of the past in the midst of present questions' (Disch 1993: 694). For an interpretation of Arendt's conception of judgment that ties it more closely to practical reasoning, see Wellmer (1997).

13. It is here, of course, that Arendt departs from Kantian ethics. Kant's publicity criterion for moral judgment rests ultimately upon the monological basis of a universalisable logic that can be grasped by any rational being. For Arendt, it is a matter of reflective judgment and needs an actual test, a particular case to which it can be applied, rather than appealing to a question of a priori reasoning grounded in the principle of non-contradiction (Arendt 1982: 49). For Arendt, action is judged not with respect to general categories but in the light of the idea of 'greatness', which can

only, by definition, be established in the particular. In this way, political judgment is comparable with what Kant thought of as aesthetic judgment (Arendt 1958: 205). See also Hansen (1993: 212–17).

14. If they did, they might potentially provide the basis for an action-guiding ethical blue-print that would transcend the perlocutionary conditions of appearance and reception that characterise the public realm. For an interesting discussion of the relevance of motives, aims and goals in Arendt's theory, see Knauer (1980).

15. On this point, see also Hammer (2002).

16. Arendt says that political theory has nothing to say about violence as such, as it is not within its province, although it may have something to say about specific justifica-tions for violence in particular contexts, thereby giving a political relevance to what itself is not political (Arendt 1973: 19).

17. On this point, see Grunenberg (2002).

18. Caruth argues that the traditional lie, committed for a specific purpose, may itself be thought of as a form of action, whereas systematic lying turns against the realm of action which depends upon the context of a common reality (Caruth 2010).

19. Machiavelli (1970: 114). Zmora problematises this issue in relation to Machiavelli's thought. His own preference for the more tumultuous Roman polity must be balanced against the superiority, on his own terms, of the 'quiet' examples of Venice and Sparta (Zmora 2007: 463).

20. For an interesting discussion of appearance and the conception of the self in Arendt, see Jacobitti (1997).

21. As Hulliung puts it, Machiavelli believed that 'the human drama is a never-ending performance of the same play' (Hulliung 1983: 173).

22. This was an exemplification, for Arendt, of the distinction that we noted earlier between the 'traditional' lie, specific in its aim and scope, and the systematic and sustained blurring of the boundaries between truth and falsehood.

23. For a critical commentary on Arendt in this respect, see Wolin (1994). Brunkhorst sees Arendt as returning to 'the elitism of an aristocratic republicanism', although he thinks that she offers us 'tools' to counter this in the form of an egalitarian republican-ism (Brunkhorst 2000: 196). But this analysis combines an idealised image of repub-lican politics with a utopian solution to the problems posed by that image. Neither, ultimately, answers to the sense of historically contextualised judgment that Arendt brings to political theory.

24. The problem with respect to elites in modern politics is not the idea of an elite itself. The general problem lies in the lack of a broader political culture, 'the conspicuous lack of interest of large parts of the population in political matters as such'. And this corresponds with the more specific problem of a lack of participatory public forums that would provide points of entry 'from which an elite could be selected, or rather, where it could select itself' (Arendt 1973: 277). As a result, the elites we have take on the character of professional 'ruling' elites whose claim is based not upon partici-patory support but instead upon managerial expertise in the light of social ends, and so 'according to standards and criteria which are themselves profoundly unpolitical' (Arendt 1973: 277).

25. An exemplar here again, for Arendt, is John Adams, for whom the 'passion for distinction' was central to the political impulse and it is 'action not rest that is our pleasure' (Arendt 1973: 34).

26. It could be argued that there are cases that look troubling with respect to the argument here. One could point, for example, to regimes that receive approbation but which nevertheless would appear morally deficient. The question arises as to what we are meant to say about such cases. If regimes of this sort are based upon denials of freedom or otherwise on the use of systematic violence and lying, then Arendt's account provides a basis for condemning them as anti-political. They can therefore be judged as inhumane on the basis of an appeal to political criteria. That they may nevertheless receive local approbation only points out that, on the one hand, the ability of citizens to make reliable judgments on their own polity and, on the other, the health of the political culture, are factors that tend to stand or fall together. Most of these troubling cases would fall foul of Arendt's immediate political criteria. If there are any that do not but which we would nevertheless want to say are morally unacceptable, then this may only mark a limit to the relevance of judgments across polities. We might find reason to object to such regimes on the basis of deep moral convictions, but this is different from an objection on the basis of political standards – and such deep moral convictions, like the operation of conscience, may be thought to hover in the background with respect to political life, rather than playing a direct part in it.

CHAPTER 8

The Role of the Theorist

In keeping with her method more generally, Arendt's conception of political ethics draws us back to the experiential field of politics itself and invites us to engage theoretically in a manner proximate with the contingent realm of appearances. The fact that this constitutes a form of intellectual resistance to both pre-political and supra-political criteria for establishing ethical precepts applicable to the public realm does not, however, entail the abandonment of any critical vocabulary. What is implied here is an immanent critical voice, demonstrating a greater modal proximity to the political itself, the kind of proximity that we have seen to be established in Arendt's methodological mediations to the theoretical voice. Commensurately, the critical judgments supplied by this theoretical approach are cognate with the field of judgment and with the standpoint of the reflective citizen rather than with that associated with what Arendt takes to be the traditionally accented voice of the philosopher. Answering as it does to our most recent experiences, this standpoint incorporates a general concern that is to be understood not in reference to an overarching principle or blueprint but rather by reference to a recognition of the political and of how, as a practice defined by its contingency, the political can decline and the capacities upon which it draws may atrophy. Accordingly, the general concern embodied in the critical perspective that Arendt's approach makes available focuses upon the possibilities for the enactment of the political and the conditions for its sustainability – the common world that provides us with grounds of common sense and terms within which we can interact coherently. We have seen how this concern makes itself apparent in Arendt's search for examples that draw our attention to the possibilities of the political, to the maintenance of a commitment to the world in 'dark times' and also in her explorations of the factors that may contribute to the emasculation of politics.

We noted in the previous chapter Arendt's extensive and critical explorations particularly of American politics in the 1960s and early 1970s, with respect to the nature of modern governance, the issues surrounding the Vietnam War, the civil rights movement, as well as the character of social policy and its ramifications for politics. These are examples of how Arendt addressed specific contemporary issues. They illustrate, more generally, how her critical concerns cash out with respect to the manner in which the theorist, as a partisan of the political, may engage with the issues to be faced. The specific modes of engagement here cannot be resolved into a ready recipe. The particular ways in which a concern for politics works out with respect to contemporary political events will depend upon the character of the events themselves, and in politics the unexpected is a central feature. But if we were tempted to think of an illustrative set of broad concerns that indicate the spirit of the critical standpoints to which Arendt's approach points us, they could be itemised as follows. First, we might maintain a concern with the ideological terms of contemporary political debate: we saw in Chapter 4 that Arendt's conception of ideology is specific and related to the emergence of totalitarianism; but we might also attend to ideological positions more broadly conceived, as action-guiding theoretical positions in politics, not least because we need to be aware of the potential of such positions to become pathological, exerting an agenda-setting dominance that marginalises plurality. Second, we may need to attend to the character of the prevailing political discourse and its rhetorical qualities. Arendt takes it that the art of rhetoric constitutes a legitimate, and indeed essential, element in the context of the realm of appearances. However, there is a need for judgment as to the point at which rhetorical presentation of political arguments and positions decline into obfuscation or sheer mendacity. A sensitivity to the distinction here allows us not only to make critical judgments about corrupted rhetorical formulations but may equally provide a point of resistance to the 'prejudicial' view, noted in the previous chapter, that all political discourse is to be regarded as mendacious. Related to this, we need to be aware of, and make judgments about, the tendency for the moral justifications for political agency and the contextual appeals to principle that these involve, to lapse either into decontextualised references to abstract formulae that unduly mitigate moral complexity or

155

into casuistry. Third, we may need to attend closely to political agendas and the particular manifestations they contain, of the tendency, associated with and highlighted by our modern experience, of the potential for freedom to be conceded to the overarching managerial concerns of the social. This amounts, in Arendt's terms, to retaining and articulating a sense of the autonomy of the political in the face of social agendas that arise accompanied by powerful and appealing instrumental arguments.

This is indicative and by no means an exhaustive account of the critical concerns that Arendt's approach might imply. The particular concerns that might be harboured in this spirit are contextualised and so, again, depart in their origin and form from the eternal preoccupations that traditional political philosophy sought to identify and problematise. This indicates, by the same token, the need to sustain active critical thinking. Whilst there is much to complain about in respect to modern politics, for Arendt, the imperative to sustain a fidelity to the autonomous sphere of action constitutes simultaneously a form of resistance to the tendency for critical thinking to ossify into routine oppositional agendas answering to non-negotiable ideological positions. In the context of modern politics, the tendency to de-problematise the political issues that we face may be as strong in 'oppositional' camps as it is in 'establishment' ones. In critical terms, this marks the continuing relevance of the theorist; and the theorist's inclination, in the spirit of the Socratic view examined in Chapter 2, consistently to re-problematise the sense of our experience in respect of our political life and the debates that animate it. It may also allow a more proximate engagement, again, with problems such as civic disengagement, cynicism and gullibility that more abstracted approaches in political theory tend to find too contingent to address directly. So an approach respecting the autonomy of the political need not exclude the possibility of critical judgments in relation to the threadbare nature of our contemporary political culture, and does not prevent the theorist, who is after all a citizen, from making claims as to what should or should not be done. It does imply, however, that judgments and claims of this sort should be discursively orientated and should answer to an awareness that, in politics, nothing is final.

THE RESPONSIBILITY OF THE THEORIST

So the theorist, as exemplified in Arendt's account, has a potentially important critical role with respect to our political life. But how are we to think of the orientation required here? In Arendt's view, this role cannot be seen in terms of the traditional disengaged scholar, concerned with philosophical reflection for its own sake and attending to the political only in so far as the questions raised can be generalised to a point where they can be subsumed under general philosophical categories. At the same time, Arendt is resistant to the modern idea of the 'engaged' intellectual, who enters the fray in the service of a specific 'cause'. And part of the point here is that the intellectual who pursues a cause puts the activity of thinking to a wholly extraneous purpose; in this sense, and in light of modern experience, that purpose may just as easily be one that serves the requirements of a depoliticised sociopolitical agenda as it does a 'radical' aim.

The more general point that Arendt brings out here is through her distinction between the more recent notion of the 'intellectual' and the historically retrieved image, stemming from the experience of the eighteenth century, of the *hommes de lettres*. This is a distinction, for Arendt, to be drawn out in respect of differing attitudes toward society, the 'hybrid realm' that is characteristic of modernity and which compromises the previously recognised distinction between the public and the private. The intellectual is the theorist who is part of society, whatever point of view they might adopt. Whether intellectuals' labours are of a 'conservative' or a 'progressive' stripe, they nevertheless represent labours that are actually or potentially 'needed by the ever expanding bureaucracies of modern government' (Arendt 1973: 121). By contrast, the image of the 'man of letters' implies a sense of withdrawal from society and a 'freely chosen seclusion' that puts one 'at a calculated distance from the social as well as the political . . . in order to look at both in perspective' (Arendt 1973: 122).

The particular challenge for the 'men of letters' was that they worked in a context where the political and the social were becoming increasingly conflated. The problem, in that context, consisted of the question of how one 'stands back' and creates theoretical distance, particularly when the requirements here depend upon whether one takes as one's object the social or the political. The achievement of the 'men of letters' in this particularly challenging circumstance was that they adopted a mode of theoretical distancing that retained a fidelity to the political, rather than succumbing to the theoretical modalities that would look appropriate to the social as the object, where the formulation of transcendent theoretical blueprints of one sort or another seems required – whether historical, sociological, psychological or some amalgam of these. Instead, the 'men of letters' studied historical examples not for the sake of whatever 'eternal wisdom' they might acquire 'but almost exclusively in order to learn about political institutions . . . it was their search for political freedom, not their quest for truth that led them back to antiquity, and their reading served to give them the concrete elements with which to think and dream of such freedom' (Arendt 1973: 123).

As the 'men of letters' took examples from the past, so they now provide examples for us. As we noted in Chapter 7, for Arendt, the point of examples is emulation rather than imitation. And this is particularly so in that the political thinker now faces new circumstances and has new experiences to take into account. Reflection on the character of the political now takes place in the context of the experience of totalitarianism and the sense of historical rupture that it has introduced, the sense which itself *leads* us to the idea of emulation rather than imitation. It also takes place in circumstances where the amalgamation of the political and the social is more complete and its consequences clearer. These circumstances combine to create a sense that we are thrown back on our own resources and that we cannot rely upon the past to provide us with solutions to present problems. This is a situation where problems of this kind carry an urgency in that at stake is not only the search for an understanding of political freedom and how it can be experienced but, augmenting this, a concern with the very possibility of politics; with the question of its retrieval or its loss. In circumstances of this kind, the theorist may be required to be less sanguine about the idea of 'withdrawal' into a broader conceptual universe, a withdrawal that inevitably takes one away from the contingencies and circumstantial urgencies of one's times. The responsibility of the theorist, which Arendt felt strongly, is to remain orientated to the concerns of the political; and it is a responsibility that we have seen Arendt seeking to maintain through a method that incorporates, in its essence, both temporal awareness and discursive engagement. We noted at the outset that although thinking and acting are wholly different engagements, thinking can be seen, for Arendt, as a kind of action in dark times.[1] The impact of thinking in dark times consists in the act of withdrawal from the process-like circumstances of everyday living and the effecting of an interruption, where questions about meaning can unsettle otherwise ossified convictions and norms. In the light of this, the task of the thinker is to maintain the autonomy of the experience of thinking itself, avoiding placing it at the service of extraneous ends. In describing her reflections, Arendt refers to 'exercises' undertaken in gaining experience of 'how to think', exercises cognate with the political as she sees it (Arendt 1977: 14). In terms of the objects of political thinking, it becomes advisable in our times, when worldly space is jeopardised, to attend to the experiences most associated with the condition of plurality. The thinker now has the responsibility for thinking not 'in order to' but 'for the sake of', and politically, one thinks for the sake of the world: the responsibility to reflect upon political things in their full particularity; to bring to bear illumination provided by partially recoverable experiences of the past; to offer contestable insights which anticipate insertion into a plural conversation. The responsibility, then, is to think in a politically orientated manner, avoiding the temptation to resort to abstraction and so leaving the realm of action to its own unreflective devices.

The Burden of the Theorist

In the course of her discussion of the *hommes de lettres*, Arendt notes that the distance at which they put themselves from worldly events in order to cultivate their understanding of the political and society was a burden rather than a blessing. They did not seek or enjoy the kind of freedom from worldly concerns that has been the aim of the philosophers of the tradition 'in order to pursue activities they deemed to be higher than those which engage men in pubic business' (Arendt 1973: 123). So their preoccupations remained worldly but they were themselves, albeit voluntarily, excluded from the public happiness that comes with direct engagement in 'public business'.

If, as I have suggested, Arendt's sense of the responsibilities of the political theorist in the contemporary world implies a greater proximity to the actual, circumstantial field of politics, embodied modally in her mediated approach, it may be that it somewhat mitigates the above sense of sacrifice. This is not to say, however, that the sense of a concern with the political, as it shapes Arendt's framing of the task of the theorist, does not imply its own kind of burden. Thinking is always a withdrawal, no matter how far it retains a modal proximity to the circumstances of the political; and the experiential gulf between thinking and acting remains, providing an index against which to characterise the inevitable (if productive) tensions involved in thinking politically. As in the case of the *hommes de lettres*, where the aim was 'to cultivate their minds in freely chosen seclusion', the issue might have been frustration with respect to non-participation. But where, in the light of the proximity that Arendt suggests between the realm of thinking and the realm of acting – where thinking engages with the contingent concerns of the public realm – the terms of the burden involved might be understood, as it were, with a reverse polarity: if the requirement to think in seclusion can frustrate the intrinsically worldly concern with politics, so equally, the requirement to think and speak in a way that engages formally and in substance with the political might frustrate the inclination of those drawn toward thinking for peace and quiet, for a refuge from the publicity that comes with participation. Arendt frames the experience of the *hommes de lettres* in a way that focuses attention on what she takes to be the contemporary experience of the political theorist (and certainly of her own experience). They craved the experience of political action but felt an obligation to be thinkers. For the political theorist in contemporary circumstances, a commensurate obligation arises: that the one who craves the life of the mind must nevertheless engage with the public realm in the light of the realisation, noted at the outset, that they can no longer be a bystander.

We noted in Chapter 2 that one of Arendt's principal models is Socrates, drawn from antiquity with respect to the activity of worldly thinking, predating the tradition and so providing a reference point for the post-traditional thinker. The importance of the example provided by Socrates is that he appears to integrate the

> apparently contradictory passions, for thinking and acting – not in the sense of being eager to apply his thoughts or establish theoretical standards for action but in the much more relevant sense of being equally at home in both spheres and able to move from one sphere to another with the greatest apparent ease. (Arendt 1981/I: 167)

His example makes us aware of the effect of thinking in unfreezing accepted norms, releasing an inclination, and indeed an enthusiasm, for bringing thinking to the marketplace. Equally, lacking any political ambition himself, his thinking remained entirely for its own sake. In this sense, Socrates provides us with an example of how to dwell within the paradoxical situation of being capable of withdrawal, in thought, from the plural world of appearance without ever being able to escape from that world.

However, the conditions that we now face, and the implications that they carry for political theory, mean that the burden entailed is magnified. This is in part because we know what happened to Socrates and, more broadly, we are aware of the implications of his fate for a sense of the difficulties that are inherent in the relation between thinking and the world. As an exemplary image, as we noted earlier, Socrates provides a sense of insouciance that is made possible by the lack of any sense of a problem to do with the relation between thinking and acting, a sense that the fate of the worldly realm may create responsibilities for the thinker and may problematise how, or from what standpoint, one thinks. Socrates could display a lack of concern as to how his thinking was received in the public realm: whilst he did not, after the fashion of the tradition, elevate and appeal to a separate ontological realm over and above the phenomenal realm, he certainly felt disposed to prioritise his *own* life, and the enjoyment of thinking that defined it, over and against worldly concerns. The fate of Socrates rendered this disposition problematic and the philosophical tradition sought, in a variety of specific guises, to solve this problem by elevating the life of the mind to a position *above* the world and, correspondingly authoritative with respect to it. We now think, Arendt wants to say, from a position after the tradition that Socrates predated (but which his death in part prompted), giving us a vantage point from which we can see the 'solutions' that the tradition offered as nugatory. In view of this, a 'post-traditional' standpoint renders the relationship between thinking and acting against the benchmarks of the tradition as newly negotiable or problematised.

Furthermore, and wholly related to this, we are now aware of the fragility of the world as a coherent space in which we can act, an experiential awareness that, as we have seen, can readily be associated with the danger of thinking and acting losing all contact with one another: where actors become unthinking and thinkers disengaged. In view of this, Socrates' insouciance is no longer available: we can no longer take the sustainability of the worldly realm for granted as Socrates felt able to do. The thinker must now share a common concern with the actor – albeit from a different experiential perspective – a concern with the world and with its unguaranteed active maintenance.[2] Thinking, at least as it is manifest in the engagement of political theory, is thinking for the sake of the world; and the thinker must attend to and care for it in a way that Socrates did not. This does not mean that Socrates does not still carry exemplary relevance. The motifs that we have seen Arendt attaching to Socrates' approach – the unfreezing of fixed ideas, the stimulation of reflection and the unsettling of assumptions – remain suggestive. However, the original and contingent questions posed by the Socratic thinker come to have, in the contemporary context, a character that appears more cognate with the interruptions to processes that authentic principled action embodies and which constitute equally contingent enactments of human freedom. So we now see thinking as neither independent of nor wholly at one with worldly experience; a realisation that arises together with a recognition of the utter contingency of both.

In light of this, to the extent that thinking now seems implicated in the fate of the world, it must attend to the phenomena of the world and take upon itself a responsibility with respect to worldly concerns.[3] For this reason, in our dark times, thinking must become *conspicuous*; its pertinence to the realm of appearances means that it takes on a visibility that traditionally it did not have. And so some of the conditions pertinent to action come to attend thinking. The responsibility of the political theorist with respect to the political and the proximity it acquires to the public realm creates a burden of exposure. Conspicuousness runs counter to a basic disposition of the thinker (without even the consolation of the 'traditional' promise of a superior way of life); the disposition of one who is 'inconspicuous . . . by definition and profession' (Arendt 1981/I: 72). Whereas those disposed to find the realisation and confirmation of their identity directly in and through the realm of action find consummation in leaving behind the concerns of the private realm and a sheltered way of life, the thinker, in becoming conspicuous, requires the exposure of the activity that, by the inclination that draws one to that activity, they would seek to enjoy in solitude, the condition of true 'free thinking'. One is required, in this sense, to come out of hiding – out of the obscurity that the thinker prefers.

The exposure involved in undertaking political theory in a manner that recognises a commitment to the political is something that Arendt herself undoubtedly experienced. The position she adopted gave her a high profile and a controversial one, placing her at odds with academic orthodoxy. Arendt was suspicious of orthodoxies that tend, she thought, to compromise independent dialogue and to turn debate into factionalism: she felt happier falling 'between all stools', even if this could be a lonely place. This led on occasion to summary dismissal of her work.[4] If the perceived contrarian character of Arendt's thinking sometimes led to controversy in the context of academia, it also set her at odds with established ideological standpoints, a position again that she found it satisfactory to occupy: 'nothing . . . compromises the understanding of political issues and their meaningful debate today more seriously than the automatic thought-reactions conditioned by the beaten paths of ideologies' (Arendt 1973: 223).[5] This provides us with a sense of the conspicuousness that Arendt herself experienced and which, more generally, we can expect to attend the kind of discursive and politically orientated approach that a fidelity to the terrain of politics itself in political theory entails. To act, for Arendt, is always at the same time to suffer in the sense of exposure to the contingent judgments of others, through which meaning is conferred upon action. When thinking is exposed in this way, the burden involved can be considered acute. Whereas the actor enters the public realm by leaving private existence decisively behind, for the thinker becoming conspicuous involves exposing the activity that they would prefer to enjoy in private. The proximity that Arendt's method of doing political theory generates between thinking and the public realm in no way denies the element of withdrawal that thinking involves (and indeed, as we have seen, presupposes it). This ineradicable element in thinking experience – the element that the philosophical tradition recognised and drew upon – does mean that the results of thinking arise from a hidden and personalised dialogue of the self with the self, where the integrity of one's own inner thought processes is a principal motif. Because of this, the risk that the thinker takes in submitting to public exposure is of being misunderstood and so being misrepresented or perhaps being informally disqualified from the conversation of which they seek to be a part (cf. Canovan 1990: 164–5). This differs in a sense from the position of the exposed actor who cannot, at least in the same sense, be misunderstood. We have seen that, for Arendt, the origins of action lie in the realm of appearances and its meaning lies with spectators: actors act into a web of human relations, becoming part of our always unfinished story, and in doing so they are revealed as agents but not as the authors or producers of the story. The meaning disclosed in the story, and the actor's part in it, are established through spectatorship and arise, therefore, wholly out of the condition of plurality.

We have also noted the central requirement of courage attending the actor's disclosures in the public realm – leaving the relative predictability and security of the private and making the move into a condition of exposure, suffering judgment. The thinker's foray into the public realm also requires courage, and indeed courage of an augmented sort, measured against the additional burden that comes with the exposure of a private engagement. In the interview mentioned at the very start of this study, Arendt commented that, had it not been for the need to provide herself with *aides memoires*, she may well have written nothing (Arendt 1994: 3).

163

This remark seems puzzling, even disingenuous: after all, if this was the purpose of writing, why publish? But it is a comment that implicates the model of Socrates and draws our attention back to the evident experiential divide between thinking and acting, a divide which underwrites a sense of a commensurate gulf in terms of the dispositions that are engaged by a commitment to each. Later in the same interview, Arendt talks of the responsibility to 'speak out'; but this now appears in the context of a sense of the burden that speaking out might carry for the thinker, whose lone quest for meaning does not, intrinsically, *need* exposure and is likely to be discomfited by it. In this sense, resuming the contrast with the burden born by the actor, it becomes apparent that the compensations for the actor are not available to the thinker. The actor's compensation for the risk and uncertainty of exposure lies in the 'public happiness' that we have seen, for Arendt, goes with participation in the public realm in and of itself, finding a consummation and satisfaction in appearance. However, the thinker's disposition is such that worldly exposure does not carry the same kind of consummation or reward for the courageous step taken.

The risk of misunderstanding or misrepresentation has always attended the exposure of thinking in the world; in a sense, the death of Socrates was the result of misunderstanding (Arendt 1990: 78–9). The tradition of political philosophy made it possible to see this risk as carrying its own kind of compensation, or at least consolation, through reference to a truth beyond the realm of appearances. It was possible, in the light of this reference point, to view the inability of others to understand as indicative only of the fact that the thinker speaks a language of the eternal incomprehensible to the many (or alternatively, in a more recent formulation, speaks a language of history that, one day, all will understand). In either case, this was a consolation that could potentially translate into a guarantee of immunity to risk if the right political conditions were in place. But in light of what we now know, under conditions following the collapse of the tradition, neither this form of consolation nor the escape to a hiding place that it also appeared to imply can be contemplated. We now know that the world of appearances which provides all the stability that is available to us, is contingent, standing in need of maintenance both practically and theoretically; and, as a consequence, to think politically in a way that is profitable must involve running the risk that comes with exposure.

In terms of the place and disposition of the thinker, Arendt took inspiration from exemplars such as Gotthold Lessing, whose writings embodied a rejection of orthodoxy and the search for concrete, contestable meanings, anticipating insertion into public debate. This approach demonstrated, for Arendt, genuine 'free thinking', providing illumination in dark times without definitive answers (Arendt 1968b: 3–31). The appreciation of independence of mind, as we have already noted, also provided the intellectual basis of Arendt's long friendship with Karl Jaspers: she did not identify with his substantive position, frequently disagreeing strongly with him; but she found in Jaspers a genuine public intellectual for whom and with whom open-ended dialogue was the point.[6]

Arendt thinks and speaks self-consciously in a context where a confidence in the authority of a univocally articulated mode of thinking with respect to the public realm is no longer possible in fact or ideal. It is a way of thinking and speaking that is given sense through the recognition of a multi-vocal world, where the possibility of meaning depends upon the conditions for, and commitment to, authentic communication. This recognition, and the care for the world that it prompts, makes bearing the burden of appearance, with its uncompensated risks, a requirement. And this explains Arendt's view that the 'advantage' that the political theorist now has, of the opportunity of free-thinking unshackled by the tradition, is 'difficult to enjoy' (Arendt 1968b: 10). The challenge thus presented, which defines the required commitment on the part of the theorist in our times, underlies Arendt's work as a whole, in terms both of its form and its content.

Concluding Remarks: Arendt and Contemporary Political Theory

The conclusions that we can draw from Arendt's approach to political theory can be framed in both a negative and a positive way, which are nevertheless related.[7] Putting it in a negative light, we have seen that Arendt, in the way she formulates the engagement of political theory, provides us with a potent challenge to the traditional way of approaching the task of thinking practically. In contemporary terms, the challenge presented here is principally to the 'mainstream' political theory that seeks to provide, through an appeal to a foundational conception of universal rationality, a recipe for a political ideal, an ideal that cannot ultimately do without the support of a corresponding social plan.[8] Theoretical approaches of this sort, in Arendt's terms, collude with the conflation of politics with the social that she takes to be a defining tendency in the

modern world. Equally, the ideal formulations that they proffer are sufficiently distanced from the actual terrain of politics as to prove somewhat
nugatory in political terms.

The character of the alternative that Arendt presents here, and broad-
ening some of the points made in Chapter 7, can be brought out in formal
terms through a distinction between political theory that embodies the
ambition for completeness and, by contrast, theory that seeks to be consummate rather than complete. Mainstream theories of justice aim at
completeness in that the foundational appeals upon which they rest can
be shown to imply directly (if not simply) a set of social requirements
that embody an ideal of justice. They are complete, then, in the sense
of providing an answer to what is taken to be the fundamental question
that defines the engagement of political theory: the question of the conditions that secure a system of justice. What such theories promise, at least
under ideal conditions, is a system of rule according to required principles
and within suitable institutional arrangements; and in a context of this
kind, we can leave the politics, as it were, to take care of itself. This sense
of completeness, which potentially allows us to be sanguine about the
engagement of politics itself is, however, grounded in a purely theoretical
solution to an equally theoretically defined sense of what the question
with respect to political theory really is.[9] The theoretical finality offered
is bought at the expense of abstraction away from politics, where nothing
is ever final. From the point of view of this theoretical position, which
embodies in contemporary form the traditional assimilation of political
acting and making with realising and sustaining a preconceived end that
is morally validated, Arendt's own approach looks incomplete. But her
aim is not completeness in this sense. What she does seek, however, is a
consummate political theory: the epistemological and temporal mediations to the theoretical standpoint that we have identified in her work
answer to this aspiration. The challenge that Arendt therefore presents
lies in an alternative that resists the consolation offered by a 'solution' to
the 'problem' of politics.

The form of Arendt's theory answers to, and allows us to confront fully,
new and unprecedented experiences that draw us back to the political as
an autonomous and contingent mode of experience. Her theory therefore
answers fully to its object and, in doing so, generates a proximity to the
terrain of political experience that gives political theory its purpose: it
reconfirms the importance of the political, and it does so not in the form
of an abstract message or an injunction but rather by reflecting upon polit-

ical experience in a manner that offers discursively orientated meanings that themselves serve to stimulate our capacity to think and speak in ways that are orientated toward, and help sustain, the political realm. These meanings are, in the sense mentioned above, decidedly incomplete; but it is just this that gives them their potency.

It is worth noting here that Arendt's challenge to mainstream theories of justice in their various forms simultaneously constitutes a challenge to the most prominent alternatives to that tradition, which are generally, by now, to be regarded as dissenting elements within the mainstream. We noted also, in Chapter 7, that Arendt's approach cannot be assimilated with the communitarian alternative to dominant foundational theories. On the face of it, there may be an apparent similarity to be asserted here on the grounds that communitarian theories share with Arendt the resistance to completeness that foundationalist theories seek. But this sense of a similarity is superficial: the resistance to theoretical completion that communitarian theory mounts comprises a rejection of the claims to universality that mainstream foundational theories tend to make, grounding basic sociopolitical claims instead upon shared convictions that vary culturally. But Arendt's quarrel with foundationalist theory is of a different sort. The communitarian complaint with respect to foundationalism is that it makes a spurious appeal to universal principles grounded, generally, in rationality which transcend (and fatally ignore) specific, shared cultural beliefs, abstracting away from the real grounds of political agreement. Arendt's complaint, however, invokes a problem not with the transcending of cultural specificity but with the transcending of the political realm as itself a source of agreement. There is a certain confluence, then, between Arendt's thinking and a communitarian position in that they accept the possibility of difference with respect to the character of political agreements. But the grounds of this acceptance are distinct, and decisively so: Arendt emphasises contingent political agreements that are themselves constitutive of a political realm, contrasting with cultural agreements. The appeal to culture, whilst resisting universalism, shares with mainstream theories an appeal to something beyond the political as a guarantee, in theory, of a political settlement, and so carries its own form of completion.[10]

When it comes to other theoretical dissent from this traditional concern with completion, Arendt also poses an alternative. This takes us back to a theme raised initially in Chapter 2, where we noted dissenting views with respect to the tradition, such as those to be found in Marxism and existentialism, which, in Arendt's view, fail ultimately to transcend the broad terms of the tradition itself: Marx and Sartre represent rebels whose revolt, as we saw, was that of the philosopher against philosophy. They sought to reverse the established hierarchy of thinking and acting, but they retained the traditional sense of hierarchy itself. Thinking comes to stand in the service of action; but this philosophically established hierarchy equally insinuates a sense of what action may achieve, whether in terms of revolutionary realisation of the non-alienated society or the achievement of personal authenticity. So whilst the priority afforded to action here again carries a superficial resemblance to Arendt's key concern, the comparison goes no further. Experiential hierarchies established philosophically and in the abstract still answer, in their inception, to the lone experience of the thinker, internal to the self, the motif of which, correspondingly, is unity rather than plurality. In this sense, the privileging of action nevertheless compromises the character of action itself by linking it to a sense of a unitary resolution, whether, again, mapped out in terms of self or society. Arendt, by contrast, rejects the presupposition of an experiential hierarchy on the grounds that it is not borne out by experience. This, as we have seen, permits her to problematise the relation between thinking and acting in a sense that hierarchical conceptions dissolve in theory and distort in practice: this problematisation, in itself of political significance, allows a sense of the potential mutual relevance of the two experiences, bringing the capacity for thinking into greater proximity, formally and substantively, with the realm of action. It is a proximity emblematised in the experience of reflective judgment, so long neglected by the tradition.

It is also worth noting here that Arendt's resistance to philosophical solutions also puts her at odds with postmodernist approaches in political theory. We can say again here that there are prima facie parallels to be drawn between Arendt's approach and that of postmodernism, broadly conceived. The latter is consciously anti-traditional, questioning the faith in definitive solutions, whether in terms of philosophical truth capable of providing a solution to the question of the best political order, or in terms of rational historical progress toward a commensurate solution. Equally, and in light of this, it promotes a deliberately discursive voice, resistant to closure. However, whilst the questioning of modernity and of its metaphysically underwritten narratives may be forceful and provocative it remains, in Arendt's terms, a distinctively philosophical questioning. It does not escape, in this sense, the terms set by the lone experience of the thinker. This is reflected in the thematic emphasis in postmodernism upon the individual experience of questioning and resistance in the face of impositions made by dominant discourses. However pertinent these may be, the ability to doubt and to question that they thematise reproduce as fundamental the opposition between individual and society; and in doing so they also reproduce the emphasis upon the liberty of the thinker or questioner as defined in contrast with collective social and intellectual structures. Framed in this way, the challenge presented by postmodern thinking entails a lack of distinction between the political and the social: it discovers a threat in all collective institutions, including those which, in Arendt's terms, prove to be sources of collective self-empowerment. If our shared language is perceived to be a 'prison house', then the key resource upon which we draw to act and to judge is to be treated with suspicion. It is as a result of this that postmodern theory, in Arendtian terms, neglects the empowering collective engagement of the political and reproduces, in its own way, the age-old suspicion that the thinker harbours in respect of worldly experiences and concerns.

These challenges that Arendt's thinking presents to contemporary political theory may be together understood as salutary with respect to the tendency of theory to abstract away from its stated object in favour of philosophical positions that transcend the contingent fabric of the political. In keeping with the consummate or internally consistent character of Arendt's approach, this challenge amounts at the same time to a warning against complacency with respect to the maintenance of a political culture, a complacency to which recent historical experience has drawn our attention and has placed permanently on our theoretical and political agenda.

If these salutary promptings can be seen to constitute the negative impact of Arendt's thought in relation to our contemporary inclinations as to how to theorise politically, we may also learn commensurate positive lessons here, even if some circumspection is appropriate. We can make extrapolations from Arendt's theoretical orientation and from its substantiation in terms of what she had to say about contemporary events and issues and draw conclusions as to how her thinking might apply to events and issues that we face now.[11] At the same time, we need to be aware of the danger of reifying Arendt's work, of treating it as a pseudo-theological text and scouring it for answers.[12] More appropriately, what we can find in Arendt's work and in the approach she takes is something exemplary. From this point of view, what Arendt presents to us is an example of courage; of an intellectual courage in being prepared to challenge the tradition of political philosophy in its various guises, and a courage that translated, for Arendt, into reluctant public appearance, in the name of 'speaking out'. Accordingly, Arendt provides us with a methodological approach which, in its mediated and discursively orientated form, is exemplary with respect to thinking for the sake of politics, a requirement that we now know is urgent. To think in this way is to think for oneself in the light of the condition of plurality. It is an exemplar that is challenging to us, as exemplars ought to be, if they are to prompt emulation rather than simply imitation.

Arendt does not tell us what to think and, in the spirit of the temporally mediated character of her approach, she would have recognised that we may later have to contemplate circumstances with which she was unfamiliar. In this sense, her work does not provide us with a blueprint that might allow us to think, as it were, unreflectively about what we now confront. What she does supply, however, is an exemplification of how to think in a manner that is reflexive with respect to its relation with action. It is an example that is summed up in her injunction, which encapsulates both the critical potential of her approach and also its fidelity to the political, in times when the political is under threat: that we should think what we are doing.

NOTES

1. This relates to an awareness, again, of the experience of totalitarianism and the burden this places upon the thinker: when we now think about the past, we must do so in a way that involves 'never denying its existence nor submitting meekly to its weight' (Arendt 1973: 211). Cf. Spyros Draenos (1979).

2. This also relates to Socrates' lack of interest in confronting problems of evil. Cf. Young-Bruehl (1994) and Villa (1999: ch. 9).

3. Herzog emphasises the sense of Arendt's distanced but proximate formulation of the position of the political theorist in terms of the 'distanced citizen' (Herzog 2001).

4. For such a dismissal, see Berlin (1992: 81–5). Stuart Hampshire was similarly dismissive – see Young-Bruehl (1982: 471). Arendt found the major universities where she taught frequently alienating, both personally and intellectually, and found no place amongst the various academic factions that she encountered. And this was not only true in America: in post-war Germany, she found the cliques and fads in universities distressing, particularly in respect of the 'cult' she saw as developing around Heidegger (Young-Bruehl 1982: 295, 305).

5. She was embroiled in a whole range of intellectual controversies: her perspective upon Zionism and other aspects of Jewish politics, including her advocacy of Jewish-Arab co-operation, caused her to be intellectually isolated and subject to *ad hominem*

responses, resulting in her being accused of promoting (albeit unintentionally) anti-Semitic views (see Young-Bruehl 1982: 223–30). Her commentary on the Federal policy of integration of black students in predominantly white schools, which she saw as an unfortunate exercise in social engineering, also caused controversy, resulting both in editorial disapproval and disappointment amongst her liberal readers. For a commentary on this debate, see Bohman (1997). We have also already noted the controversy over her remarks upon the Eichmann case. Villa notes, in relation to this case, that even if the independent judge need not be a martyr like Socrates, one may have to accept becoming a pariah. Although, in assimilating Arendt with Strauss, Villa presents Arendt as more radically 'estranged' than she might be thought to have been. Whilst he is correct to say that Arendt has in common with Strauss that neither seeks to 'guide us into the light' in the form of some 'comprehensive perspective', there can be no doubt that Arendt's perspective on modern politics remains proximate to contemporary events, involving an attempt to speak discursively about them, in a manner that contrasts sharply with Strauss's appeal to the philosophical and moral authority of the ancients. See Villa (1999: 106). For reflections on pariahdom with respect to the public realm, see Ring (1991).

6. See Arendt and Jaspers (1992).

7. In this section, I characterise some approaches in modern political theory in necessarily broad-brush terms, doing no justice to the internal variety and debate within these standpoints. The broad characterisations here serve only as markers in order to try and bring out the distinctiveness of Arendt's approach.

8. For influential examples, amongst others, see Rawls (1973) and Habermas (1979).

9. We have noted before Arendt's suspicion of the enchantment that pure logical reasoning may exercise and which compromises our ability to reflect freely on our experience.

10. The fact that, in these different but cognate ways, Arendt's position entails a rejection of both foundational and communitarian modes of political theorising suggests equally that her position involves a departure from more recent amalgamations of those approaches. That Arendt appears to fall between the universalist claims of foundationalist theorist and the relativist standpoint of communitarian thought does not mean that she can be assimilated with those formulations seeking to bring the two together – see for example Walzer (1983) and Raz (1986) – or indeed with more recent 'republican' formulations of this amalgam – for example Pettit (1997). The point here is that these variations on a theme retain a fundamental and traditional commitment to seeking prescriptive formulae that might, if put to work, solve the political problem.

11. For an account of the contemporary relevance of Arendt, see Young-Bruehl (2006).

12. On this point, see Waldron (2007).

Bibliography

Arendt, H. (1957), *Rahel Varnhagen: the Life of a Jewess*, London: East West Library.

Arendt, H. (1958), *The Human Condition*, Chicago, IL: University of Chicago Press.

Arendt, H. (1965), *Eichmann in Jerusalem: a Report on the Banality of Evil*, New York, NY: Viking.

Arendt, H. (1968a), *The Origins of Totalitarianism*, New York, NY: Harvest.

Arendt, H. (1968b), *Men in Dark Times*, New York, NY: Harvest.

Arendt, H. (1971), 'Thinking and moral considerations: a lecture', *Social Research*, 38 (3), 416–46.

Arendt, H. (1972), *Crises of the Republic*, New York, NY: Harcourt Brace Jovanovich.

Arendt, H. (1973), *On Revolution*, London: Penguin.

Arendt, H. (1977), *Between Past and Future: Eight Exercises in Political Thought*, London: Penguin.

Arendt, H. (1978), *Jew as Pariah*, ed. R. H. Feldman, New York, NY: Grove Press.

Arendt, H. (1979), 'On Hannah Arendt', in M. Hill (ed.), *Hannah Arendt: the Recovery of the Public World*, New York, NY: St. Martin's Press, pp. 303–39.

Arendt, H. (1981), *The Life of the Mind: I/Thinking, II/Willing*, New York, NY: Harcourt Brace Jovanovich.

Arendt, H. (1982), *Lectures on Kant's Political Philosophy*, ed. R. Beiner, Brighton: Harvester.

Arendt, H. (1990), 'Philosophy and politics', *Social Research*, 57, 73–103.

Arendt, H. (1994), *Essays in Understanding 1930–1954: Formation, Exile and Totalitarianism*, ed. J. Kohn, New York, NY: Schocken Books.

Arendt, H. (2003), *Responsibility and Judgment*, ed. J. Kohn, New York, NY: Schocken Books.

Arendt, H. (2005), *The Promise of Politics*, New York, NY: Schocken Books.

Arendt, H. and Jaspers, K. (1992), *Hannah Arendt-Karl Jaspers Correspondence*, ed. L. Kohler and H. Saner, New York, NY: Harcourt Brace Jovanovich.

Austin, J. L. (1975), *How to Do Things with Words*, Oxford: Oxford University Press.

Baehr, P. (2010), *Hannah Arendt, Totalitarianism and the Social Sciences*, Stanford, CA: Stanford University Press.

Ball, T. (1995), *Reappraising Political Theory*, Oxford: Clarendon Press.

Bauer, Y. (1978), *The Holocaust in Historical Perspective*, London: Sheldon Press.

Beiner, R. (1994), 'Judging in a world of appearances', in L. Hinchman and S. Hinchman (eds), *Hannah Arendt: Critical Essays*, Albany, NY: State University of New York Press, pp. 365–88.

Benhabib, S. (1988), 'Judgment and the moral foundations of politics in Arendt's thought', *Political Theory*, 16 (1), 29–51.

Benhabib, S. (1996), *The Reluctant Modernism of Hannah Arendt*, London: Sage.

Benhabib, S. (2000), 'Arendt's *Eichmann in Jerusalem*', in D. Villa (ed.), *The Cambridge Companion to Hannah Arendt*, Cambridge: Cambridge University Press, pp. 65–85.

Berlin, I. (1992), *Conversations with Isaiah Berlin*, ed. R. Jahanbegloo, London: Phoenix.

Bernstein, R. (1997), 'Did Hannah Arendt change her mind? From radical evil to the banality of evil', in L. May and J. Kohn (eds), *Hannah Arendt: Twenty Years Later*', London: MIT Press, pp. 127–46.

Bernstein, R. (2000), 'Arendt on thinking', in D. Villa (ed.), *The Cambridge Companion to Hannah Arendt*, Cambridge: Cambridge University Press, pp. 277–92.

Bernstein, R. (2010), 'Is evil banal? A misleading question', in R. Berkowitz *et al.* (eds), *Thinking in Dark Times: Hannah Arendt on Ethics and Politics*, New York, NY: Fordham University Press, pp. 131–6.

Biskowski, L. (1993), 'Practical foundations for judgment', *Journal of Politics*, 55 (4), 867–87.

Black, M. (1962), *Models and Metaphors: Studies in Language and Philosophy*, Ithaca, NY: Cornell University Press.

Bohman, J. (1997), 'The moral costs of political pluralism: the dilemmas of difference and equality in Arendt's "Reflections on Little Rock"', in J. May and L. Kohn (eds), *Hannah Arendt: Twenty Years Later*, London: MIT Press, pp. 53–80.

Brunkhorst, H. (2000), 'Equality and elitism in Arendt', in D. Villa (ed.), *The Cambridge Companion to Hannah Arendt*, Cambridge: Cambridge University Press, pp. 178–98.

Burks, V. (2002), 'The political faculty: Arendt's "Ariadne thread" of common sense', *Theory and Event*, 6 (1), 1–27.

Canovan, M. (1990), 'Socrates or Heidegger? Arendt's reflections on philosophy and politics', *Social Research*, 57, 135–65.

Canovan, M. (1992), *Hannah Arendt: a Reinterpretation of her Political Thought*, Cambridge: Cambridge University Press.

Canovan, M. (1997), 'Hannah Arendt as a conservative thinker', in L. May and J. Kohn (eds), *Hannah Arendt: Twenty Years Later*, London: MIT Press, pp. 11–32.

Canovan, M. (2000), 'Arendt's theory of totalitarianism', in D. Villa (ed.), *The Cambridge Companion to Hannah Arendt*, Cambridge: Cambridge University Press, pp. 25–43.

Caruth, C. (2010), 'Lying and history', in R. Berkowitz *et al.* (eds), *Thinking in Dark Times: Hannah Arendt on Ethics and Politics*, New York, NY: Fordham University Press, pp. 78–92.

Crick, B. (1970), 'Introduction', in N. Machiavelli, *The Discourses*, Harmondsworth: Penguin.

Culbert, J. (2010), 'Judging the events of our time', in R. Berkowitz *et al.* (eds), *Thinking In Dark Times: Hannah Arendt on Ethics and Politics*, New York, NY: Fordham University Press, pp. 145–52.

Curtis, K. (1997), 'Aesthetic foundations of democratic politics in the work of Hannah Arendt', in C. Calhoun and J. McGowan (eds), *Hannah Arendt and the Meaning of Politics*, Minneapolis, MN: University of Minnesota Press, pp. 27–52.

Dietz, M. (2000), 'Arendt and the Holocaust', in D. Villa (ed.), *The Cambridge Companion to Hannah Arendt*, Cambridge: Cambridge University Press, pp. 86–109.

Disch, L. J. (1993), 'More truth than fact: storytelling as critical understanding in the writings of Hannah Arendt', *Political Theory*, 21 (4), 665–94.

Disch, L. J. (1994), *Hannah Arendt and the Limits of Philosophy*, Ithaca, NY: Cornell University Press.

Dolan, F. (2000), 'Arendt on philosophy and politics', in D. Villa (ed.), *The Cambridge Companion to Hannah Arendt*, Cambridge: Cambridge University Press, pp. 261–76.

Dunn, J. (1990), *Interpreting Political Responsibility*, Cambridge: Polity.

Ferrara, A. (1998), 'Judgment, identity and authenticity: a reconstruction of Hannah Arendt's interpretation of Kant', *Philosophy and Social Criticism*, 24 (2), 113–36.

Grunenberg, A. (2002), 'Totalitarian lies and post-totalitarian guilt: the question of ethics in democratic politics', *Social Research*, 69 (2), 359–79.

Habermas, J. (1979), *Communication and the Evolution of Society*, London: Heinemann.

Hammer, D. (2002), 'Hannah Arendt and Roman political thought: the practice of theory', *Political Theory*, 30 (1), 124–49.

Hansen, P. (1993), *Hannah Arendt: Politics, History and Citizenship*, Cambridge: Polity.

Herzog, A. (2001), 'Marginal thinking or communication: Hannah Arendt's model of the political thinker', *European Legacy*, 6 (5), 577–94.

Honig, B. (1991), *Political Theory and the Displacement of Politics*, Ithaca, NY: Cornell University Press.

Horkheimer, M. and Adorno, M. (1979), *Dialectic of Enlightenment*, London: Verso.

Hulliung, M. (1983), *Citizen Machiavelli*, Princeton, NJ: Princeton University Press.

Jacobitti, S. (1997), 'Thinking about the self', in L. May and J. Kohn (eds), *Hannah Arendt: Twenty Years On*, London: MIT Press, pp. 199–219.

Jay, M. (and Botstein, L.) (1978), 'Hannah Arendt: opposing views', *Partisan Review*, 45, 348–80.

Kateb, G. (1983), *Hannah Arendt: Politics, Conscience, Evil*, Oxford: Martin Robertson.

Kateb, G. (2000), 'Political action: its nature and advantages', in D. Villa (ed.), *The Cambridge Companion to Hannah Arendt*, Cambridge: Cambridge University Press, pp. 130–48.

Kateb, G. (2002), 'Ideology and storytelling', *Social Research*, 69 (2), 321–57.

Knauer, J. (1980), 'Motive and goal in Hannah Arendt's concept of political action', *American Political Science Review*, 74 (3), 721–33.

Kohn, J. (1997), 'Evil and plurality: Hannah Arendt's way to *the Life of the Mind, I*', in L. May and J. Kohn (eds), *Hannah Arendt: Twenty Years On*, London: MIT Press, pp. 147–78.

Langer, L. (1991), *Holocaust Testimonies: the Ruins of Memory*, New Haven, CT: Yale University Press.

Levi, P. (1989), *The Drowned and the Saved*, London: Abacus.

Lispstadt, D. (1994), *Denying the Holocaust: the Growing Assault on Truth and Memory*, New York, NY: Plume.

Machiavelli, N. (1970), *The Discourses*, Harmondsworth: Penguin.

Machiavelli, N. (1981), *The Prince*, Harmondsworth: Penguin.

May, L. (1997), 'Socialization and institutional evil', in L. May and J. Kohn (eds), *Hannah Arendt: Twenty Years On*, London: MIT Press, pp. 83–106.

Nelson, J. (1978), 'Politics and truth: Arendt's problematic', *American Journal of Political Science*, 22 (2), 270–301.

Parrikko, T. (1999), 'Committed to think, judge and act: Hannah Arendt's ideal-typical approach to human faculties', in J. Hermson *et al.* (eds), *The Judge and the Spectator: Hannah Arendt's Political Philosophy*, Leuven: Peeters, pp. 110–30.

Pettit, P. (1997), *Republicanism: a Theory of Freedom and Government*, Oxford: Clarendon.

Pitkin, H. (1998), *The Attack of the Blob: Hannah Arendt's Conception of the Social*, Chicago, IL: Chicago University Press.

Rawls, J. (1973), *A Theory of Justice*, Oxford: Oxford University Press.

Raz, J. (1986), *The Morality of Freedom*, Oxford: Oxford University Press.

Ring, J. (1991), 'The pariah as hero: Hannah Arendt's political actor', *Political Theory*, 19 (3), 433–52.

Rotenstreich, N. (1981), 'Postscript', in Y. Bauer and N. Rotenstreich (eds), *The Holocaust in Historical Experience*, London: Holmes and Meier.

Söllner, A. (2004), 'Hannah Arendt's *Origins of Totalitarianism* in its original context', *European Journal of Political Theory*, 3 (2), 219–30.

Spyros Draenos, S. (1979), 'Thinking without a ground: Hannah Arendt and the contemporary situation of understanding', in M. Hill (ed.), *Hannah Arendt: the Recovery of the Public World*, London: St. Martin's Press, pp. 209–24.

Steinberger, P. (1990), 'Hannah Arendt on judgment', *American Journal of Political Science*, 34 (3), 803–21.

Taylor, D. (2002), 'Hannah Arendt on judgement; thinking for politics', *International Journal of Philosophical Studies*, 10 (2), 151–69.

Tsao, R. (2002), 'Arendt against Athens: re-reading *The Human Condition*', *Political Theory*, 30 (1), 97–123.

Vidal-Naquet, P. (1992), *Assassins of Memory: Essays on the Denial of the Holocaust*, New York, NY: Columbia University Press.

Villa, D. (1997), 'The banality of philosophy: Arendt on Heidegger and Eichmann', in L. May and J. Kohn (eds), *Hannah Arendt: Twenty Years Later*, London: MIT Press, pp. 179–96.

Villa, D. (1999), *Politics, Philosophy, Terror: Essays in the Thought of Hannah Arendt*, Princeton, NJ: Princeton University Press.

Villa, D. (2000), 'Introduction: the development of Arendt's political thought', in D. Villa (ed.), *The Cambridge Companion to Hannah Arendt*, Cambridge: Cambridge University Press, pp. 1–21.

Vollrath, E. (1977), 'Hannah Arendt and the method of political thinking', *Social Research*, 44 (1), 160–82.

Waldron, J. (2000), 'Arendt's constitutional politics', in D. Villa (ed.), *The Cambridge Companion to Hannah Arendt*, Cambridge: Cambridge University Press, pp. 201–19.

Waldron, J. (2007), 'What would Hannah say?', *New York Review of Books*, 15 March.

Walzer, M. (1983), *Spheres of Justice: a Defense of Pluralism and Equality*, New York, NY: Basic Books.

Wellmer, A. (1997), 'Hannah Arendt on judgment: the unwritten doctrine of reason', in L. May and J. Kohn (eds) *Hannah Arendt: Twenty Years Later*, London: MIT Press, pp. 33–52.

Wolin, S. (1994), 'Hannah Arendt: democracy and the political', in L. Hinchman and S. Hinchman (eds), *Hannah Arendt: Critical Essays*, Albany, NY: State University of New York Press, pp. 289–306.

Young-Bruehl, E. (1982), *Hannah Arendt: For Love of the World*, London: Yale University Press.

Young-Bruehl, E. (1994), 'Reflections on Hannah Arendt's *The Life of the Mind*', in L. Hinchman and S. Hinchman (eds), *Hannah Arendt: Critical Essays*, Albany, NY: State University of New York Press, pp. 335–64.

Young-Bruehl, E. (2006), *Why Arendt Matters*, London: Yale University Press.

Zerrilli, L. (2005), 'We feel our freedom: imagination and judgment in the thought of Hannah Arendt', *Political Theory*, 33 (2), 158–88.

Zmora, H. (2007), 'A world without a saving grace: glory and immortality in Machiavelli', *History of Political Thought*, 28 (3), 449–68.

Index

179